ISBN 978-1-330-17807-2
PIBN 10045421

This book is a reproduction of an important historical work. Forgotten Books uses
state-of-the-art technology to digitally reconstruct the work, preserving the original format
whilst repairing imperfections present in the aged copy. In rare cases, an imperfection in
the original, such as a blemish or missing page, may be replicated in our edition. We do,
however, repair the vast majority of imperfections successfully; any imperfections that
remain are intentionally left to preserve the state of such historical works.

1 MONTH OF
FREE
READING

at

www.ForgottenBooks.com

By purchasing this book you are eligible for one month membership to ForgottenBooks.com, giving you unlimited access to our entire collection of over 700,000 titles via our web site and mobile apps.

To claim your free month visit:

www.forgottenbooks.com/free45421

English
Français
Deutsche
Italiano
Español
Português

www.forgottenbooks.com

Mythology Photography **Fiction**
Fishing Christianity **Art** Cooking
Essays Buddhism Freemasonry
Medicine **Biology** Music **Ancient
Egypt** Evolution Carpentry Physics
Dance Geology **Mathematics** Fitness
Shakespeare **Folklore** Yoga Marketing
Confidence Immortality Biographies
Poetry **Psychology** Witchcraft
Electronics Chemistry History **Law**
Accounting **Philosophy** Anthropology
Alchemy Drama Quantum Mechanics
Atheism Sexual Health **Ancient History**
Entrepreneurship Languages Sport
Paleontology Needlework Islam
Metaphysics Investment Archaeology
Parenting Statistics Criminology
Motivational

OLIVER GOLDSMITH

(SIR JOSHUA REYNOLDS)

OXFORD EDITION

THE BEE

AND OTHER ESSAYS BY

OLIVER GOLDSMITH

TOGETHER WITH

THE LIFE OF NASH

HUMPHREY MILFORD

OXFORD UNIVERSITY PRESS

· LONDON EDINBURGH ·GLASGOW

NEW YORK TORONTO MELBOURNE BOMBAY

1914

OXFORD : HORACE HART

PRINTER TO THE UNIVERSITY

CONTENTS

676594

THE

B E E.

BEING

ESSAYS

ON THE MOST

INTERESTING SUBJECTS.

Floriferis ut Apes in faltibus omnia libant,
Omnia Nos itidem.

L O N D O N:

Printed for J. WILKIE, at the *Bible*, in *St. Paul's Church-Yard.* MDCCLIX.

[In the following reprint of *The Bee*, the pieces subsequently revised and included in *Essays*, 1765 (ed. 2, 1766) are omitted, being given in their later form under ' Essays '. The following pieces are also omitted : Four translations from Voltaire ; ' The Sentiments of a Frenchman on the Temper of the English,' reprinted with altera- tions from the English translation (1747) of Le Blanc's *Lettres* ; ' On Deceit and Falsehood,' reprinted with alterations from *The Humourist,* 1720; and ' An Account of the Augustan Age of England ' (of doubtful authorship). Five poems are also omitted, which will be found in the companion volume of Goldsmith's Poems.]

THE BEE

NUMBER I. SATURDAY, *October* 6, 1759.

REMARKS ON OUR THEATRES

OUR theatres are now opened, and all Grub Street is preparing its advice to the managers; we shall undoubtedly hear learned disquisitions on the structure of one actor's legs, and another's eyebrows. We shall be told much of enunciations, tones, and attitudes, and shall have our lightest pleasures commented upon by didactic dullness. We shall, it is feared, be told, that Garrick is a fine actor, but then, as a manager, so avaricious! That Palmer is a most promising genius, and Holland likely to do well, in a particular cast of character. We shall have them giving Shuter instructions to amuse us by rule, and deploring over the ruins of desolated majesty in Covent Garden. As I love to be advising too, for advice is easily given, and bears a show of wisdom and superiority, I must be permitted to offer a few observations upon our theatres and actors, without, on this trivial occasion, throwing my thoughts into the formality of method.

There is something in the deportment of all our players infinitely more stiff and formal than among the actors of other nations. Their action sits uneasy upon them; for as the English use very little gesture in ordinary conversation, our English-bred actors are obliged to supply stage gestures by their imagination alone. A French comedian finds proper models of action

in every company and in every coffee-house he enters.
An Englishman is obliged to take his models from the
stage itself ; he is obliged to imitate nature from an
imitation of nature. I know of no set of men more likely
to be improved by travelling than those of the theatrical
profession. The inhabitants of the Continent are less
reserved than here ; they may be seen through upon
a first acquaintance ; such are the proper models to draw
from ; they are at once striking, and are found in great
abundance.

Though it would be inexcusable in a comedian to add
anything of his own to the poet's dialogue, yet as to
action he is entirely at liberty. By this he may show
the fertility of his genius, the poignancy of his humour,
and the exactness of his judgement ; we scarce see a
coxcomb or a fool in common life that has not some
peculiar oddity in his action. These peculiarities it is
not in the power of words to represent, and depend
solely upon the actor. They give a relish to the humour
of the poet, and make the appearance of nature more
illusive ; the Italians, it is true, mask some characters,
and endeavour to preserve the peculiar humour by the
make of the mask ; but I have seen others still preserve
a great fund of humour in the face without a mask ; one
actor, particularly, by a squint which he threw into some
characters of low life, assumed a look of infinite solidity.
This, though upon reflection we might condemn, yet,
immediately, upon representation, we could not avoid
being pleased with. To illustrate what I have been saying
by the plays I have of late gone to see : In *The Miser*,
which was played a few nights ago at Covent Garden,
Lovegold appears through the whole in circumstances
of exaggerated avarice ; all the player's action, therefore,
should conspire with the poet's design, and represent
him as as epitome of penury. The French comedian,

in this character, in the midst of one of his most violent passions, while he appears in an ungovernable rage, feels the demon of avarice still upon him, and stoops down to pick up a pin, which he quilts into the flap of his coat-pocket with great assiduity. Two candles are lighted up for his wedding ; he flies and turns one of them into the socket ; it is, however, lighted up again ; he then steals to it, and privately crams it into his pocket. *The Mock-Doctor* was lately played at the other house. Here again the comedian had an opportunity of heightening the ridicule by action. The French player sits in a chair with a high back, and then begins to show away by talking nonsense, which he would have thought Latin by those whom he knows do not understand a syllable of the matter. At last he grows enthusiastic, enjoys the admiration of the company, tosses his legs and arms about, and in the midst of his raptures and vocifera-tion, he and the chair fall back together. All this appears dull enough in the recital, but the gravity of Cato could not stand it in the representation. In short, there is hardly a character in comedy to which a player of any real humour might not add strokes of vivacity that could not fail of applause. But instead of this we too often see our fine gentlemen do nothing, through a whole part, but strut, and open their snuff-box ; our pretty fellows sit indecently with their legs across, and our clowns pull up their breeches. These, if once, or even twice, repeated, might do well enough ; but to see them served up in every scene, argues the actor almost as barren as the character he would expose.

The magnificence of our theatres is far superior to any others in Europe where plays only are acted. The great care our performers take in painting for a part, their exactness in all the minutiae of dress, and other

little scenical proprieties, have been taken notice of
by Ricoboni, a gentleman of Italy, who travelled Europe
with no other design but to remark upon the stage ;
but there are several apparent improprieties still con-
tinned, or lately come into fashion. As, for instance,
spreading a carpet punctually at the beginning of the
death scene, in order to prevent our actors from spoiling
their clothes ; this immediately apprises us of the
tragedy to follow ; for laying the cloth is not a more
sure indication of dinner, than laying the carpet of bloody
work at Drury Lane. Our little pages also with unmeaning faces, that bear up the train of a weeping
princess, and our awkward lords in waiting, take off
much from her distress. Mutes of every kind divide
our attention, and lessen our sensibility ; but here it
is entirely ridiculous, as we see them seriously employed in doing nothing. If we must have dirty-
shirted guards upon the theatres, they should be taught
to keep their eyes fixed on the actors, and not roll them
round upon the audience, as if they were ogling the
boxes.

Beauty, methinks, seems a requisite qualification in
an actress. This seems scrupulously observed elsewhere,
and for my part I could wish to see it observed at home.
I can never conceive a hero dying for love of a lady
totally destitute of beauty. I must think the part
unnatural, for I cannot bear to hear him call that face
angelic, when even paint cannot hide its wrinkles. I
must condemn him of stupidity, and the person whom
I can accuse for want of taste will seldom become the
object of my affections or admiration. But if this be
a defect, what must be the entire perversion of scenical
decorum, when, for instance, we see an actress that might
act the Wapping Landlady without a bolster, pining
in the character of Jane Shore, and, while unwieldy

with fat, endeavouring to convince the audience that she is dying with hunger.

For the future, then, I could wish that the parts of the young or beautiful were given to performers of suitable figures ; for I must own, I could rather see the stage filled with agreeable objects, though they might sometimes bungle a little, than see it crowded with withered or misshapen figures, be their emphasis, as I think it is called, ever so proper. The first may have the awkward appearance of new-raised troops, but in viewing the last, I cannot avoid the mortification of fancying myself placed in an hospital of invalids.

A LETTER FROM A TRAVELLER

(The sequel of this correspondence to be continued occasionally. I shall alter nothing either in the style or substance of these letters, and the reader may depend on their being genuine.)

CRACOW, *Aug.* 2, 1758.

My DEAR WILL,

You see, by the date of my letter, that I am arrived in Poland. When will my wanderings be at an end ? When will my restless disposition give me leave to enjoy the present hour ? When at Lyons, I thought all happiness lay beyond the Alps ; when in Italy, I found myself still in want of something, and expected to leave solicitude behind me by going into Roumelia ; and now you find me turning back, still expecting ease everywhere but where I am. It is now seven years since I saw the face of a single creature who cared a farthing whether I was dead or alive. Secluded from all the comforts of confidence, friendship, or society, I feel the solitude of a hermit, but not his ease.

The Prince of * * * has taken me in his train, so that I am in no danger of starving for this bout. The prince's governor is a rude ignorant pedant, and his tutor a battered rake : thus, between two such characters, you may imagine he is finely instructed. I made some attempts to display all the little knowledge I had acquired by reading or observation ; but I find myself regarded as an ignorant intruder. The truth is, I shall never be able to acquire a power of expressing myself with ease in any language but my own ; and, out of my own country, the highest character I can ever acquire, is that of being a philosophic vagabond.

When I consider myself in the country which was once so formidable in war, and spread terror and desolation over the whole Roman empire, I can hardly account for the present wretchedness and pusillanimity of its inhabitants ; a prey to every invader ; their cities plundered without an enemy ; their magistrates seeking redress by complaints, and not by vigour. Everything conspires to raise my compassion for their miseries, were not my thoughts too busily engaged by my own. The whole kingdom is in strange disorder ; when our equipage, which consists of the prince and thirteen attendants, had arrived at some towns, there were no conveniences to be found, and we were obliged to have girls to conduct us to the next. I have seen a woman travel thus on horseback before us for thirty miles, and think herself highly paid, and make twenty reverences, upon receiving, with ecstasy, about twopence for her trouble. In general, we were better served by the women than the men on those occasions. The men seemed directed by a low sordid interest alone ; they seemed mere machines, and all their thoughts were employed in the care of their horses. If we gently desired them to make more speed, they took not the least notice ; kind language was what they had by no means been used to. It was proper to speak to them in the tones of anger, and sometimes it was even necessary to use blows, to excite them to their duty. How different these from the common people of England, whom \ a blow might induce to return the affront sevenfold. These poor people, however, from being brought up to vile usage, lose all the respect which they should have for themselves. They have contracted a habit of regarding constraint as the great rule of their duty. When they were treated with mildness, they no longer continued to perceive a superiority. They fancied themselves our equals, and a continuance of our humanity might probably have rendered them insolent ; but the imperious tone, menaces, and blows, at once changed their sensations and their ideas : their ears and their shoulders taught their souls to shrink back into servitude, from which they had for some moments fancied themselves disengaged.

The enthusiasm of liberty an Englishman feels is never so strong as when presented by such prospects as these. I must own, in all my indigence, it is one of my comforts (perhaps, indeed, it is my only boast) that I am of that happy country ; though I scorn to starve there ; though I do not choose to lead a life of wretched dependence, or be an object for my former acquaintance to point at. While you enjoy all the ease and elegance of prudence and virtue, your old friend wanders over the world, without a single anchor to hold by, or a friend, except you, to confide in.

Yours, &c.

A SHORT ACCOUNT OF THE LATE MR. MAUPERTUIS

Mr. Maupertuis, lately deceased, was the first to whom the English philosophers owed their being particularly admired by the rest of Europe. The romantic system of Des Cartes was adapted to the taste of the superficial and the indolent ; the foreign universities had embraced it with ardour, and such are seldom convinced of their error till all others give up such false opinions as untenable. The philosophy of Newton, and the metaphysics of Locke appeared, but, like all new truths, they were at once received with opposition and contempt. The English, 'tis true, studied, understood, and consequently admired them ; it was very different on the Continent. Fontenelle, who seemed to preside over the republic of letters, unwilling to acknowledge that all his life had been spent in erroneous philosophy, joined in the universal disapprobation, and the English philosophers seemed entirely unknown.

Maupertuis, however, made them his study; he thought he might oppose the physics of his country, and yet still be a good citizen; he defended our countrymen, wrote in their favour, and, at last, as he had truth on his side, carried his cause. Almost all the learning of the English, till very lately, was conveyed in the language of France. The writings of Maupertuis spread the reputation of his master Newton, and by a happy fortune have united his fame with that of our human prodigy.

The first of his performances, openly, in vindication of the Newtonian system, is his treatise entituled, *Sur la figure des Astres*, if I remember right ; a work at once expressive of a deep geometrical knowledge, and the most happy manner of delivering abstruse science with ease. This met with violent opposition from a people, though fond of novelty in everything else, yet, however, in matters of science, attached to ancient opinions with bigotry. As the old and the obstinate fell away, the youth of France embraced the new opinions, and now seem more eager to defend Newton than even his countrymen.

That oddity of character which great men are sometimes remarkable for, Maupertuis was not entirely free from. It is certain he was extremely whimsical. Though born to a large fortune, when employed in mathematical inquiries, he disregarded his person to such a degree, and loved retirement so much, that he has been more than once put on the list of modest beggars by the curates of Paris, when he retired to some private quarter of the town, in order to enjoy his meditations without interruption. The character given of him by one of Voltaire's antagonists, if it can be depended upon, is much to his honour. ' You,' says this writer to Mr. Voltaire, ' you ' were entertained by the King of Prussia as a buffoon, ' but Maupertuis as a philosopher.' It is certain that the preference which this royal scholar gave to Maupertuis was the cause of Voltaire's disagreement with him. Voltaire could not bear to see a man, whose talents he had no great opinion of, preferred before him as president of the Royal Academy. His *Micromegas* was designed to ridicule Maupertuis ; and probably it has brought more disgrace on the author than the subject. Whatever absurdities men of letters have indulged, and how fantastical soever the modes of science have been, their anger is still more subject to ridicule.

NUMBER II. SATURDAY, *October* 13, 1759.

SOME PARTICULARS RELATIVE TO CHARLES XII NOT COMMONLY KNOWN

STOCKHOLM.

SIR,

I cannot resist your solicitations, though it is possible I shall be unable to satisfy your curiosity. The polite of every country seem to have but one character. A gentleman of Sweden differs but little, except in trifles, from one of any other country. It is among the vulgar we are to find those distinctions which characterize a people, and from them it is that I take my picture of the Swedes.

Though the Swedes in general appear to languish under oppression, which often renders others wicked, or of malignant dispositions, it has not, however, the same influence upon them, as they are faithful, civil, and incapable of atrocious crimes. Would you believe that in Sweden highway robberies are not so much as heard of ? For my part, I have not in the whole country seen a gibbet or a gallows. They pay an infinite respect to their ecclesiastics, whom they suppose to be the privy councillors of Providence, who, on their part, turn this credulity to their own advantage, and manage their parishioners as they please. In general, however, they seldom abuse their sovereign authority. Hearkened to as oracles, regarded as the dispensers of eternal rewards and punishments, they readily influence their hearers into justice, and make them practical philosophers without the pains of study.

As to their persons they are perfectly well made, and the men particularly have a very engaging air. The greatest part of the boys which I saw in the country had very white hair. They were as beautiful as Cupids, and there was something open and entirely happy in their little chubby faces. The girls, on the contrary, have neither such fair nor such even complexions, and their features are much less delicate, which is a circumstance different from that of almost every other country. Besides this, it is observed that the women are generally afflicted with the itch, for which Scania is particularly remarkable. I had an instance of this in one of the inns on the road. The hostess was one of the most beautiful women I have ever seen ; she had so fine a complexion, that I could not avoid admiring it. But what was my surprise, when she opened her bosom in order to suckle her child, to perceive that seat of delight all covered with this disagreeable distemper. The careless manner in which she exposed to our eyes so disgusting an object, sufficiently testifies that they regard it as no very extraordinary malady, and seem to take no pains to conceal it. Such are the remarks, which probably you may think trifling enough, I have made in my journey to Stockholm, which, to take it altogether, is a large, beautiful, and even populous city.

The arsenal appears to me one of its greatest curiosities; it is an handsome spacious building, but, however, illy stored with the implements of war. To recompense this defect, they have almost filled it with trophies, and other marks of their former military glory. I saw there several chambers filled with Danish, Saxon, Polish, and Russian standards. There was at least enough to suffice half a dozen armies ; but new standards are more easily made than new armies can be enlisted. I saw, besides, some very rich furniture, and some of the crown jewels of great value ; but what principally engaged my attention, and touched me with passing melancholy, were the bloody, yet precious, spoils of the two greatest heroes the North ever produced. What I mean are the clothes in which the great Gustavus Adolphus, and the intrepid Charles XII died, by a fate not usual to kings. The first, if I remember, is a sort of a buff waistcoat, made antique fashion, very plain, and without the least ornaments ; the second, which was even more remarkable, consisted only of a coarse blue cloth coat, a large hat of less value, a shirt of coarse linen, large boots, and buff gloves made to cover a great part of the arm. His saddle, his pistols, and his sword, have nothing in them remarkable ; the meanest soldier was in this respect no way inferior to his gallant monarch. I shall use this opportunity to give you some particulars of the life of a man already so well known, which I had from persons who knew him when a child, and who now, by a fate not unusual to courtiers, spend a life of poverty and retirement, and talk over in raptures all the actions of their old victorious king, companion, and master.

Courage and inflexible constancy formed the basis of this monarch's character. In his tenderest years he gave instances of both. When he was yet scarce seven years old, being at dinner with the queen his mother, intending to give a bit of bread to a great dog he was fond of, this hungry animal snapped too greedily at the morsel, and bit his hand in a terrible manner. The wound bled copiously, but our young hero, without offering to cry, or taking the least notice of his misfortune, endeavoured to conceal what had happened, lest his dog should be brought into trouble, and wrapped his bloody hand in the napkin. The queen, perceiving that he did not eat, asked him the reason. He contented himself with replying, that he thanked her, he was not hungry. They thought he was taken ill, and so repeated their solicitations. But all was in vain, though the poor child was already grown pale with the loss of blood. An officer who attended at table at last perceived it ; for Charles would sooner have died than betrayed his dog, who, he knew, intended no injury.

At another time, when in the small-pox, and his case appeared dangerous, he grew one day very uneasy in his bed, and a gentleman who watched him, desirous of covering him up close, received from the patient a violent box on his ear. Some hours after, observing the prince more calm, he entreated to know how he had incurred his displeasure, or what he had done to have merited a blow. ' A blow,' replied Charles, ' I don't remember ' anything of it ; I remember, indeed, that I thought ' myself in the battle of Arbela, fighting for Darius, ' where I gave Alexander a blow, which brought him to ' the ground.'

What great effects might not these two qualities of courage and constancy have produced, had they at first received a just direction. Charles, with proper instruction, thus naturally disposed, would have been the delight and the glory of his age. Happy those princes, who are educated by men who are at once virtuous and wise, and have been for some time in the school of affliction ; who weigh happiness against glory, and teach their royal pupils the real value of fame ; who are ever showing the superior dignity of man to that of royalty ; that a peasant who does his duty is a nobler character than a king of even middling reputation. Happy, I say, were princes, could such men be found to instruct them ; but those to whom such an education is generally entrusted, are men who themselves have acted in a sphere too high to know mankind. Puffed up themselves with ideas of false grandeur, and measuring merit by adventitious circumstances of greatness, they generally communicate those fatal prejudices to their pupils, confirm their pride by adulation, or increase their ignorance by teaching them to despise that wisdom which is found among the poor.

But not to moralize when I only intend a story,— what is related of the journeys of this prince is no less astonishing. He has sometimes been on horseback for four and twenty hours successively, and thus traversed the greatest part of his kingdom. At last none of his officers were found capable of following him ; he thus consequently rode the greatest part of these journeys quite alone, without taking a moment's repose, and without any other subsistence but a bit of bread. In one of these rapid courses he underwent an adventure singular enough. Riding thus post one day, all alone, he had the misfortune to have his horse fall dead under him. This might have embarrassed an ordinary man, but it gave Charles no sort of uneasiness. Sure of finding another horse, but not equally so of meeting with a good saddle and pistols, he ungirds his horse, claps the whole equipage on his own back, and thus accoutred, marches on to the next inn, which by good fortune was not far off. Entering the stable, he here found a horse entirely to his mind ; so, without further ceremony, he clapped on his saddle and housing with great composure, and was just going to mount, when the gentleman who owned the horse was apprised of a stranger's going to steal his property out of the stable. Upon asking the king, whom he had never seen, bluntly, how he presumed to meddle with his horse, Charles coolly replied, squeezing in his lips, which was his usual custom, that he took the horse because he wanted one ; ' for you see,' continued he, 'if I have none, I shall be obliged to carry the saddle ' myself.' This answer did not seem at all satisfactory to the gentleman, who instantly drew his sword. In this the king was not much behindhand with him, and to it they were going, when the guards, by this time, came

up, and testified that surprise which was natural, to
see arms in the hand of a subject against his king.
Imagine whether the gentleman was less surprised than
they at his unpremeditated disobedience. His astonishment, however, was soon dissipated by the king, who,
taking him by the hand, assured him he was a brave
fellow, and himself would take care he should be provided
for. This promise was afterwards fulfilled ; and I have
been assured the king made him a captain.

I am, Sir, &c.

ON OUR THEATRES

MADEMOISELLE CLAIRON, a celebrated actress at Paris,
seems to me the most perfect female figure I have ever
seen upon any stage. Not, perhaps, that nature has been
more liberal of personal beauty to her, than some to be
seen upon our theatres at home. There are actresses
here who have as much of what connoisseurs call statuary
grace, by which is meant elegance unconnected with
motion, as she ; but they all fall infinitely short of her,
when the soul comes to give expression to the limbs,
and animates every feature.

Her first appearance is excessively engaging ; she
never comes in staring round upon the company, as if
she intended to count the benefits of the house, or at
least to see, as well as be·seen. Her eyes are always,
at first, intently fixed upon the persons of the drama, and
she lifts them by degrees, with enchanting diffidence,
upon the spectators. Her first speech, or at least the
first part of it, is delivered with scarce any motion of
the arm ; her hands and her tongue never set out
together ; but the one prepares us for the other. She
sometimes begins with a mute, eloquent attitude ; but
never goes forward all at once with hands, eyes, head,

and voice. This observation, though it may appear of
no importance, should certainly be adverted to ; nor
do I see any one performer (Garrick only excepted)
among us, that is not, in this particular, apt to offend.
By this simple beginning she gives herself a power of
rising in the passion of the scene. As she proceeds,
every gesture, every look acquires new violence, till at
last transported, she fills the whole vehemence of the
part, and all 'the idea of the poet.

Her hands are not alternately stretched out, and then
drawn in again, as with the singing women at Sadler's
Wells ; they are employed with graceful variety, and
every moment please with new and unexpected eloquence.
Add to this, that their motion is generally from the
shoulder ; she never flourishes her hands while the upper
part of her arm is motionless, nor has she the ridiculous
appearance, as if her elbows were pinned to her hips.

But of all the cautions to be given our rising actresses,
I would particularly recommend it to them never to
take notice of the audience, upon any occasion whatsoever ; let the spectators applaud never so loudly, their
praises should pass, except at the end of the epilogue,
with seeming inattention. I can never pardon a lady
on the stage who, when she draws the admiration of the
whole audience, turns about to make them a low curtsy
for their applause. Such a figure no longer continues
Belvidera, but at once drops into Mrs. Cibber. Suppose
a sober tradesman, who once a year takes his shillings-
worth at Drury Lane, in order to be delighted with the
figure of a queen, the Queen of Sheba for instance, or
any other queen : this honest man has no other idea of
the great but from their superior pride and impertinence :
suppose such a· man placed among the spectators, the
first figure that presents on the stage is the queen herself,
curtsying and cringing to all the company ; how can

he fancy her the haughty favourite of King Solomon the wise, who appears actually more submissive than the wife of his bosom. We are all tradesmen of a nicer relish in this respect, and such a conduct must disgust every spectator who loves to have the illusion of nature strong upon him.

Yet, while I recommend to our actresses a skilful attention to gesture, I would not have them study it in the looking-glass. This, without some precaution, will render their action formal ; by too great an intimacy with this, they become stiff and affected. People seldom improve, when they have no other model but themselves to copy after. I remember to have known a notable performer of the other sex, who made great use of this flattering monitor ; and yet was one of the stiffest figures I ever saw. I am told his apartment was hung round with looking-glass, that he might see his person twenty times reflected upon entering the room ; and I will make bold to say, he saw twenty very ugly fellows whenever he did so.

NUMBER III. SATURDAY, *October* 20, 1759.

THE HISTORY OF HYPATIA

MAN, when secluded from society, is not a more solitary being than the woman who leaves the duties of her own sex to invade the privileges of ours. She seems, in such circumstances, like one in banishment ; she appears like a neutral being between the sexes ; and though she may have the admiration of both, she finds true happiness from neither.

Of all the ladies of antiquity, I have read of none who was ever more justly celebrated than the beautiful Hypatia, the daughter of Theon the philosopher. This most accomplished of women was born at Alexandria, in the reign of Theodosius the younger. Nature was never more lavish of its gifts than it had been to her, endued as she was with the most exalted understanding, and the happiest turn to science. Education completed what nature had begun, and made her the prodigy not only of her age, but the glory of her sex.

From her father she learned geometry and astronomy ; she collected from the conversation and schools of the other philosophers, for which Alexandria was at that time famous, the principles of the rest of the sciences.

What cannot be conquered by natural penetration and a passion for study ? The boundless knowledge which, at that period of time, was required to form the character of a philosopher no way discouraged her ; she delivered herself up to the study of Aristotle and Plato, and soon not one in all Alexandria understood so perfectly as she all the difficulties of these two philosophers.

But not their systems alone, but those of every other sect, were quite familiar to her ; and to this knowledge she added that of polite learning, and the art of oratory. All the learning which it was possible for the human mind to contain, being joined to a most enchanting eloquence, rendered this lady the wonder not only of the populace, who easily admire, but of philosophers themselves, who are seldom fond of admiration.

The city of Alexandria was every day crowded with strangers, who came from all parts of Greece and Asia to see and hear her. As for the charms of her person, they might not probably have been mentioned, did she not join to a beauty the most striking, a virtue that might repress the most assuming ; and though in the whole capital, famed for charms, there was not one who could equal her in beauty ; though in a city, the resort of all the learning then existing in the world, there was not one who could equal her in knowledge ; yet, with such accomplishments, Hypatia was the most modest of her sex. Her reputation for virtue was not less than her virtues ; and, though in a city divided between two factions, though visited by the wits and the philosophers of the age, calumny never dared to suspect her morals, or attempt her character. Both the Christians and the Heathens who have transmitted her history and her misfortunes, have but one voice, when they speak of her beauty, her knowledge, and her virtue. Nay, so much harmony reigns in their accounts of this prodigy of perfection, that, in spite of the opposition of their faith, we should never have been able to judge of what religion was Hypatia, were we not informed, from other circumstances, that she was a heathen. Providence had taken so much pains in forming her, that we are almost induced to complain of its not having endeavoured to make her a Christian ; but from this complaint we are deterred by a thousand contrary observations, which lead us to reverence its inscrutable mysteries.

This great reputation, which she so justly was possessed of, was at last, however, the occasion of her ruin.

The person who then possessed the patriarchate of Alexandria was equally remarkable for his violence, cruelty, and pride. Conducted by an ill-grounded zeal for the Christian religion, or perhaps desirous of augmenting his authority in the city, he had long meditated the banishment of the Jews. A difference arising between them and the Christians with respect to some public games, seemed to him a proper juncture for putting his ambitious designs into execution. He found no difficulty in exciting the people, naturally disposed to revolt. The prefect who, at that time, commanded the city, interposed on this occasion, and thought it just to put one of the chief creatures of the patriarch to the

torture, in order to discover the first promoter of the
conspiracy. The patriarch, enraged at the injustice he
thought offered to his character and dignity, and piqued
at the protection which was offered to the Jews, sent
for the chiefs of the synagogue, and enjoined them to
renounce their designs, upon pain of incurring his highest
displeasure.

The Jews, far from fearing his menaces, excited new
tumults, in which several citizens had the misfortune
to fall. The patriarch could no longer contain : at the
head of a numerous body of Christians, he flew to the
synagogues, which he demolished, and drove the Jews
from a city, of which they had been possessed since the
times of Alexander the Great. It may be easily imagined
that the prefect could not behold, without pain, his
jurisdiction thus insulted, and the city deprived of a
number of its most industrious inhabitants.

The affair was therefore brought before the emperor.
The patriarch complained of the excesses of the Jews,
and the prefect of the outrages of the patriarch. At
this very juncture, five hundred monks of Mount Nitria,
imagining the life of their chief to be in danger, and that
their religion was threatened in his fall, flew into the
city with ungovernable rage, attacked the prefect in the
streets, and, not content with loading him with reproaches,
wounded him in several places.

The citizens had by this time notice of the fury of the
monks ; they, therefore, assembled in a body, put the
monks to flight, seized on him who had been found
throwing a stone, and delivered him to the prefect,
who caused him to be put to death without farther delay.

The patriarch immediately ordered the dead body,
which had been exposed to view, to be taken down,
procured for it all the pomp and rites of burial, and went
even so far as himself to pronounce the funeral oration,

in which he classed a seditious monk among the martyrs. This conduct was by no means generally approved of ; the most moderate even among the Christians perceived and blamed his indiscretion ; but he was now too far advanced to retire. He had made several overtures towards a reconciliation with the prefect, which not succeeding, he bore all those an implacable hatred whom he imagined to have any hand in traversing his designs ; but Hypatia was particularly destined to ruin. She could not find pardon, as she was known to have a most refined friendship for the prefect ; wherefore the populace were incited against her. Peter, a reader of the principal church, one of those vile slaves by which men in power are too frequently attended—wretches ever ready to commit any crime which they hope may render them agreeable to their employer,—this fellow, I say, attended by a crowd of villains, waited for Hypatia, as she was returning from a visit, at her own door, seized her as she was going in, and dragged her to one of the churches called Cesarea, where, stripping her in the most inhuman manner, they exercised the most inhuman cruelties upon her, cut her into pieces, and burnt her remains to ashes. Such was the end of Hypatia, the glory of her own sex, and the astonishment of ours.

SOME PARTICULARS RELATING TO FATHER FREIJO

Primus mortales tollere contra
Est oculos ausus, primusque assurgere contra.
LUCR.

THE Spanish nation has, for many centuries past, been remarkable for the grossest ignorance in polite literature, especially in point of natural philosophy ; a science so useful to mankind, that her neighbours have ever esteemed it a matter of the greatest importance to endeavour, by repeated experiments, to strike a light out of the chaos in which truth seemed to be confounded. Their curiosity, in this respect, was so indifferent, that, though they had discovered new worlds, they were at a loss to explain the phenomena of their own, and their pride so unaccountable, that they disdained to borrow from others that instruction which their natural indolence permitted them not to acquire.

It gives me, however, a secret satisfaction to behold an extraordinary genius now existing in that nation, whose studious endeavours seem calculated to undeceive the superstitious, and instruct the ignorant : I mean the celebrated Padre Freijo. In unravelling the mysteries of nature, and explaining physical experiments, he takes an opportunity of displaying the concurrence of second causes, in those very wonders which the vulgar ascribe to supernatural influence.

An example of this kind happened a few years ago, in a small town of the kingdom of Valencia. Passing through at the hour of mass, he alighted from his mule, and proceeded to the parish church, which he found extremely crowded, and there appeared on the faces of the faithful a more than usual alacrity. The sun, it seems, which had been for some minutes under a cloud, had begun to shine on a large crucifix, that stood on the middle of the altar, studded with several precious stones. The reflection from these, and from the diamond eyes of some silver saints, so dazzled the multitude, that they unanimously cried out, 'A miracle ! a miracle!' whilst the priest at the altar, with seeming consternation, continued his heavenly conversation. Padre Freijo soon dissipated the charm, by tying his handkerchief round the head of one of the statues, for which he was arraigned by the Inquisition ; whose flames, however, he has had the good fortune hitherto to escape.

MISCELLANEOUS

WERE I to measure the merit of my present undertaking by its success, or the rapidity of its sale, I might be led to form conclusions by no means favourable to the pride of an author. Should I estimate my fame by its extent, every newspaper and every magazine would leave me far behind. Their fame is diffused in a very wide circle—that of some as far as Islington, and some yet farther still ; while mine, I sincerely believe, has hardly travelled beyond the sound of Bow bell ; and while the works of others fly like unpinioned swans, I find my own move as heavily as a new-plucked goose.

Still, however, I have as much pride as they who have ten times as many readers. It is impossible to repeat all the agreeable delusions in which a disappointed author is apt to find comfort. I conclude, that what my reputation wants in extent, is made up by its solidity. *Minus juvat Gloria lata quam magna.* I have great satisfaction in considering the delicacy and discernment of those readers I have, and in ascribing my want of popularity to the ignorance or inattention of those I have not. All the world may forsake an author, but vanity will never forsake him.

Yet notwithstanding so sincere a confession, I was once induced to show my indignation against the public, by discontinuing my endeavours to please ; and was bravely resolved, like Raleigh, to vex them, by burning my manuscript in a passion. Upon recollection, however, I considered what set or body of people would be displeased at my rashness. The sun, after so sad an accident, might shine next morning as bright as usual ; men might laugh and sing the next day, and transact business

as before, and not a single creature feel any regret but
myself.

I reflected upon the story of a minister, who, in the
reign of Charles II, upon a certain occasion resigned
all his posts, and retired into the country in a fit of
resentment. But as he had not given the world entirely
up with his ambition, he sent a messenger to town, to
see how the courtiers would bear his resignation. Upon
the messenger's return, he was asked whether there
appeared any commotions at court? To which he
replied, 'There were very great ones.' 'Aye,' says the
minister, 'I knew my friends would make a bustle;
'all petitioning the king for my restoration, I presume?'
'No, Sir,' replied the messenger, 'they are only petitioning
'his majesty to be put in your place.' In the same
manner, should I retire in indignation, instead of having
Apollo in mourning, or the Muses in a fit of the spleen;
instead of having the learned world apostrophizing at
my untimely decease, perhaps all Grub Street might
laugh at my fall, and self-approving dignity might never
be able to shield me from ridicule. In short, I am
resolved to write on, if it were only to spite them. If
the present generation will not hear my voice, hearken,
O posterity, to you I call, and from you I expect redress!
What rapture will it not give to have the Scaligers,
Daciers, and Warburtons of future times commenting
with admiration upon every line I now write, working
away those ignorant creatures who offer to arraign my
merit with all the virulence of learned reproach. Aye,
my friends, let them feel it; call names; never spare
them; they deserve it all, and ten times more. I have
been told of a critic, who was crucified, at the command
of another, to the reputation of Homer. That, no doubt,
was more than poetical justice, and I shall be perfectly
content if those who criticize me are only clapped in the

pillory, kept fifteen days upon bread and water, and obliged to run the gantlope through Paternoster Row. The truth is, I can expect happiness from posterity either way. If I write ill, happy in being forgotten; if well, happy in being remembered with respect.

Yet, considering things in a prudential light, perhaps I was mistaken in designing my paper as an agreeable relaxation to the studious, or a help to conversation among the gay; instead of addressing it to such, I should have written down to the taste and apprehension of the many, and sought for reputation on the broad road. Literary fame, I now find, like religious, generally begins among the vulgar. As for the polite, they are so very polite, as never to applaud upon any account. One of these, with a face screwed up into affectation, tells you, that fools may *admire*, but men of sense only *approve*. Thus, lest he should rise into rapture at anything new, he keeps down every passion but pride and self-importance; approves with phlegm, and the poor author is damned in the taking a pinch of snuff. Another has written a book himself, and being condemned for a dunce, he turns a sort of king's evidence in criticism, and now becomes the terror of every offender. A third, possessed of full-grown reputation, shades off every beam of favour from those who endeavour to grow beneath him, and keeps down that merit, which, but for his influence, might rise into equal eminence. While others, still worse, peruse old books for their amusement, and new books only to condemn; so that the public seem heartily sick of all but the business of the day, and read everything new with as little attention as they examine the faces of the passing crowd.

From these considerations I was once determined to throw off all connexions with taste, and fairly address my countrymen in the same engaging style and manner with other periodical pamphlets, much more in vogue than probably mine shall ever be. To effect this, I had thoughts of changing the title into that of the ROYAL BEE, the ANTI-GALLICAN BEE, or the BEE'S MAGAZINE. I had laid in a proper stock of popular topics, such as encomiums on the King of Prussia, invectives against the Queen of Hungary and the French, the necessity of a militia, our undoubted sovereignty of the seas, reflections upon the present state of affairs, a dissertation upon liberty, some seasonable thoughts upon the intended bridge of Blackfriars, and an address to Britons. The history of an old woman, whose teeth grew three inches long, an ode upon our victories, a rebus, an acrostic upon Miss Peggy P., and a journal of the weather. All this, together with four extraordinary pages of *letter-press*, a beautiful map of England, and two prints curiously coloured from nature, I fancied might touch their very souls. I was actually beginning an address to the people, when my pride at last overcame my prudence, and determined me to endeavour to please by the goodness of my entertainment, rather than by the magnificence of my sign.

The *Spectator*, and many succeeding essayists, frequently inform us of the numerous compliments paid them in the course of their lucubrations ; of the frequent encouragements they met to inspire them with ardour, and increase their eagerness to please. I have received *my letters* as well as they ; but alas ! not congratulatory ones ; not assuring me of success and favour ; but pregnant with bodings that might shake even fortitude itself.

One gentleman assures me, he intends to throw away no more threepences in purchasing the BEE ; and what is still more dismal, he will not recommend me as a poor author wanting encouragement to his neighbourhood, which it seems is very numerous. Were my soul set upon threepences, what anxiety might not such a denunciation produce ! But such does not happen to be the present motive of publication : I write partly to show my good nature, and partly to show my vanity ; nor will I lay down the pen till I am satisfied one way or another.

Others have disliked the title and the motto of my paper ; point out a mistake in the one, and assure me the other has been consigned to dullness by anticipation. All this may be true ; *but what is that to me ?* Titles and mottoes to books are like escutcheons and dignities in the hands of a king. The wise sometimes condescend to *accept* of them ; but none but a fool will imagine them of any real importance. We ought to depend upon intrinsic merit, and not the slender helps of title. *Nam quae non fecimus ipsi, vix ea nostra voco.*

For my part, I am ever ready to mistrust a promising title, and have, at some expense, been instructed not to hearken to the voice of an advertisement, let it plead never so loudly, or never so long. A countryman coming one day to Smithfield, in order to take a slice of Bartholomew Fair, found a perfect show before every booth. The drummer, the fire-eater, the wire-walker, and the salt-box, were all employed to invite him in. *Just a going ; the court of the King of Prussia in all his glory ; pray, gentlemen, walk in and see.* From people who generously gave so much away, the clown expected a monstrous bargain for his money when he got in. He steps up, pays his sixpence, the curtain is drawn ; when, too late, he finds that he had the best part of the show for nothing at the door.

A FLEMISH TRADITION

EVERY country has its traditions, which, either too minute or not sufficiently authentic to receive historical sanction, are handed down among the vulgar, and serve at once to instruct and amuse them. Of this number the adventures of Robin Hood, the hunting of Chevy Chace, and the bravery of Johnny Armstrong, among the English; of Kaul Dereg, among the Irish; and Creighton, among the Scots, are instances. Of all the traditions, however, I remember to have heard, I do not recollect any more remarkable than one still current in Flanders; a story generally the first the peasants tell their children, when they bid them behave like Bidderman the wise. It is by no means, however, a model to be set before a polite people for imitation; since if, on the one hand, we perceive in it the steady influence of patriotism; we, on the other, find as strong a desire of revenge. But, to waive introduction, let us to the story.

When the Saracens overran Europe with their armies, and penetrated as far even as Antwerp, Bidderman was lord of a city, which time has since swept into destruction. As the inhabitants of this country were divided under separate leaders, the Saracens found an easy conquest, and the city of Bidderman, among the rest, became a prey to the victors.

Thus dispossessed of his paternal city, our unfortunate governor was obliged to seek refuge from the neighbouring princes, who were as yet unsubdued, and he for some time lived in a state of wretched dependence among them.

Soon, however, his love to his native country brought him back to his own city, resolved to rescue it from the enemy, or fall in the attempt: thus, in disguise, he went among the inhabitants, and endeavoured, but in vain, to excite them to a revolt. Former misfortunes lay so heavily on their minds, that they rather chose to suffer the most cruel bondage, than attempt to vindicate their former freedom.

As he was thus one day employed, whether by information or from suspicion is not known, he was apprehended by a Saracen soldier as a spy, and brought before the very tribunal at which he once presided. The account he gave of himself was by no means satisfactory. He could produce no friends to vindicate his character ; wherefore, as the Saracens knew not their prisoner, and as they had no direct proofs against him, they were content with condemning him to be publicly whipped as a vagabond.

The execution of this sentence was accordingly performed with the utmost rigour. Bidderman was bound to the post, the executioner seeming disposed to add to the cruelty of the sentence, as he received no bribe for lenity. Whenever Bidderman groaned under the scourge, the other, only redoubling his blows, cried out, *Does the villain murmur ?* If Bidderman entreated but a moment's respite from torture, the other only repeated his former exclamation, *Does the villain murmur ?*

From this period, revenge, as well as patriotism, took entire possession of his soul. His fury stooped so low as to follow the executioner with unremitting resentment. But, conceiving that the best method to attain these ends was to acquire some eminence in the city, he laid himself out to oblige its new masters, studied every art, and practised every meanness, that serve to promote the needy, or render the poor pleasing ; and by these means, in a few years, he came to be of some note in the city, which justly belonged entirely to him.

The executioner was, therefore, the first object of his

resentment, and he even practised the lowest fraud to
gratify the revenge he owed him. A piece of plate,
which Bidderman had previously stolen from the Saracen
governor, he privately conveyed into the executioner's
house, and then gave information of the theft. They
who are any way acquainted with the rigour of the
Arabian laws, know that theft is punished with immediate
death. The proof was direct in this case ; the executioner had nothing to offer in his own defence, and he
was therefore condemned to be beheaded upon a scaffold
in the public market-place. As there was no executioner
in the city but the very man who was now to suffer,
Bidderman himself undertook this, to him, most agreeable office. The criminal was conducted from the
judgement-seat, bound with cords. The scaffold was
erected, and he placed in such a manner as he might lie
most convenient for the blow.

But his death alone was not sufficient to satisfy the
resentment of this extraordinary man, unless it was
aggravated with every circumstance of cruelty. Wherefore, coming up the scaffold, and disposing everything
in readiness for the intended blow, with the sword in
his hand he approached the criminal, and whispering
in a low voice, assured him, that he himself was the
very person that had once been used with so much
cruelty ; that to his knowledge, he died very innocently,
for the plate had been stolen by himself, and privately
conveyed into the house of the other.

' O, my countrymen,' cried the criminal, ' do you
' hear what this man says ? '——*Does the villain murmur ?*
replied Bidderman, and immediately, at one blow,
severed his head from his body.

Still, however, he was not content till he had ample
vengeance of the governors of the city, who condemned
him. To effect this, he hired a small house, adjoining

to the town wall, under which he every day dug, and carried out the earth in a basket. In this unremitting labour, he continued several years, every day digging a little, and carrying the earth unsuspected away. By this means he at last made a secret communication from the country into the city, and only wanted the appearance of an enemy, in order to betray it. This opportunity, at length, offered ; the French army came into the neighbourhood, but had no thoughts of sitting down before a town which they considered as impregnable. Bidderman, however, soon altered their resolutions, and, upon communicating his plan to the General, he embraced it with ardour. Through the private passage above mentioned, he introduced a large body of the most resolute soldiers, who soon opened the gates for the rest, and the whole army rushing in, put every Saracen that was found to the sword.

THE SAGACITY OF SOME INSECTS

To the Author of the Bee

Sir,

Animals, in general, are sagacious in proportion as they cultivate society. The elephant and the beaver show the greatest signs of this when united ; but when man intrudes into their communities, they lose all their spirit of industry, and testify but a very small share of that sagacity, for which, when in a social state, they are so remarkable.

Among insects, the labours of the bee and the ant have employed the attention and admiration of the naturalist ; but their whole sagacity is lost upon separation, and a single bee or ant seems destitute of every degree of industry, is the most stupid insect

imaginable, languishes for a time in solitude, and soon
dies.

Of all the solitary insects I have ever remarked, the
spider is the most sagacious ; and its actions to me, who
have attentively considered them, seem almost to exceed
belief. This insect is formed by nature for a state of
war, not only upon other insects, but upon each other.
For this state nature seems perfectly well to have
formed it. Its head and breast are covered with a strong
natural coat of mail, which is impenetrable to the
attempts of every other insect, and its belly is enveloped
in a soft pliant skin, which eludes the sting even of
a wasp. Its legs are terminated by strong claws, not
unlike those of a lobster, and their vast length, like
spears, serves to keep every assailant at a distance.

Not worse furnished for observation than for an attack
or a defence, it has several eyes, large, transparent, and
covered with a horny substance, which, however, does
not impede its vision. Besides this, it is furnished with
a forceps above the mouth, which serves to kill or secure
the prey already caught in its claws or its net.

Such are the implements of war with which the body
is immediately furnished ; but its net to entangle the
enemy seems what it chiefly trusts to, and what it
takes most pains to render as complete as possible.
Nature has furnished the body of this little creature
with a glutinous liquid, which, proceeding from the anus,
it spins into a thread, coarser or finer as it chooses to
contract or dilate its sphincter. In order to fix its
thread when it begins to weave, it emits a small drop of
its liquid against the wall, which, hardening by degrees,
serves to hold the thread very firmly. Then receding
from the first point, as it recedes the thread lengthens ;
and when the spider has come to the place where the
other end of the thread should be fixed, gathering up

with its claws the thread which would otherwise be too slack, it is stretched tightly, and fixed in the same manner to the wall as before.

In this manner it spins and fixes several threads parallel to each other, which, so to speak, serve as the warp to the intended web. To form the woof, it spins in the same manner its thread, transversely fixing one end to the first thread that was spun, and which is always the strongest of the whole web, and the other to the wall. All these threads, being newly spun, are glutinous, and therefore stick to each other wherever they happen to touch, and in those parts of the web most exposed to be torn, our natural artist strengthens them, by doubling the threads sometimes sixfold.

Thus far naturalists have gone in the description of this animal; what follows is the result of my own observation upon that species of the insect called a *House-Spider*. I perceived about four years ago, a large spider in one corner of my room, making its web; and though the maid frequently levelled her fatal broom against the labours of the little animal, I had the good fortune then to prevent its destruction; and I may say, it more than paid me by the entertainment it afforded.

In three days the web was, with incredible diligence, completed; nor could I avoid thinking that the insect seemed to exult in its new abode. It frequently traversed it round, examined the strength of every part of it, retired into its hole, and came out very frequently. The first enemy, however, it had to encounter, was another and a much larger spider, which, having no web of its own, and having probably exhausted all its stock in former labours of this kind, came to invade the property of its neighbour. Soon then a terrible encounter ensued, in which the invader seemed to have the victory, and the laborious spider was obliged to take refuge in its hole. Upon this I perceived the victor using every art to draw the enemy from his stronghold. He seemed to go off, but quickly returned ; and when he found all arts vain, began to demolish the new web without mercy. This brought on another battle, and, contrary to my expectations, the laborious spider became conqueror, and fairly killed his antagonist.

Now, then, in peaceable possession of what was justly its own, it waited three days with the utmost patience, repairing the breaches of its web, and taking no sustenance that I could perceive. At last, however, a large blue fly fell into the snare, and struggled hard to get loose. The spider gave it leave to entangle itself as much as possible, but it seemed to be too strong for the cobweb. I must own I was greatly surprised when I saw the spider immediately sally out, and in less than a minute weave a new net round its captive, by which the motion of its wings was stopped ; and when it was fairly hampered in this manner, it was seized, and dragged into the hole.

In this manner it lived, in a precarious state ; and nature seemed to have fitted it for such a life, for upon a single fly it subsisted for more than a week. I once put a wasp into the net; but when the spider came out in order to seize it as usual, upon perceiving what kind of an enemy it had to deal with, it instantly broke all the bands that held it fast, and contributed all that lay in its power to disengage so formidable an antagonist. When the wasp was at liberty, I expected the spider would have set about repairing the breaches that were made in its net, but those it seems were irreparable, wherefore the cobweb was now entirely forsaken, and a new one begun, which was completed in the usual time.

I had now a mind to try how many cobwebs a single

spider could furnish ; wherefore I destroyed this, and the insect set about another. When I destroyed the other also, its whole stock seemed entirely exhausted, and it could spin no more. The arts it made use of to support itself, now deprived of its great means of subsistence, were indeed surprising. I have seen it roll up its legs like a ball, and lie motionless for hours together, but cautiously watching all the time ; when a fly happened to approach sufficiently near, it would dart out all at once, and often seize its prey.

Of this life, however, it soon began to grow weary, and resolved to invade the possession of some other spider, since it could not make a web of its own. It formed an attack upon a neighbouring fortification with great vigour, and at first was as vigorously repulsed. Not daunted, however, with one defeat, in this manner it continued to lay siege to another's web for three days, and, at length, having killed the defendant, actually took possession. When smaller flies happen to fall into the snare, the spider does not sally out at once, but very patiently waits till it is sure of them ; for, upon his immediately approaching, the terror of his appearance might give the captive strength sufficient to get loose : The manner then is to wait patiently till, by ineffectual and impotent struggles, the captive has wasted all its strength, and then he becomes a certain and an easy conquest.

The insect I am now describing lived three years ; every year it changed its skin, and got a new set of legs. I have sometimes plucked off a leg, which grew again in two or three days. At first, it dreaded my approach to its web, but at last it became so familiar as to take a fly out of my hand, and upon my touching any part of the web, would immediately leave its hole, prepared either for a defence or an attack.

To complete this description, it may be observed, that the male spiders are much less than the female, and that the latter are oviparous. When they come to lay, they spread a part of their web under the eggs, and then roll them up carefully, as we roll up things in a cloth, and thus hatch them in their hole. If disturbed in their holes, they never attempt to escape without carrying this young brood in their forceps away with them, and thus frequently are sacrificed to their parental affection.

As soon as ever the young ones leave their artificial covering, they begin to spin, and almost sensibly seem to grow bigger. If they have the good fortune, when even but a day old, to catch a fly, they fall to with good appetites ; but they live sometimes three or four days without any sort of sustenance, and yet still continue to grow larger, so as every day to double their former size. As they grow old, however, they do not still continue to increase, but their legs only continue to grow longer ; and when a spider becomes entirely stiff with age, and unable to seize its prey, it dies at length of hunger.

THE CHARACTERISTICS OF GREATNESS

In every duty, in every science in which we would wish to arrive at perfection, we should propose for the object of our pursuit some certain station even beyond our abilities ; some imaginary excellence, which may amuse and serve to animate our inquiry. In deviating from others, in following an unbeaten road, though we, perhaps, may never arrive at the wished-for object, yet it is possible we may meet several discoveries by the way ; and the certainty of small advantages, even while we travel with security, is not so amusing as the hopes of great rewards, which inspire the adventurer. *Evenit nonnunquam*, says Quintilian, *ut aliquid grande inveniat qui semper quaerit quod nimium est.*

This enterprising spirit is, however, by no means the character of the present age ; every person who should now leave received opinions, who should attempt to be more than a commentator upon philosophy, or an imitator in polite learning, might be regarded as a chimerical projector. Hundreds would be ready not only to point out his errors, but to load him with reproach. Our probable opinions are now regarded as certainties ; the difficulties hitherto undiscovered, as utterly inscrutable ; and the writers of the last age inimitable, and therefore the properest models of imitation.

One might be almost induced to deplore the philosophic spirit of the age, which in proportion as it enlightens the mind, increases its timidity, and represses the vigour of every undertaking. Men are now content with being prudently in the right ; which, though not the way to make new acquisitions, it must be owned, is the best method of securing what we have. Yet this is certain, that the writer who never deviates, who never hazards a new thought, or a new expression, though his friends may compliment him upon his sagacity, though criticism lifts her feeble voice in his praise, will seldom arrive at any degree of perfection. The way to acquire lasting esteem, is not by the fewness of a writer's faults, but the greatness of his beauties ; and our noblest works are generally most replete with both.

An author, who would be sublime, often runs his thought into burlesque ; yet I can readily pardon his mistaking ten times for once succeeding. True Genius walks along a line ; and, perhaps, our greatest pleasure is in seeing it so often near falling, without being ever actually down.

Every science has its hitherto undiscovered mysteries,

after which men should travel undiscouraged by the failure of former adventurers. Every new attempt serves, perhaps, to facilitate its future invention. We may not find the Philosopher's stone, but we shall probably hit upon new inventions in pursuing it. We shall, perhaps, never be able to discover the longitude, yet, perhaps, we may arrive at new truths in the investigation.

Were any of these sagacious minds among us, (and surely no nation, or no period, could ever compare with us in this particular) were any of those minds, I say, who now sit down contented with exploring the intricacies of another's system, bravely to shake off admiration, and, undazzled with the splendour of another's reputation, to chalk out a path to fame for themselves, and boldly cultivate untried experiment, what might not be the result of their inquiries, should the same study that has made them wise, make them enterprising also ? What could not such qualities, united, produce ? But such is not the character of the English, while our neighbours of the Continent launch out into the ocean of science, without proper stores for the voyage, we fear shipwreck in every breeze, and consume in port those powers which might probably have weathered every storm.

Projectors in a state are generally rewarded above their deserts ; projectors in the republic of letters, never. If wrong, every inferior dunce thinks himself entitled to laugh at their disappointment ; if right, men of superior talents think their honour engaged to oppose, since every new discovery is a tacit diminution of their own pre-eminence.

To aim at excellence, our reputation, our friends, and our all, must be ventured ; by aiming only at mediocrity, we run no risk, and we do little service. Prudence and greatness are ever persuading us to contrary pursuits.

The one instructs us to be content with our station, and to find happiness in bounding every wish. The other impels us to superiority, and calls nothing happiness but rapture. The one directs to follow mankind, and to act and think with the rest of the world. The other drives us from the crowd, and exposes us as a mark to all the shafts of envy, or ignorance.

Nec minus periculum ex magna fama quam ex mala.—TACIT.

The rewards of mediocrity are immediately paid, those attending excellence generally paid in reversion. In a word, the little mind who loves itself, will write and think with the vulgar, but the great mind will be bravely eccentric, and scorn the beaten road, from universal benevolence.

A CITY NIGHT-PIECE

Ille dolet vere, qui sine teste dolet.—MART.

THE clock has struck two, the expiring taper rises and sinks in the socket, the watchman forgets the hour in slumber, the laborious and the happy are at rest, and nothing now wakes but guilt, revelry and despair. The drunkard once more fills the destroying bowl, the robber walks his midnight round, and the suicide lifts his guilty arm against his own sacred person.

Let me no longer waste the night over the page of antiquity, or the sallies of contemporary genius, but pursue the solitary walk, where vanity, ever changing, but a few hours past, walked before me, where she kept up the pageant, and now, like a froward child, seems hushed with her own importunities.

What a gloom hangs all around! the dying lamp feebly emits a yellow gleam, no sound is heard but of the chiming clock, or the distant watch-dog. All the bustle of human pride is forgotten, and this hour may well display the emptiness of human vanity.

There may come a time when this temporary solitude may be made continual, and the city itself, like its inhabitants, fade away, and leave a desert in its room.

What cities, as great as this, have once triumphed in existence, had their victories as great as ours, joy as just, and as unbounded as we, and with short-sighted presumption, promised themselves immortality. Posterity can hardly trace the situation of some. The sorrowful traveller wanders over the awful ruins of others, and as he beholds, he learns wisdom, and feels the transience of every sublunary possession.

Here stood their citadel, but now grown over with weeds ; there their senate-house, but now the haunt of every noxious reptile ; temples and theatres stood here, now only an undistinguished heap of ruin. They are fallen, for luxury and avarice first made them feeble. (The rewards of state were conferred on amusing and not on useful members of society.) Thus true virtue languished, their riches (and opulence) invited the plunderer, who, though once repulsed, returned again, and at last swept the defendants into undistinguished destruction.

How few appear in those streets, which but some few hours ago were crowded ; and those who appear, no longer now wear their daily mask, nor attempt to hide their lewdness or their misery.

But who are those who make the streets their couch, and find a short repose from wretchedness at the doors of the opulent ? These are strangers, wanderers, and orphans, whose circumstances are too humble to expect redress, and their distresses too great even for pity. Some are without the covering even of rags, and others emaciated with disease ; the world seems to have disclaimed them ; society turns its back upon their distress, and has given them up to nakedness and hunger. (These poor shivering females have once seen happier days, and been flattered into beauty.) They have been prostituted to the gay luxurious villain, and are now turned out to meet the severity of winter in the streets. Perhaps, now lying at the doors of their betrayers, they sue to wretches whose hearts are insensible to calamity, or debauchees who may curse, but will not relieve them.)

Why, why was I born a man, and yet see the sufferings of wretches I cannot relieve ! Poor houseless creatures ! the world will give you reproaches, but will not give you relief. The slightest misfortunes, the most imaginary uneasinesses of the rich, are aggravated with all the power of eloquence, and engage our attention ; while you weep unheeded, persecuted by every subordinate species of tyranny, and finding enmity in every law. (Why was this heart of mine formed with so much sensibility ! or why was not my fortune adapted to its impulse !)Tenderness, without a capacity of relieving, only makes the heart that feels it more wretched than the object which sues for assistance.

But let me turn from a scene of such distress to the sanctified hypocrite, *who has been talking of virtue till the time of bed*, and now steals out, to give a loose to his vices under the protection of midnight ; vices more atrocious, because he attempts to conceal them. See how he pants down the dark alley, and, with hastening steps, (fears an acquaintance in every face.) He has passed the whole day in company he hates, and now goes to prolong the night among company that as heartily hate him. May his vices be detected ; may the morning rise upon his shame ; yet I wish to no purpose ; villany, when detected, never gives up, but boldly adds impudence to imposture.

NUMBER V.   SATURDAY, *November* 3, 1759.

UPON POLITICAL FRUGALITY

FRUGALITY has ever been esteemed a virtue as well among Pagans as Christians : there have been even heroes who have practised it. However, we must acknowledge, that it is too modest a virtue, or, if you will, too obscure a one to be essential to heroism; few heroes have been able to attain to such a height. Frugality agrees much better with politics ; it seems to be the base, the support, and, in a word, seems to be the inseparable companion of a just administration.

However this be, there is not, perhaps, in the world a people less fond of this virtue than the English; and of consequence there is not a nation more restless, more exposed to the uneasinesses of life, or less capable of providing for particular happiness. We are taught to despise this virtue from our childhood ; our education is improperly directed, and a man who has gone through the politest institutions, is generally the person who is least acquainted with the wholesome precepts of frugality. We every day hear the elegance of taste, the magnificence of some, and the generosity of others, made the subject of our admiration and applause. All this we see represented not as the end and recompense of labour and desert, but as the actual result of genius, as the mark of a noble and exalted mind.

In the midst of these praises bestowed on luxury, for which elegance and taste are but another name, perhaps it may be thought improper to plead the cause of frugality. It may be thought low, or vainly declamatory, to exhort our youth from the follies of dress, and of every other superfluity; to accustom themselves, even with mechanic meanness, to the simple necessaries of life. Such sort of instructions may appear antiquated ; yet, however, they seem the foundations of all our virtues, and the most efficacious method of making mankind useful members of society. Unhappily, however, such discourses are not fashionable among us, and the fashion seems every day growing still more obsolete, since the press, and every other method of exhortation, seems disposed to talk of the luxuries of life as harmless enjoyments. I remember, when a boy, to have remarked, that those who in school wore the finest clothes, were pointed at as being conceited and proud. At present, our little masters are taught to consider dress betimes, and they are regarded, even at school, with contempt, who do not appear as genteel as the rest. Education should teach us to become useful, sober, disinterested, and laborious members of society ; but does it not at present point out a different path ! It teaches us to multiply our wants, by which means we become more eager to possess, in order to dissipate, a greater charge to ourselves, and more useless or obnoxious to society.

If a youth happens to be possessed of more genius than fortune, he is early informed that he ought to think of his advancement in the world ; that he should labour to make himself pleasing to his superiors ; that he should shun low company (by which is meant the company of his equals) ; that he should rather live a little above than below his fortune ; that he should think of becoming great ; but he finds none to admonish him to become frugal, to persevere in one single design, to avoid every pleasure and all flattery, which however seeming to conciliate the favour of his superiors, never conciliate their esteem. There are none to teach him that the best way of becoming happy in himself, and useful to others, is to continue in the state in which fortune at first placed him, without making too hasty strides to advancement ; that greatness may be attained, but should not be expected ; and that they who most impatiently expect advancement, are seldom possessed of their wishes.] He has few, I say, to teach him this lesson, or to moderate his youthful passions ; yet, this experience may say, that a young man, who but for six years of the early part of his life, could seem divested of all his passions, would certainly make, or considerably increase his fortune, and might indulge several of his favourite inclinations in manhood with the utmost security.

The efficaciousness of these means is sufficiently known and acknowledged ; but as we are apt to connect a low idea with all our notions of frugality, the person who would persuade us to it, might be accused of preaching up avarice.

Of all vices, however, against which morality dissuades, there is not one more undetermined than this of avarice. Misers are described by some, as men divested of honour, sentiment, or humanity ; but this is only an ideal picture, or the resemblance at least is found but in a few.   In truth, they who are generally called misers, are some of the very best members of society.   The sober, the laborious, the attentive, the frugal, are thus styled by the gay, giddy, thoughtless, and extravagant.   The first set of men do society all the good, and the latter all the evil that is felt.   Even the excesses of the first no way injure the commonwealth ; those of the latter are the most injurious that can be conceived.

The ancient Romans, more rational than we in this particular, were very far from thus misplacing their admiration or praise ; instead of regarding the practice of parsimony as low or vicious, they made it synonymous even with probity.   They esteemed those virtues so inseparable, that the known expression of *Vir Frugi* signified, at one and the same time, a sober and managing man, an honest man, and a man of substance.

The Scriptures, in a thousand places, praise economy; and it is everywhere distinguished from avarice. But in spite of all its sacred dictates, a taste for vain pleasures and foolish expense is the ruling passion of the present times. Passion, did I call it? rather the madness which at once possesses the great and the little, the rich and the poor; even some are so intent upon acquiring the superfluities of life, that they sacrifice its necessaries in this foolish pursuit.

To attempt the entire abolition of luxury, as it would be impossible, so it is not my intent. The generality of mankind are too weak, too much slaves to custom and opinion, to resist the torrent of bad example. But if it be impossible to convert the multitude, those who have received a more extended education, who are enlightened and judicious, may find some hints on this subject useful. They may see some abuses, the suppression of which would by no means endanger public liberty; they may be directed to the abolition of some unnecessary expenses, which have no tendency to promote happiness or virtue, and which might be directed to better purposes. Our fireworks, our public feasts and entertainments, our entries of ambassadors, &c., what mummery all this; what childish pageants, what millions are sacrificed in paying tribute to custom, what an unnecessary charge at times when we are pressed with real want, which cannot be satisfied without burdening the poor!

Were such suppressed entirely, not a single creature in the state would have the least cause to mourn their suppression, and many might be eased of a load they now feel lying heavily upon them. If this were put in practice, it would agree with the advice of a sensible writer of Sweden, who, in the *Gazette de France*, 1753, thus expressed himself on that subject. 'It were 'sincerely to be wished,' says he, 'that the custom were

'established amongst us, that in all events which cause
'a public joy, we made our exultations conspicuous
'only by acts useful to society. We should then quickly
'see many useful monuments of our reason, which would
'much better perpetuate the memory of things worthy
'of being transmitted to posterity, and would be much
'more glorious to humanity than all these tumultuous
'preparations of feasts, entertainments, and other
'rejoicings used upon such occasions.'

The same proposal was long before confirmed by
a Chinese emperor, who lived in the last century, who,
upon an occasion of extraordinary joy, forbade his
subjects to make the usual illuminations, either with
a design of sparing their substance, or of turning them
to some more durable indication of joy, more glorious
for him, and more advantageous to his people.

After such instances of political frugality, can we then
continue to blame the Dutch ambassador at a certain
court, who, receiving, at his departure, the portrait of
the king, enriched with diamonds, asked what this
fine thing might be worth ? Being told that it might
amount to about two thousand pounds : ' And why,'
cries he, ' cannot his majesty keep the picture, and
' give me the money ? ' This simplicity may be ridiculed
at first ; but, when we come to examine it more closely,
men of sense will at once confess that he had reason in
what he said, and that a purse of two thousand guineas
is much more serviceable than a picture.

Should we follow the same method of state frugality
in other respects, what numberless savings might not be
the result ! How many possibilities of saving in the
administration of justice, which now burdens the subject,
and enriches some members of society, who are useful
only from its corruption !

It were to be wished, that they who govern kingdoms,

would imitate artisans. When at London a new stuff has been invented, it is immediately counterfeited in France. How happy were it for society, if a first minister would be equally solicitous to transplant the useful laws of other countries into his own. We are arrived at a perfect imitation of porcelain ; let us endeavour to imitate the good to society that our neighbours are found to practise, and let our neighbours also imitate those parts of duty in which we excel.

There are some men, who, in their garden, attempt to raise those fruits which nature has adapted only to the sultry climates beneath the line. We have at our very doors a thousand laws and customs infinitely useful ; these are the fruits we should endeavour to transplant ; these the exotics that would speedily become naturalized to the soil. They might grow in every climate, and benefit every possessor.

The best and the most useful laws I have ever seen, are generally practised in Holland. When two men are determined to go to law with each other, they are first obliged to go before the reconciling judges, called the *peacemakers*. If the parties come attended with an advocate or a solicitor, they are obliged to retire, as we take fuel from the fire we are desirous of extinguishing.

The peacemakers then begin advising the parties, by assuring them, that it is the height of folly to waste their substance, and make themselves mutually miserable, by having recourse to the tribunals of justice : ‘ Follow ‘ but our direction, and we will accommodate matters ‘ without any expense to either.’ If the rage of debate is too strong upon either party, they are remitted back for another day, in order that time may soften their tempers, and produce a reconciliation. They are thus sent for twice or thrice ; if their folly happens to be incurable, they are permitted to go to law, and as we give up to amputation such members as cannot be cured by art, justice is permitted to take its course.

It is unnecessary to make here long declamations, or calculate what society would save, were this law adopted. I am sensible, that the man who advises any reformation, only serves to make himself ridiculous. 'What!' mankind will be apt to say, 'adopt the 'customs of countries that have not so much real liberty 'as our own? our present customs, what are they to any 'man? we are very happy under them! This must be 'a very pleasant fellow, who attempts to make us 'happier than we already are! Does he not know that 'abuses are the patrimony of a great part of the nation? 'Why deprive us of a malady by which such numbers 'find their account?' This I must own is an argument to which I have nothing to reply.

What numberless savings might there not be made in both arts and commerce, particularly in the liberty of exercising trade, without the necessary prerequisites of freedom! Such useless obstructions have crept into every state, from a spirit of monopoly, a narrow selfish spirit of gain, without the least attention to general society. Such a clog upon industry frequently drives the poor from labour, and reduces them, by degrees, to a state of hopeless indigence. We have already a more than sufficient repugnance to labour; we should by no means increase the obstacles, or make excuses in a state for idleness. Such faults have ever crept into a state, under wrong or needy administrations.

Exclusive of the masters, there are numberless faulty expenses among the workmen; clubs, garnishes, freedoms, and such-like impositions, which are not too minute even for law to take notice of, and which should be abolished without mercy, since they are ever the inlets to excess and idleness, and are the parent of all those outrages which naturally fall upon the more useful part of society. In the towns and countries I have seen, I never saw a city or a village yet, whose miseries were not in proportion to the number of its public-houses. In Rotterdam, you may go through eight or ten streets without finding a public-house. In Antwerp, almost every second house seems an ale-house. In the one city, all wears the appearance of happiness and warm affluence ; in the other, the young fellows walk about the streets in shabby finery, their fathers sit at the door darning or knitting stockings, while their ports are filled with dunghills.

Ale-houses are ever an occasion of debauchery and excess, and either in a religious or political light, it would be our highest interest to have the greatest part of them suppressed. They should be put under laws of not continuing open beyond a certain hour, and harbouring only proper persons. These rules, it may be said, will diminish the necessary taxes ; but this is false reasoning, since what was consumed in debauchery abroad, would, if such a regulation took place, be more justly, and, perhaps, more equitably for the workman's family, spent at home ; and this cheaper to them, and without loss of time. On the other hand, our ale-houses being ever open, interrupt business ; the workman is never certain who frequents them, nor can the master be sure of having what was begun, finished at the convenient time.

A habit of frugality among the lower orders of mankind is much more beneficial to society than the unreflecting might imagine. The pawnbroker, the attorney, and other pests of society, might, by proper management, be turned into serviceable members ; and, were their trades abolished, it is possible the same avarice that conducts the one, or the same chicanery that characterizes the

other, might, by proper regulations, be converted into
frugality, and commendable prudence.

But some have made the eulogium of luxury, have
represented it as the natural consequence of every
country that is become rich. ' Did we not employ our
' extraordinary wealth in superfluities,' say they, ' what
' other means would there be to employ it in ? '   To
which it may be answered, If frugality were established
in the state, if our expenses were laid out rather in the
necessaries than the superfluities of life, there might be
fewer wants, and even fewer pleasures, but infinitely
more happiness. The rich and the great would be better
able to satisfy their creditors ; they would be better able
to marry their children, and, instead of one marriage at
present, there might be two, if such regulations took place.

The imaginary calls of vanity, which in reality
contribute nothing to our real felicity, would not then
be attended to, while the real calls of nature might
be always and universally supplied. The difference of
employment in the subject is what, in reality, produces
the good of society. If the subject be engaged in
providing only the luxuries, the necessaries must be
deficient in proportion. If, neglecting the produce of
our own country, our minds are set upon the productions
of another, we increase our wants, but not our means ;
and every new imported delicacy for our tables, or orna-
ment in our equipage, is a tax upon the poor.

The true interest of every government is to cultivate
the necessaries, by which is always meant every happiness our own country can produce ; and suppress all
the luxuries, by which is meant, on the other hand,
every happiness imported from abroad. Commerce
has therefore its bounds ; and every new import,
instead of encouragement, should be first examined
whether it be conducive to the interest of society.

Among the many publications with which the press is every day burdened, I have often wondered why we never had, as in other countries, an *Economical Journal,* which might at once direct to all the useful discoveries in other countries, and spread those of our own. As other journals serve to amuse the learned, or what is more often the case, to make them quarrel, while they only serve to give us the history of the mischievous world, for so I call our warriors ; or the idle world, for so may the learned be called ; they never trouble their heads about the most useful part of mankind, our peasants and our artisans ; were such a work carried into execution with proper management and just direction, it might serve as a repository for every useful improvement, and increase that knowledge which learning often serves to confound.

Sweden seems the only country where the science of economy seems to have fixed its empire. In other countries, it is cultivated only by a few admirers, or by societies which have not received sufficient sanction to become completely useful ; but here there is founded a royal academy, destined to this purpose only, composed of the most learned and powerful members of the state ; an academy which declines everything which only terminates in amusement, erudition, or curiosity, and admits only of observations tending to illustrate husbandry, agriculture, and every real physical improvement. In this country nothing is left to private rapacity, but every improvement is immediately diffused, and its inventor immediately recompensed by the state. Happy were it so in other countries ; by this means every impostor would be prevented from ruining or deceiving the public with pretended discoveries or nostrums, and every real inventor would not, by this means, suffer the inconveniences of suspicion.

In short, true economy, equally unknown to the prodigal and avaricious, seems to be a just mean between both extremes ; and to a transgression of this at present decried virtue, it is that we are to attribute a great part of the evils which infest society. A taste for superfluity, amusement, and pleasure bring effeminacy, idleness, and expense in their train. But a thirst of riches is always proportioned to our debauchery, and the greatest prodigal is too frequently found to be the greatest miser ; so that the vices which seem the most opposite, are frequently found to produce each other ; and, to avoid both, it is only necessary to be frugal.

Virtus est medium duorum vitiorum et utrinque reductum.—HOR.

A REVERIE

SCARCE a day passes in which we do not hear compliments paid to Dryden, Pope, and other writers of the last age, while not a month comes forward that is not loaded with invective against the writers of this. Strange, that our critics should be fond of giving their favours to those who are insensible of the obligation, and their dislike to these who, of all mankind, are most apt to retaliate the injury.

Even though our present writers had not equal merit with their predecessors, it would be politic to use them with ceremony. Every compliment paid them would be more agreeable, in proportion as they least deserved it. Tell a lady with a handsome face that she is pretty, she only thinks it her due ; it is what she has heard a thousand times before from others, and disregards the compliment : but assure a lady, the cut of whose visage is something more plain, that she looks killing to-day, she instantly bridles up and feels the force of the well-timed flattery the whole day after. Compliments which we think are deserved, we only accept, as debts, with indifference ; but those which conscience informs us we do not merit, we receive with the same gratitude that we do favours given away.

Our gentlemen, however, who preside at the distribution of literary fame, seem resolved to part with praise neither from motives of justice, or generosity ; one would think, when they take pen in hand, that it was only to blot reputations, and to put their seals to the packet which consigns every new-born effort to oblivion.

Yet, notwithstanding the republic of letters hangs at present so feebly together ; though those friendships which once promoted literary fame seem now to be discontinued ; though every writer who now draws the quill seems to aim at profit, as well as applause, many among them are probably laying in stores for immortality, and are provided with a sufficient stock of reputation to last the whole journey.

As I was indulging these reflections, in order to eke out the present page, I could not avoid pursuing the metaphor, of going a journey, in my imagination, and formed the following Reverie, too wild for allegory, and too regular for a dream.

I fancied myself placed in the yard of a large inn, in which there were an infinite number of wagons and stage-coaches, attended by fellows who either invited the company to take their places, or were busied in packing their baggage. Each vehicle had its inscription, showing the place of its destination. On one I could read, *The pleasure stage-coach* ; on another, *The wagon of industry* ; on a third, *The vanity whim* ; and on a fourth, *The landau of riches*. I had some inclination to step into each of these, one after another ; but, I know not by what means, I passed them by, and at last fixed my eye upon a small carriage, Berlin fashion, which seemed the most convenient vehicle at a distance in the world ; and, upon my nearer approach, found it to be *The fame machine*.

I instantly made up to the coachman, whom I found to be an affable and seemingly good-natured fellow. He informed me, that he had but a few days ago returned from the temple of fame, to which he had been carry-ing Addison, Swift, Pope, Steele, Congreve, and Colley Cibber ; that they made but indifferent company by the way ; and that he once or twice was going to empty his berlin of the whole cargo : ' However,' says he, ' I got them all safe home, with no other damage than ' a black eye, which Colley gave Mr. Pope, and am now ' returned for another coachful.' ' If that be all, friend,' said I, ' and if you are in want of company, I'll make ' one with all my heart. Open the door ; I hope the ' machine rides easy.' ' Oh ! for that, sir, extremely ' easy.' But still keeping the door shut, and measuring me with his eye, ' Pray, sir, have you no luggage ? ' You seem to be a good-natured sort of a gentleman ; ' but I don't find you have got any luggage, and I never ' permit any to travel with me but such as have some-' thing valuable to pay for coach-hire.' Examining my pockets, I own I was not a little disconcerted at this unexpected rebuff ; but considering that I carried a number of the BEE under my arm, I was resolved to open it in his eyes, and dazzle him with the splendour of the page. He read the title and contents, however, without any emotion, and assured me he had never heard of it before. ' In short, friend,' said he, now losing all his former respect, ' you must not come in. I ' expect better passengers ; but, as you seem a harmless ' creature, perhaps, if there be room left, I may let you ' ride a while for charity.'

I now took my stand by the coachman at the door, and since I could not command a seat, was resolved to be as useful as possible, and earn by my assiduity, what I could not by my merit.

The next that presented for a place, was a most whimsical figure indeed. He was hung round with papers of his own composing, not unlike those who sing ballads in the streets, and came dancing up to the door with all the confidence of instant admittance. The volubility of his motion and address prevented my being able to read more of his cargo than the word *Inspector*, which was written in great letters at the top of some of the papers. He opened the coach-door himself without any ceremony, and was just slipping in, when the coachman, with as little ceremony, pulled him back. Our figure seemed perfectly angry at this repulse, and demanded gentleman's satisfaction. ' Lord, sir ! ' replied the coachman, ' instead of proper luggage, by ' your bulk you seem loaded for a West India voyage. ' You are big enough, with all your papers, to crack ' twenty stage-coaches. Excuse me, indeed, sir, for you ' must not enter.' Our figure now began to expostulate ; he assured the coachman, that though his baggage seemed so bulky, it was perfectly light, and that he would be contented with the smallest corner of room. But Jehu was inflexible, and the carrier of the *Inspectors* was sent to dance back again, with all his papers fluttering in the wind. We expected to have no more trouble from this quarter, when, in a few minutes, the same figure changed his appearance, like harlequin upon the stage, and with the same confidence again made his approaches, dressed in lace, and carrying nothing but a nosegay. Upon coming near, he thrust the nosegay to the coachman's nose, grasped the brass, and seemed now resolved to enter by violence. I found the struggle

soon begin to grow hot, and the coachman, who was
a little old, unable to continue the contest; so, in order
to ingratiate myself, I stepped in to his assistance, and our
united efforts sent our literary Proteus, though worsted,
unconquered still, clear off, dancing a rigadoon, and
smelling to his own nosegay.

The person who after him appeared as candidate for
a place in the stage, came up with an air not quite so
confident, but somewhat, however, theatrical ; and,
instead of entering, made the coachman a very low bow,
which the other returned, and desired to see his baggage ;
upon which he instantly produced some farces, a tragedy,
and other miscellany productions. The coachman,
casting his eye upon the cargo, assured him, at present
he could not possibly have a place, but hoped in time he
might aspire to one, as he seemed to have read in the
book of nature, without a careful perusal of which none
ever found entrance at the temple of fame. ' What !
' (replied the disappointed poet) shall my tragedy, in
' which I have vindicated the cause of liberty and
' virtue——' ' Follow nature, (returned the other) and
' never expect to find lasting fame by topics which only
' please from their popularity. Had you been first in
' the cause of freedom, or praised in virtue more than
' an empty name, it is possible you might have gained
' admittance ; but at present I beg, sir, you will stand
' aside for another gentleman whom I see approaching.'

This was a very grave personage, whom at some
distance I took for one of the most reserved, and even
disagreeable figures I had seen ; but as he approached,
his appearance improved, and when I could distinguish
him thoroughly, I perceived, that, in spite of the severity
of his brow, he had one of the most good-natured
countenances that could be imagined. Upon coming to
open the stage door, he lifted a parcel of folios into the

seat before him, but our inquisitorial coachman at once shoved them out again. 'What, not take in my dic-
'tionary!' exclaimed the other in a rage. 'Be patient,
'sir, (replied the coachman) I have drove a coach, man and
'boy, these two thousand years ; but I do not remember
'to have carried above one dictionary during the whole
'time. That little book which I perceive peeping from
'one of your pockets, may I presume to ask what it
'contains ?' 'A mere trifle, (replied the author) it is
'called the *Rambler.*' 'The *Rambler*! (says the coach-
'man) I beg, sir, you'll take your place ; I have heard
'our ladies in the court of Apollo frequently mention
'it with rapture ; and Clio, who happens to be a little
'grave, has been heard to prefer it to the *Spectator* ;
'though others have observed, that the reflections, by
'being refined, sometimes become minute.'

This grave gentleman was scarce seated, when another, whose appearance was something more modern, seemed willing to enter, yet afraid to ask. He carried in his hand a bundle of essays, of which the coachman was curious enough to inquire the contents. 'These
'(replied the gentleman) are rhapsodies against the
'religion of my country.' 'And how can you expect
'to come into my coach, after thus choosing the wrong
'side of the question ?' 'Aye, but I am right (replied
'the other ;) and if you give me leave, I shall in a few
'minutes state the argument.' 'Right or wrong (said
'the coachman) he who disturbs religion is a blockhead,
'and he shall never travel in a coach of mine.' 'If then
'(said the gentleman, mustering up all his courage) if
'I am not to have admittance as an essayist, I hope
'I shall not be repulsed as an historian ; the last volume
'of my history met with applause.' 'Yes, (replied the
'coachman) but I have heard only the first approved at
'the temple of fame ; and as I see you have it about you,

'enter without further ceremony.' My attention was now diverted to a crowd, who were pushing forward a person that seemed more inclined to the *stage-coach of riches*; but by their means he was driven forward to the same machine, which he, however, seemed heartily to despise. Impelled, however, by their solicitations, he steps up, flourishing a voluminous history, and demanding admittance. 'Sir, I have formerly heard 'your name mentioned (says the coachman) but never 'as an historian. Is there no other work upon which 'you may claim a place?' 'None (replied the other) 'except a romance; but this is a work of too trifling 'a nature to claim future attention.' 'You mistake '(says the inquisitor), a well-written romance is no such 'easy task as is generally imagined. I remember 'formerly to have carried Cervantes and Segrais; and 'if you think fit, you may enter.'

Upon our three literary travellers coming into the same coach, I listened attentively to hear what might be the conversation that passed upon this extraordinary occasion; when, instead of agreeable or entertaining dialogue, I found them grumbling at each other, and each seemed discontented with his companions. Strange! thought I to myself, that they who are thus born to enlighten the world, should still preserve the narrow prejudices of childhood, and, by disagreeing, make even the highest merit ridiculous. Were the learned and the wise to unite against the dunces of society, instead of sometimes siding into opposite parties with them, they might throw a lustre upon each other's reputation, and teach every rank of subordinate merit, if not to admire, at least not to avow dislike.

In the midst of these reflections, I perceived the coach-man, unmindful of me, had now mounted the box. Several were approaching to be taken in, whose pretensions I was sensible were very just ; I therefore desired him to stop, and take in more passengers ; but he replied, as he had now mounted the box, it would be improper to come down ; but that he should take them all, one after the other, when he should return. So he drove away, and, for myself, as I could not get in, I mounted behind, in order to hear the conversation on the way.

[*To be continued.*]

A WORD OR TWO ON THE LATE FARCE CALLED 'HIGH LIFE BELOW STAIRS'

JUST as I had expected, before I saw this farce, I found it, formed on too narrow a plan to afford a pleasing variety. The sameness of the humour in every scene could not at last fail of being disagreeable. The poor, affecting the manners of the rich, might be carried on through one character or two at the most, with great propriety ; but to have almost every personage on the scene almost of the same character, and reflecting the follies of each other, was unartful in the poet to the last degree.

The scene was also almost a continuation of the same absurdity ; and my Lord Duke and Sir Harry (two foot-men who assume these characters) have nothing else to *do* but to talk like their masters, and are only introduced to speak, and to show themselves. Thus, as there is a sameness of character, there is a barrenness of incident, which, by a very small share of address, the poet might have easily avoided.

From a conformity to critic rules, which, perhaps, on the whole, have done more harm than good, our author has sacrificed all the vivacity of the dialogue to nature ; and though he makes his characters talk like servants, they are seldom absurd enough, or lively enough, to make us merry. Though he is always natural, he happens seldom to be humorous.

The satire was well intended, if we regard it as being masters ourselves ; but, probably, a philosopher would rejoice in that liberty which Englishmen give their domestics ; and, for my own part, I cannot avoid being pleased at the happiness of those poor creatures, who, in some measure, contribute to mine. The Athenians, the politest and best-natured people upon earth, were the kindest to their slaves ; and if a person may judge, who has seen the world, our English servants are the best treated, because the generality of our English gentlemen are the politest under the sun.

But not to lift my feeble voice among the pack of critics, who, probably, have no other occupation but that of cutting up everything new, I must own, there are one or two scenes that are fine satire, and sufficiently humorous ; particularly the first interview between the two footmen, which, at once, ridicules the manners of the great, and the absurdity of their imitators.

Whatever defects there might be in the composition, there were none in the action ; in this the performers showed more humour than I had fancied them capable of. Mr. Palmer and Mr. King were entirely what they desired to represent ; and Mrs. Clive (but what need I talk of her, since, without the least exaggeration, she has more true humour than any actor or actress upon the English or any other stage I have seen)—she, I say, did the part all the justice it was capable of. And, upon the whole, a farce, which has only this to recommend it, that the author took his plan from the volume of nature, by the sprightly manner in which it was performed, was, for one night, a tolerable entertainment. Thus much may be said in its vindication, that people of fashion seemed more pleased in the representation than the subordinate ranks of people.

UPON UNFORTUNATE MERIT

EVERY age seems to have its favourite pursuits, which serve to amuse the idle, and relieve the attention of the industrious. Happy the man who is born excellent in the pursuit in vogue, and whose genius seems adapted to the times he lives in. How many do we see, who might have excelled in arts or sciences, and who seem furnished with talents equal to the greatest discoveries, had the road not been already beaten by their predecessors, and nothing left for them, except trifles to discover, while others, of very moderate abilities, become famous, because happening to be first in the reigning pursuit.

Thus, at the renewal of letters in Europe, the taste was not to compose new books, but to comment on the old ones. It was not to be expected that new books should be written, when there were so many of the Ancients, either not known or not understood. It was not reasonable to attempt new conquests, while they had such an extensive region lying waste for want of cultivation. At that period, criticism and erudition were the reigning studies of the times ; and he, who had only an inventive genius, might have languished in hopeless obscurity. When the writers of antiquity were sufficiently explained and known, the learned set about imitating them : from hence proceeded the number of Latin orators, poets and historians, in the reigns of Clement the Seventh and Alexander the Sixth. This passion for antiquity lasted for many years, to the utter exclusion of every other pursuit, till some began to find, that those works which were imitated from nature, were more like the writings of antiquity, than even those written in express imitation. It was then modern language began to be cultivated with assiduity, and our poets and orators poured forth their wonders upon the world.

As writers become more numerous, it is natural for readers to become more indolent ; from whence must necessarily arise a desire of attaining knowledge with the greatest possible ease. No science or art offers its instruction and amusement in so obvious a manner as statuary and painting. From hence we see, that a desire of cultivating those arts generally attends the decline of science. Thus the finest statues, and the most beautiful paintings of antiquity, preceded but a little the absolute decay of every other science. The statues of Antoninus, Commodus, and their contemporaries, are the finest productions of the chisel, and appeared but just before learning was destroyed by comment, criticism, and barbarous invasions.

What happened in Rome may probably be the case with us at home. Our nobility are now more solicitous in patronizing painters and sculptors than those of any other polite profession ; and from the lord, who has his gallery, down to the 'prentice, who has his twopenny copperplate, all are admirers of this art. The great, by their caresses, seem insensible to all other merit but that of the pencil; and the vulgar buy every book rather from the excellence of the sculptor than the writer.

How happy were it now, if men of real excellence in that profession were to arise ! Were the painters of Italy now to appear, who once wandered like beggars from one city to another, and produce their almost breathing figures, what rewards might they not expect ! But many of them lived without rewards, and therefore rewards alone will never produce their equals. We have often found the great exert themselves, not only without promotion, but in spite of opposition. We have found them flourishing, like medicinal plants, in a region of savageness and barbarity, their excellence unknown, and their virtues unheeded.

They who have seen the paintings of Caravagio are sensible of the surprising impression they make ; bold, swelling, terrible to the last degree ; all seems animated, and speaks him among the foremost of his profession ; yet this man's fortune and his fame seemed ever in opposition to each other.

Unknowing how to flatter the great, he was driven from city to city in the utmost indigence, and might truly be said to paint for his bread.

Having one day insulted a person of distinction, who refused to pay him all the respect which he thought his due, he was obliged to leave Rome, and travel on foot, his usual method of going his journeys down into the country, without either money or friends to subsist him.

After he had travelled in this manner as long as his strength would permit, faint with famine and fatigue, he at last called at an obscure inn by the wayside. The host knew, by the appearance of his guest, his indifferent circumstances, and refused to furnish him a dinner without previous payment.

As Caravagio was entirely destitute of money, he took down the innkeeper's sign, and painted it anew for his dinner.

Thus refreshed, he proceeded on his journey, and left the innkeeper not quite satisfied with this method of payment. Some company of distinction, however, coming soon after, and struck with the beauty of the new sign, bought it at an advanced price, and astonished the innkeeper with their generosity; he was resolved, therefore, to get as many signs as possible drawn by the same artist, as he found he could sell them to good advantage; and accordingly set out after Caravagio, in order to bring him back. It was nightfall before he came up to the place, where the unfortunate Caravagio lay dead by the roadside, overcome by fatigue, resentment, and despair.

NUMBER VI. SATURDAY, *November* 10, 1759.

SOME ACCOUNT OF THE ACADEMIES OF ITALY

THERE is not, perhaps, a country in Europe, in which learning is so fast upon the decline as in Italy; yet not one in which there are such a number of academies instituted for its support. There is scarce a considerable town in the whole country which has not one or two institutions of this nature, where the learned, as they are pleased to call themselves, meet to harangue, to compliment each other, and praise the utility of their institution.

Jarchius has taken the trouble to give us a list of those clubs, or academies, which amount to five hundred and fifty, each distinguished by somewhat whimsical in the name. The academicians of Bologna, for instance, are divided into the Abbandonati, the Ausiosi, Ociosio, Arcadi, Confusi, Dubbiosi, &c. There are few of these who have not published their transactions, and scarce a member who is not looked upon as the most famous man in the world, at home.

Of all those societies, I know of none whose works are worth being known out of the precincts of the city in which they were written, except the Cicalata Academica (or, as we might express it, the Tickling Society) of Florence. I have just now before me a manuscript oration, spoken by the late Tomaso Crudeli, at that society, which will, at once, serve to give a better picture of the manner in which men of wit amuse themselves in that country, than anything I could say upon the occasion. The oration is this :

'The younger the nymph, my dear companions, the more happy the lover. From fourteen to seventeen, you are sure of finding love for love ; from seventeen to twenty-one, there is always a mixture of interest and affection. But when that period is past, no longer expect to receive, but to buy. No longer expect a nymph who gives, but who sells, her favours. At this age, every glance is taught its duty ; not a look, not a sigh, without design ; the lady, like a skilful warrior, aims at the heart of another, while she shields her own from danger.

'On the contrary, at fifteen, you may expect nothing but simplicity, innocence, and nature. The passions are then sincere ; the soul seems seated in the lips ; the dear object feels present happiness, without being anxious for the future ; her eyes brighten if her lover approaches ; her smiles are borrowed from the Graces, and her very mistakes seem to complete her desires.

'Lucretia was just sixteen. The rose and lily took possession of her face, and her bosom, by its hue and its coldness, seemed covered with snow. So much beauty, and so much virtue, seldom want admirers. Orlandino, a youth of sense and merit, was among the number. He had long languished for an opportunity of declaring his passion, when Cupid, as if willing to indulge his happiness, brought the charming young couple by mere accident to an arbour, where every prying eye, but that of love, was absent. Orlandino talked of the sincerity of his passion, and mixed flattery with his addresses ; but it was all in vain. The nymph was pre-engaged, and had long devoted to heaven those charms for which he sued. "My dear Orlandino," said she, "you know I have long been dedicated to "St. Catherine, and to her belongs all that lies below "my girdle ; all that is above, you may freely possess, "but farther I cannot, must not, comply. The vow is "passed; I wish it were undone, but now it is impossible." You may conceive, my companions, the embarrassment our young lovers felt upon this occasion. They kneeled to St. Catherine, and though both despaired, both implored her assistance. Their tutelar saint was entreated to show some expedient, by which both might continue to love, and yet both be happy. Their petition was sincere. St. Catherine was touched with compassion; for lo, a miracle ! Lucretia's girdle unloosed, as if without hands ; and though before bound round her middle, fell spontaneously down to her feet, and gave Orlandino the possession of all those beauties which lay above it.'

NUMBER VII. SATURDAY, *November* 17, 1759.

OF ELOQUENCE

OF all kinds of success, that of an orator is the most pleasing. Upon other occasions, the applause we deserve is conferred in our absence, and we are insensible of the pleasure we have given ; but in eloquence, the victory and the triumph are inseparable. We read our own glory in the face of every spectator, the audience is moved, the antagonist is defeated, and the whole circle bursts into unsolicited applause.

The rewards which attend excellence in this way are so pleasing, that numbers have written professed treatises to teach us the art ; schools have been established with no other intent ; rhetoric has taken place among the institutions ; and pedants have ranged under proper heads, and distinguished with long learned names, *some* of the strokes of nature, or of passion, which orators have used. I say only *some*, for a folio volume could not contain all the figures which have been used by the truly eloquent ; and scarce a good speaker or writer but makes use of some that are peculiar or new.

Eloquence has preceded the rules of rhetoric, as languages have been formed before grammar. Nature renders men eloquent in great interests, or great passions. He that is sensibly touched, sees things with a very different eye from the rest of mankind. All nature to him becomes an object of comparison and metaphor, without attending to it ; he throws life into all, and inspires his audience with a part of his own enthusiasm.

It has been remarked, that the lower parts of mankind generally express themselves most figuratively, and that tropes are found in the most ordinary forms of conversation. Thus, in every language, the heart burns ; the courage is roused ; the eyes sparkle ; the spirits are cast down ; passion inflames ; pride swells, and pity sinks the soul. Nature, everywhere, speaks in those strong images, which, from their frequency, pass unnoticed.

Nature it is which inspires those rapturous enthusiasms, those irresistible turns ; a strong passion, a pressing danger, calls up all the imagination, and gives the orator irresistible force. Thus, a captain of the first caliphs, seeing his soldiers fly, cried out, ' Whither do you run ? ' the enemy are not there ! You have been told that the ' caliph is dead ; but God is still living. He regards the ' brave, and will reward the courageous. Advance ! '

A man, therefore, may be called eloquent, who transfers the passion or sentiment with which he is moved himself, into the breast of another ; and this definition appears the more just, as it comprehends the graces of silence, and of action. An intimate persuasion of the truth to be proved, is the sentiment and passion to be transferred ; and he who effects this, is truly possessed of the talent of eloquence.

I have called eloquence a talent, and not an art, as so many rhetoricians have done, as art is acquired by exercise and study, and eloquence is the gift of nature. Rules will never make either a work or a discourse eloquent ; they only serve to prevent faults, but not to introduce beauties ; to prevent those passages which are truly eloquent, and dictated by nature, from being blended with others which might disgust or, at least, abate our passion.

What we clearly conceive, (says Boileau) we can clearly express. I may add, that what is felt with emotion, is expressed also with the same movements; the words arise as readily to paint our emotions, as to express our thoughts with perspicuity. The cool care an orator takes to express passions which he does not feel, only prevents his rising into that passion he would seem to feel. In a word, to feel your subject thoroughly, and to speak without fear, are the only rules of eloquence, properly so called, which I can offer. Examine a writer of genius on the most beautiful parts of his work, and he will always assure you that such passages are generally those which have given him the least trouble, for they came as if by inspiration. To pretend that cold and didactic precepts will make a man eloquent, is only to prove that he is incapable of eloquence.

But, as in being perspicuous, it is necessary to have a full idea of the subject, so in being eloquent, it is not sufficient, if I may so express it, to feel by halves. The orator should be strongly impressed, which is generally

the effects of a fine and exquisite sensibility, and not that
transient and superficial emotion, which he excites in
the greatest part of his audience. It is even impossible
to affect the hearers in any great degree without being
affected ourselves. In vain it will be objected, that
many writers have had the art to inspire their readers with
a passion for virtue, without being virtuous themselves;
since it may be answered, that sentiments of virtue
filled their minds at the time they were writing. They
felt the inspiration strongly, while they praised justice,
generosity, or good nature ; but, unhappily for them,
these passions might have been discontinued, when they
laid down the pen. In vain will it be objected again,
that we can move without being moved, as we can
convince without being convinced. It is much easier to
deceive our reason than ourselves ; a trifling defect in
reasoning may be overseen, and lead a man astray; for
it requires reason and time to detect the falsehood, but our
passions are not so easily imposed upon,—our eyes, our
ears, and every sense, are watchful to detect the imposture.

No discourse can be eloquent that does not elevate the
mind. Pathetic eloquence, it is true, has for its only
object to affect ; but I appeal to men of sensibility,
whether their pathetic feelings are not accompanied with
some degree of elevation. We may then call eloquence
and sublimity the same thing, since it is impossible to
be one, without feeling the other. From hence it follows,
that we may be eloquent in any language, since no
language refuses to paint those sentiments with which
we are thoroughly impressed. What is usually called
sublimity of style, seems to be only an error. Eloquence
is not in the words, but in the subject; and in great
concerns, the more simply anything is expressed, it is
generally the more sublime. True eloquence does not
consist, as the rhetoricians assure us, in saying great

things in a sublime style, but in a simple style ; for
there is, properly speaking, no such thing as a sublime
style, the sublimity lies only in the things ; and when
they are not so, the language may be turgid, affected,
metaphorical, but not affecting.

What can be more simply expressed, than the following
extract from a celebrated preacher, and yet what was
ever more sublime ? Speaking of the small number of
the elect, he breaks out thus among his audience : ' Let
' me suppose that this was the last hour of us all ; that
' the heavens were opening over our heads ; that time
' was passed, and eternity begun ; that Jesus Christ in
' all His glory, that man of sorrows in all His glory,
' appeared on the tribunal, and that we were assembled
' here to receive our final decree of life or death eternal !
' Let me ask, impressed with terror like you, and not
' separating my lot from yours, but putting myself in
' the same situation in which we must all one day
' appear before God, our judge,—let me ask, if Jesus
' Christ should now appear to make the terrible separa-
' tion of the just from the unjust, do you think the
' greatest number would be saved ? Do you think the
' number of the elect would even be equal to that of
' the sinners ? Do you think, if all our works were
' examined with justice, would He find ten just persons
' in this great assembly ? Monsters of ingratitude, would
' he find one ? ' Such passages as these, are sublime in
every language. The expression may be less striking, or
more indistinct, but the greatness of the idea still
remains. In a word, we may be eloquent in every
language and in every style, since elocution is only an
assistant, but not a constitutor of eloquence.

Of what use, then, will it be said, are all the precepts
given us upon this head, both by the ancients and
moderns ? I answer, that they cannot make us eloquent,

but they will certainly prevent us from becoming ridiculous. They can seldom procure a single beauty, but they may banish a thousand faults. The true method of an orator is not to attempt always to move, always to affect, to be continually sublime, but at proper intervals to give rest both to his own and the passions of his audience. In these periods of relaxation, or of preparation rather, rules may teach him to avoid anything low, trivial, or disgusting. Thus criticism, properly speaking, is intended not to assist those parts which are sublime, but those which are naturally mean and humble, which are composed with coolness and caution, and where the orator rather endeavours not to offend, than attempts to please.

I have hitherto insisted more strenuously on that eloquence which speaks to the passions, as it is a species of oratory almost unknown in England. At the bar it is quite discontinued, and I think with justice. In the senate it is used but sparingly, as the orator speaks to enlightened judges. But in the pulpit, in which the orator should chiefly address the vulgar, it seems strange that it should be entirely laid aside.

The vulgar of England are without exception, the most barbarous and the most unknowing of any in Europe. A great part of their ignorance may be chiefly ascribed to their teachers, who, with the most pretty gentleman-like serenity, deliver their cool discourses, and address the reason of men who have never reasoned in all their lives. They are told of cause and effect, of beings self-existent, and the universal scale of beings. They are informed of the excellence of the Bangorian controversy, and the absurdity of an intermediate state. The spruce preacher reads his lucubration without lifting his nose from the text, and never ventures to earn the shame of an enthusiast.

By this means, though his audience feel not one word of all he says, he earns, however, among his acquaintance, the character of a man of sense ; among his acquaintance only, did I say ? nay, even with his bishop.

The polite of every country have several motives to induce them to a rectitude of action ; the love of virtue for its own sake, the shame of offending, and the desire of pleasing. The vulgar have but one, the enforcements of religion ; and yet those who should push this motive home to their hearts, are basely found to desert their post. They speak to the squire, the philosopher, and the pedant ; but the poor, those who really want instruction, are left uninstructed.

I have attended most of our pulpit orators, who, it must be owned, write extremely well upon the text they assume. To give them their due also, they read their sermons with elegance and propriety, but this goes but a very short way in true eloquence. The speaker must be moved. In this, in this alone, our English divines are deficient. Were they to speak to a few calm dispassionate hearers, they certainly use the properest methods of address ; but their audience is chiefly composed of the poor, who must be influenced by motives of reward and punishment, and whose only virtues lie in self-interest or fear.

How then are such to be addressed ? not by studied periods, or cold disquisitions ; not by the labours of the head, but the honest spontaneous dictates of the heart. Neither writing a sermon with regular periods and all the harmony of elegant expression ; neither reading it with emphasis, propriety, and deliberation ; neither pleasing with metaphor, simile, or rhetorical fustian ; neither arguing coolly, and untying consequences united in *a priori*, nor bundling up inductions *a posteriori* ; neither pedantic jargon, nor academical trifling, can

persuade the poor. Writing a discourse coolly in the
closet, then getting it by memory, and delivering it on
Sundays, even that will not do. What then is to be done ?
I know of no expedient to speak—to speak at once
intelligibly and feelingly—except to understand the
language : to be convinced of the truth of the object—
to be perfectly acquainted with the subject in view—
to prepossess yourself with a low opinion of your
audience—and to do the rest extempore. By this means
strong expressions, new thoughts, rising passions, and
the true declamatory style, will naturally ensue.

Fine declamation does not consist in flowery periods,
delicate allusions, or musical cadences ; but in a plain,
open, loose style, where the periods are long and obvious ;
where the same thought is often exhibited in several
points of view ; all this, strong sense, a good memory,
and a small share of experience, will furnish to every
orator ; and without these a clergyman may be called
a fine preacher, a judicious preacher, and a man of sound
sense ; he may make his hearers admire his understanding, but will seldom enlighten theirs.

When I think of the Methodist preachers among us,
how seldom they are endued with common sense, and
yet how often and how justly they affect their hearers,
I cannot avoid saying within myself, had these been bred
gentlemen, and been endued with even the meanest
share of understanding, what might they not effect !
Did our bishops, who can add dignity to their expostula-
tions, testify the same fervour, and *entreat* their hearers,
as well as *argue*, what might not be the consequence !
The vulgar, by which I mean the bulk of mankind,
would then have a double motive to love religion ; first,
from seeing its professors honoured here, and next,
from the consequences hereafter. At present, the
enthusiasms of the poor are opposed to law ; did law

conspire with their enthusiasms, we should not only be the happiest nation upon earth, but the wisest also.

Enthusiasm in religion, which prevails only among the vulgar, should be the chief object of politics. A society of enthusiasts, governed by reason among the great, is the most indissoluble, the most virtuous, and the most efficient of its own decrees that can be imagined. Every country that has any degree of strength, have had their enthusiasms, which ever serve as laws among the people. The Greeks had their *Kalokagathia*, the Romans their *Amor Patriae*, and we the truer and firmer bond of the *Protestant religion*. The principle is the same in all; how much then is it the duty of those whom the law has appointed teachers of this religion, to enforce its obligations, and to raise those enthusiasms among people, by which alone political society can subsist.

From eloquence, therefore, the morals of our people are to expect emendation; but how little can they be improved, by men who get into the pulpit rather to show their parts than convince us of the truth of what they deliver; who are painfully correct in their style, musical in their tones; where every sentiment, every expression, seems the result of meditation and deep study.

Tillotson has been commended as the model of pulpit eloquence; thus far he should be imitated, where he generally strives to convince, rather than to please: but to adopt his long, dry, and sometimes tedious discussions, which serve to amuse only divines, and are utterly neglected by the generality of mankind—to praise the intricacy of his periods, which are too long to be spoken,—to continue his cool phlegmatic manner of enforcing every truth,—is certainly erroneous. As I said before, the good preacher should adopt no model, write no sermons, study no periods; let him but understand his subject, the language he speaks, and be convinced of the truths he delivers. It is amazing to what heights eloquence of this kind may reach ! This is that eloquence the ancients represented as lightning, bearing down every opposer ; this the power which has turned whole assemblies into astonishment, admiration, and awe ; that is described by the torrent, the flame, and every other instance of irresistible impetuosity.

But to attempt such noble heights, belongs only to the truly great, or the truly good. To discard the lazy manner of reading sermons, or speaking sermons by rote ; to set up singly against the opposition of men who are attached to their own errors, and to endeavour to be great, instead of being prudent, are qualities we seldom see united. A minister of the Church of England, who may be possessed of good sense, and some hopes of preferment, will seldom give up such substantial advantages for the empty pleasure of improving society. By his present method he is liked by his friends, admired by his dependents, not displeasing to his bishop ; he lives as well, eats and sleeps as well, as if a real orator, and an eager asserter of his mission ; he will hardly, therefore, venture all this to be called, perhaps, an enthusiast ; nor will he depart from customs established by the brotherhood, when, by such a conduct, he only singles himself out for their contempt.

CUSTOM AND LAWS COMPARED

WHAT, say some, can give us a more contemptible idea of a large state than to find it mostly governed by custom ; to have few written laws, and no boundaries to mark the jurisdiction between the senate and people ? Among the number who speak in this manner is the great Montesquieu, who asserts that every nation is free in proportion to the number of its written laws, and seems to hint at a despotic and arbitrary conduct in the present King of Prussia, who has abridged the laws of his country into a very short compass.

As Tacitus and Montesquieu happen to differ in sentiment upon a subject of so much importance (for the Roman expressly asserts, that the state is generally vicious in proportion to the number of its laws), it will not be amiss to examine it a little more minutely, and see whether a state which, like England, is burdened with a multiplicity of written laws, or which, like Switzerland, Geneva, and some other republics, is governed by custom and the determination of the judge, is best.

And to prove the superiority of custom to written law, we shall at least find history conspiring. Custom, or the traditional observance of the practice of their forefathers, was what directed the Romans, as well in their public as private determinations. Custom was appealed to in pronouncing sentence against a criminal, where part of the formulary was *more majorum*. So Sallust, speaking of the expulsion of Tarquin, says, *mutato more*, and not *lege mutata* ; and Virgil, *pacisque imponere morem*. So that, in those times of the empire in which the people retained their liberty, they were governed by custom ; when they sunk under oppression and tyranny, they were restrained by new laws, and the laws of tradition abolished.

As getting the ancients on our side is half a victory, it will not be amiss to fortify the argument with an observation of Chrysostom's : *That the enslaved are the fittest to be governed by laws, and free men by custom.* Custom partakes of the nature of parental injunction ; it is kept by the people themselves, and observed with a willing obedience. The observance of it must, therefore, be a mark of freedom ; and coming originally to a state from the reverenced founders of its liberty, will be an encouragement and assistance to it in the defence of that blessing ; but a conquered people, a nation of slaves, must pretend to none of this freedom, or these happy distinctions ; having, by degeneracy, lost all right to their brave forefathers' free institutions, their masters will in policy take the forfeiture ; and the fixing a conquest must be done by giving laws which may every moment serve to remind the people enslaved of their conquerors : nothing being more dangerous than to trust a late-subdued people with old customs, that presently upbraid their degeneracy, and provoke them to revolt.

The wisdom of the Roman republic, in their veneration for custom, and backwardness to introduce a new law, was perhaps the cause of their long continuance, and of the virtues of which they have set the world so many examples. But to show in what that wisdom consists, it may be proper to observe, that the benefits of new written laws are merely confined to the consequences of their observance ; but customary laws, keeping up a veneration for the founders, engage men in the imitation of their virtues, as well as policy. To this may be ascribed the religious regard the Romans paid to their forefathers' memory, and their adhering for so many ages to the practice of the same virtues, which nothing contributed more to efface than the introduction of a voluminous body of new laws over the neck of venerable custom.

The simplicity, conciseness, and antiquity of custom gives an air of majesty and immutability that inspires awe and veneration ; but new laws are too apt to be voluminous, perplexed, and indeterminate ; from whence must necessarily arise neglect, contempt, and ignorance.

As every human institution is subject to gross imperfections, so laws must necessarily be liable to the same inconveniences, and their defects soon discovered. Thus, through the weakness of one part, all the rest are liable to be brought into contempt. But such weaknesses in a custom, for very obvious reasons, evade an examination ; besides, a friendly prejudice always stands up in their favour.

But let us suppose a new law to be perfectly equitable and necessary ; yet, if the procurers of it have betrayed a conduct that confesses by-ends and private motives, the disgust to the circumstances disposes us, unreasonably indeed, to an irreverence of the law itself ; but we are indulgently blind to the most visible imperfections of an old custom. Though we perceive the defects ourselves, yet we remain persuaded that our wise forefathers had good reasons for what they did ; and though such motives no longer continue, the benefit will still go along with the observance, though we don't know how. It is thus the Roman lawyers speak, *Non omnium quae a majoribus constituta sunt ratio reddi potest, et ideo rationes eorum quae constituuntur inquiri non oportet, aliaquin multa ex his quae certa sunt subvertuntur.*

Those laws which preserve to themselves the greatest love and observance, must needs be best ; but custom, as it executes itself, must be necessarily superior to written laws in this respect, which are to be executed by another. Thus nothing can be more certain than that numerous written laws are a sign of a degenerate community, and are frequently not the consequence of vicious morals in a state, but the causes.

From hence we see how much greater benefit it would be to the state rather to abridge than increase its laws. We every day find them increasing ; acts and reports, which may be termed the acts of judges, are every day becoming more voluminous, and loading the subject with new penalties.

Laws ever increase in number and severity, until they at length are strained so tight as to break themselves. Such was the case of the latter empire, whose laws were at length become so strict, that the barbarous invaders did not bring servitude but liberty.

OF THE PRIDE AND LUXURY OF THE MIDDLING CLASS OF PEOPLE

OF all the follies and absurdities which this great metropolis labours under, there is not one, I believe, at present, appears in a more glaring and ridiculous light than the pride and luxury of the middling class of people ; their eager desire of being seen in a sphere far above their capacities and circumstances, is daily— nay hourly—instanced by the prodigious numbers of mechanics, who flock to the races, and gaming-tables, (brothels) and all public diversions this fashionable town affords.

You shall see a grocer or a tallow-chandler sneak from behind the counter, clap on a laced coat and a bag, fly to the E. O. table, throw away fifty pieces with some sharping man of quality, while his industrious wife is selling a pennyworth of sugar, or a pound of candles, to support her fashionable spouse in his extravagances.

I was led into this reflection by an odd adventure, which happened to me the other day at Epsom races, where I went, not through any desire, I do assure you, of laying bets, or winning thousands ; but at the earnest request of a friend who had long indulged the curiosity of seeing the sport, very natural for an Englishman. When we had arrived at the course, and had taken several turns to observe the different objects that made up this whimsical group, a figure suddenly darted by us, mounted and dressed in all the elegance of those polite gentry who come to show you they have a little money, and rather than pay their just debts at home, generously come abroad to bestow it on gamblers and pickpockets. As I had not an opportunity of viewing his face till his return, I gently walked after him, and met him as he came back, when, to my no small surprise, I beheld, in this gay Narcissus, the visage of Jack Varnish, a humble vender of prints. Disgusted at the sight, I pulled my friend by the sleeve, pressed him to return home, telling him all the way, that I was so enraged at the fellow's impudence, I was resolved never to lay out another penny with him.

And now, pray, sir, let me beg of you to give this a place in your paper, that Mr. Varnish may understand he mistakes the thing quite, if he imagines horse-racing commendable in a tradesman ; and that he who is revelling every night in the arms of a common strumpet (though blessed with an indulgent wife) when he ought to be minding his business, will never thrive in this world. He will find himself soon mistaken, his finances decrease, his friends shun him, customers fall off, and himself thrown into a jail. I would earnestly recommend this adage to every mechanic in London, ' Keep your shop, and your shop will keep you.' A strict observance of these words will, I am sure, in time, gain them estates. Industry is the road to wealth, and honesty to happiness ; and he who strenuously endeavours to pursue them both, may never fear the critic's lash, or the sharp cries of penury and want.

SABINUS AND OLINDA

In a fair, rich, and flourishing country, whose cliffs are washed by the German Ocean, lived Sabinus, a youth formed by nature to make a conquest wherever he thought proper ; but the constancy of his disposition fixed him only with Olinda. He was, indeed, superior to her in fortune, but that defect on her side was so amply supplied by her merit, that none was thought more worthy of his regards than she. He loved her, he was beloved by her ; and, in a short time, by joining hands publicly, they avowed the union of their hearts. But, alas ! none, however fortunate, however happy, are exempt from the shafts of envy, and the malignant effects of ungoverned appetite. How unsafe, how detestable, are they who have this fury for their guide ! How certainly will it lead them from themselves, and plunge them in errors they would have shuddered at, even in apprehension. Ariana, a lady of many amiable qualities, very nearly allied to Sabinus, and highly esteemed by him, imagined herself slighted, and injuriously treated, since his marriage with Olinda. By incautiously suffering this jealousy to corrode in her breast, she began to give a loose to passion ; she forgot those many virtues for which she had been so long and so justly applauded. Causeless suspicion, and mistaken resentment, betrayed her into all the gloom of discontent ; she sighed without ceasing ; the happiness of others gave her intolerable pain ; she thought of nothing but revenge. How unlike what she was, the cheerful, the prudent, the compassionate Ariana !

She continually laboured to disturb a union so firmly, so affectionately founded, and planned every scheme which she thought most likely to disturb it.

Fortune seemed willing to promote her unjust inten-

tions : the circumstances of Sabinus had been long
embarrassed by a tedious law-suit, and the court
determining the cause unexpectedly in favour of his
opponent, it sunk his fortune to the lowest pitch of
penury from the highest affluence. From the nearness
of relationship, Sabinus expected from Ariana those
assistances his present situation required ; but she was
insensible to all his entreaties, and the justice of every
remonstrance, unless he first separated from Olinda,
whom she regarded with detestation. Upon a compliance with her desires in this respect, she promised
her fortune, her interest, and her all, should be at his
command. Sabinus was shocked at the proposal ; he
loved his wife with inexpressible tenderness, and refused
those offers with indignation which were to be purchased
at so high a price. Ariana was no less displeased to
find her offers rejected, and gave a loose to all that
warmth which she had long endeavoured to suppress.
Reproach generally produces recrimination ; the quarrel
rose to such a height, that Sabinus was marked for
destruction ; and the very next day, upon the strength
of an old family debt, he was sent to jail, with none but
Olinda to comfort him in his miseries. In this mansion
of distress they lived together with resignation, and even
with comfort. She provided the frugal meal, and he read
for her while employed in the little offices of domestic
concern. Their fellow prisoners admired their contentment, and whenever they had a desire of relaxing into
mirth, and enjoying those little comforts that a prison
affords, Sabinus and Olinda were sure to be of the party.
Instead of reproaching each other for their mutual
wretchedness, they both lightened it, by bearing each
a share of the load imposed by Providence. Whenever
Sabinus showed the least concern on his dear partner's
account, she conjured him by the love he bore her,

by those tender ties which now united them for ever,
not to discompose himself ; that, so long as his affection
lasted, she defied all the ills of fortune, and every loss
of fame or friendship ; that nothing could make her
miserable, but his seeming to want happiness ; nothing
pleased, but his sympathizing with her pleasure.] A
continuance in prison soon robbed them of the little
they had left, and famine began to make its horrid
appearance ; yet still was neither found to murmur ;
they both looked upon their little boy, who, insensible
of their or his own distress, was playing about the room,]
with inexpressible yet silent anguish] when a messenger
came to inform them that Ariana was dead, and that
her will, in favour of a very distant relation, who
was now in another country, might be easily procured,
and burnt, in which case, all her large fortune would
revert to him, as being the next heir at law.

A proposal of so base a nature filled our unhappy
couple with horror ; they ordered the messenger
immediately out of the room, and falling upon each
other's neck, indulged an agony of sorrow ; for now
even all hopes of relief were banished. The messenger
who made the proposal, however, was only a spy sent
by Ariana to sound the dispositions of a man she loved
at once and persecuted. This lady, though warped by
wrong passions, was naturally kind, judicious, and
friendly. She found that all her attempts to shake the
constancy or the integrity of Sabinus were ineffectual ;
she had, therefore, begun to reflect, and to wonder
how she could, so long, and so unprovoked, injure such
uncommon fortitude and affection.

She had, from the next room, herself heard the
reception given to the messenger, and could not avoid
feeling all the force of superior virtue ; she therefore
reassumed her former goodness of heart ; she came in

the room with tears in her eyes, and acknowledged the severity of her former treatment. She bestowed her first care in providing them all the necessary supplies, and acknowledged them as the most deserving heirs of her fortune. From this moment Sabinus enjoyed an uninterrupted happiness with Olinda, and both were happy in the friendship and assistance of Ariana, who, dying soon after, left them in possession of a large estate, and, in her last moments, confessed that virtue was the only path to true glory ; and that, however innocence may for a time be depressed, a steady perseverance will, in time, lead it to a certain victory.

NUMBER VIII. SATURDAY, *November* 24, 1759.

OF THE OPERA IN ENGLAND

THE rise and fall of our amusements pretty much resemble that of empire. They this day flourish without any visible cause for such vigour ; the next they decay away, without any reason that can be assigned for their downfall. Some years ago the Italian opera was the only fashionable amusement among our nobility. The managers of the playhouses dreaded it as a mortal enemy, and our very poets listed themselves in the opposition ; at present, the house seems deserted, the *castrati* sing to empty benches ; even Prince Vologese himself, a youth of great expectations, sings himself out of breath, and rattles his chain to no purpose.

To say the truth, the opera, as it is conducted among us, is but a very humdrum amusement ; in other countries, the decorations are entirely magnificent, the singers all excellent, and the burlettas, or interludes, quite entertaining ; the best poets compose the words, and the best masters the music ; but with us it is other-

wise ; the decorations are but trifling, and cheap ; the
singers, Matei only excepted, but indifferent. Instead of
interlude, we have those sorts of skipping dances, which
are calculated for the galleries of the theatre. Every
performer sings his favourite song, and the music is
only a medley of old Italian airs, or some meagre modern
Capricio.

When such is the case, it is not much to be wondered,
if the opera is pretty much neglected ; the lower orders
of people have neither taste nor fortune to relish such
an entertainment ; they would find more satisfaction
in the *Roast Beef of Old England* than in the finest closes
of an eunuch ; they sleep amidst all the agony of recita-
tive : On the other hand, people of fortune or taste
can hardly be pleased where there is a visible poverty
in the decorations, and an entire want of taste in the
composition.

Would it not surprise one, that when Metastasio is
so well known in England, and so universally admired,
the manager or the composer should have recourse to
any other operas than those written by him ? I might
venture to say, that *written by Metastasio,* put up in
the bills of the day, would alone be sufficient to fill a
house, since thus the admirers of sense, as well as sound,
might find entertainment.

The performers also should be entreated to sing only
their parts, without clapping in any of their own
favourite airs. I must own, that such songs are generally
to me the most disagreeable in the world. Every
singer generally chooses a favourite air, not from the
excellency of the music, but from the difficulty ; such
songs are generally chosen as surprise rather than please,
where the performer may show his compass, his breath,
and his volubility.

From hence proceed those unnatural startings, those

unmusical closings, and shakes lengthened out to a painful continuance; such, indeed, may show a voice, but it must give a truly delicate ear the utmost uneasiness. Such tricks are not music; neither Corelli nor Pergolesi ever permitted them, and they begin even to be discontinued in Italy, where they first had their rise.

And now I am upon the subject: Our composers also should affect greater simplicity, let their base clef have all the variety they can give it; let the body of the music (if I may so express it) be as various as they please, but let them avoid ornamenting a barren groundwork; let them not attempt, by flourishing, to cheat us of solid harmony.

The works of Mr. Rameau are never heard without a surprising effect. I can attribute it only to this simplicity he everywhere observes, insomuch that some of his finest harmonies are often only octave and unison. This simple manner has greater powers than is generally imagined; and were not such a demonstration misplaced, I think, from the principles of music, it might be proved to be most agreeable.

But to leave general reflection. With the present set of performers, the operas, if the conductor thinks proper, may be carried on with some success, since they have all some merit; if not as actors, at least as singers. Signora Matei is at once both a perfect actress and a very fine singer. She is possessed of a fine sensibility in her manner, and seldom indulges those extravagant and unmusical flights of voice complained of before. Cornacini, on the other hand, is a very indifferent actor; has a most unmeaning face; seems not to feel his part; is infected with a passion of showing his compass; but to recompense all these defects, his voice is melodious; he has vast compass and great volubility; his swell and shake are perfectly fine, unless that he continues the latter too long. In short, whatever the defects of his action may be, they are amply recompensed by his excellency as a singer ; nor can I avoid fancying that he might make a much greater figure in an oratorio, than upon the stage.

However, upon the whole, I know not whether ever operas can be kept up in England ; they seem to be entirely exotic, and require the nicest management and care. Instead of this, the care of them is assigned to men unacquainted with the genius and disposition of the people they would amuse, and whose only motives are immediate gain. Whether a discontinuance of such entertainments would be more to the loss or the advantage of the nation, I will not take upon me to determine, since it is as much our interest to induce foreigners of taste among us on the one hand, as it is to discourage those trifling members of society who generally compose the operatical *dramatis personae*, on the other.

E S S A Y S.

BY

OLIVER GOLDSMITH.

COLLECTA REVIRESCUNT.

The SECOND EDITION, corrected.

LONDON:

Printed for W. GRIFFIN in Catharine-Street.

MDCCLXVI.

[Two 'Essays' in Verse: 'The Double Transformation' and 'A New Simile in the Manner of Swift' are omitted. They may be found in the companion volume of Goldsmith's Poems. The titles to the Essays have for the most part been supplied from the post-humous edition of 1798. A third essay on 'Beau Tibbs', not reprinted in *Essays*, 1765 (ed. 2, 1766), will be found in an Appendix to this volume.]

THE PREFACE

THE following Essays have already appeared at different times, and in different publications. The pamphlets in which they were inserted being generally unsuccessful, these shared the common fate, without assisting the bookseller's aims, or extending the writer's reputation. The public were too strenuously employed with their own follies, to be assiduous in estimating mine; so that many of my best attempts in this way have fallen victims to the transient topic of the times; the Ghost in Cock Lane, or the siege of Ticonderago.

But though they have passed pretty silently into the world, I can by no means complain of their circulation. The magazines and papers of the day have, indeed, been liberal enough in this respect. Most of these essays have been regularly reprinted twice or thrice a year, and conveyed to the public through the kennel of some engaging compilation. If there be a pride in multiplied editions, I have seen some of my labours sixteen times reprinted, and claimed by different parents as their own. I have seen them flourished at the beginning with praise, and signed at the end with the names of Philantos, Philalethes, Philaluctheros, and Philanthropos. These gentlemen have kindly stood sponsors to my productions; and, to flatter me more, have always taken my errors on themselves.

It is time, however, at last, to vindicate my claims; and as these entertainers of the public, as they call themselves, have partly lived upon me for some years let me now try if I cannot live a little upon myself I would desire, in this case, to imitate the fat man, whom

I have somewhere read of, in a shipwreck, who, when the sailors, pressed by famine, were taking slices from his posteriors to satisfy their hunger, insisted, with great justice, on having the first cut for himself.

Yet after all, I cannot be angry with any who have taken it into their heads, to think that whatever I write is worth reprinting, particularly when I consider how great a majority will think it scarce worth reading. Trifling and superficial are terms of reproach that are easily objected, and that carry an air of penetration in the observer. These faults have been objected to the following essays ; and it must be owned, in some measure, that the charge is true. However, I could have made them more metaphysical, had I thought fit ; but I would ask whether, in a short essay, it is not necessary to be superficial ? Before we have prepared to enter into the depths of a subject, in the usual forms, we have got to the bottom of our scanty page, and thus lose the honours of a victory, by too tedious a preparation for the combat.

There is another fault in this collection of trifles, which, I fear, will not be so easily pardoned. It will be alleged, that the humour of them (if any be found) is stale and hackneyed. This may be true enough as matters now stand, but I may with great truth assert, that the humour was new when I wrote it. Since that time, indeed, many of the topics which were first started here, have been hunted down, and many of the thoughts blown upon. In fact, these Essays were considered as quietly laid in the grave of oblivion ; and our modern compilers, like sextons and executioners, think it their undoubted right to pillage the dead.

However, whatever right I have to complain of the public, they can, as yet, have no just reason to complain of me. If I have written dull Essays, they have hitherto treated them as dull Essays. Thus far we are at least upon par, and until they think fit to make me their humble debtor, by praise, I am resolved not to lose a single inch of my self-importance. Instead, therefore, of attempting to establish a credit amongst them, it will perhaps be wiser to apply to some more distant correspondent ; and as my drafts are in some danger of being protested at home, it may not be imprudent, upon this occasion, to draw my bills upon Posterity.

ESSAYS

ESSAY I

INTRODUCTORY PAPER

[Altered from ' Introduction ' in *The Bee*, No. I]

THERE is not, perhaps, a more whimsical figure in nature, than a man of real modesty, who assumes an air of impudence ; who, while his heart beats with anxiety, studies ease, and affects good humour. In this situation, however, every unexperienced writer, as I am, finds himself. Impressed with the terrors of the tribunal before which he is going to appear, his natural humour turns to pertness, and for real wit he is obliged to substitute vivacity.

For my part, as I was never distinguished for address, and have often blundered in making my bow, I am at a loss whether to be merry or sad on this solemn occasion. Should I modestly decline all merit, it is too probable the hasty reader may take me at my word. If, on the other hand, like labourers in the magazine trade, I humbly presume to promise an epitome of all the good things that were ever said or written, those readers I most desire to please may forsake me.

My bookseller, in this dilemma perceiving my embarrassment, instantly offered his assistance and advice : ' You must know, sir,' says he, ' that the republic of ' letters is at present divided into several classes. One ' writer excels at a plan, or a title-page ; another works ' away the body of the book ; and the third is a dab ' at an index. Thus a magazine is not the result of any ' single man's industry ; but goes through as many hands ' as a new pin, before it is fit for the public. I fancy, sir,'

continues he, ' I can provide an eminent hand, and upon
' moderate terms, to draw up a promising plan to smooth
' up our readers a little, and pay them, as Colonel
' Chartres paid his seraglio, at the rate of three half-
' pence in hand, and three shillings more in promises.'

He was proceeding in his advice, which, however,
I thought proper to decline, by assuring him, that, as
I intended to pursue no fixed method, so it was impossible
to form any regular plan ; determined never to be
tedious, in order to be logical, wherever pleasure presented, I was resolved to follow.

It will be improper therefore to pall the reader's
curiosity by lessening his surprise, or anticipate any
pleasure I am able to procure him, by saying what shall
come next. Happy could any effort of mine, but repress
one criminal pleasure, or but for a moment fill up an
interval of anxiety ! How gladly would I lead mankind
from the vain prospects of life, to prospects of innocence
and ease, where every breeze breathes health, and every
sound is but the echo of tranquillity.

But whatever may be the merit of his intentions,
every writer is now convinced that he must be chiefly
indebted to good fortune for finding readers willing to
allow him any degree of reputation. It has been remarked,
that almost every character which has excited either
attention or pity, has owed part of its success to merit,
and part to an happy concurrence of circumstances in
its favour. Had Caesar or Cromwell exchanged countries,
the one might have been a sergeant, and the other an
exciseman. So it is with wit, which generally succeeds
more from being happily addressed, than from its native
poignancy. A jest calculated to spread at a gaming
table, may be received with perfect indifference should
it happen to drop in a mackerel boat. We have all seen
dunces triumph in some companies, where men of real

humour were disregarded, by a general combination in favour of stupidity. To drive the observation as far as it will go, should the labours of a writer who designs his performances for readers of a more refined appetite, fall into the hands of a devourer of compilations, what can he expect but contempt and confusion ? If his merits are to be determined by judges who estimate the value of a book from its bulk, or its frontispiece, every rival must acquire an easy superiority, who with persuasive eloquence promises four extraordinary pages of letter-press, or three beautiful prints, curiously coloured from nature.

Thus then, though I cannot promise as much entertainment, or as much elegance as others have done, yet the reader may be assured he shall have as much of both as I can. He shall, at least, find me alive while I study his entertainment ; for I solemnly assure him, I was never yet possessed of the secret of writing and sleeping.

During the course of this paper, therefore, all the wit and learning I have, are heartily at his service ; which if, after so candid a confession he should, notwithstanding, still find intolerably dull, or low, or sad stuff, this I protest is more than I know. I have a clear conscience, and am entirely out of the secret.

Yet I would not have him, upon the perusal of a single paper, pronounce me incorrigible ; he may try a second, which, as there is a studied difference in subject and style, may be more suited to his taste ; if this also fails, I must refer him to a third, or even to a fourth, in case of extremity : if he should still continue refractory, and find me dull to the last, I must inform him, with Bayes in the *Rehearsal*, that I think him a very odd kind of a fellow, and desire no more of his acquaintance. But still if my readers impute the general tenor of my subject to me as a fault, I must beg leave to tell them a story.

A traveller, in his way to Italy, found himself in a country where the inhabitants had each a large excrescence depending from the chin ; a deformity which, as it was endemic, and the people little used to strangers, it had been the custom, time immemorial, to look upon as the greatest beauty. Ladies grew toasts from the size of their chins, and no men were beaux whose faces were not broadest at the bottom. It was Sunday, a country church was at hand, and our traveller was willing to perform the duties of the day. Upon his first appearance at the church door, the eyes of all were naturally fixed upon the stranger ; but what was their amazement, when they found that he actually wanted that emblem of beauty, a pursed chin. Stifled bursts of laughter, winks, and whispers, circulated from visage to visage ; the prismatic figure of the stranger's face was a fund of infinite gaiety. Our traveller could no longer patiently continue an object for deformity to point at. ' Good folks,' said he, ' I perceive that I am a very ' ridiculous figure here, but I assure you am reckoned ' no way deformed at Home.'

ESSAY II

THE STORY OF *ALCANDER AND SEPTIMIUS*

TAKEN FROM A BYZANTINE HISTORIAN

[Altered from *The Bee*, No. I]

ATHENS, long after the decline of the Roman Empire, still continued the seat of learning, politeness, and wisdom. Theodoric, the Ostrogoth, repaired the schools which barbarity was suffering to fall into decay, and continued those pensions to men of learning, which avaricious governors had monopolized.

In this city, and about this period, Aleander and

Septimius were fellow students together. The one, the most subtle reasoner of all the Lyceum ; the other, the most eloquent speaker in the academic grove. Mutual admiration soon begot a friendship. Their fortunes were nearly equal, and they were natives of the two most celebrated cities in the world ; for Aleander was of Athens, Septimius came from Rome.

In this state of harmony they lived for some time together, when Aleander, after passing the first part of his youth in the indolence of philosophy, thought at length of entering into the busy world ; and, as a step previous to this, placed his affections on Hypatia, a lady of exquisite beauty. The day of their intended nuptials was fixed ; the previous ceremonies were performed ; and nothing now remained but her being conducted in triumph to the apartment of the intended bridegroom.

Alcander's exultation in his own happiness, or being unable to enjoy any satisfaction without making his friend Septimius a partner, prevailed upon him to introduce Hypatia to his fellow student ; which he did with all the gaiety of a man who found himself equally happy in friendship and love. But this was an interview fatal to the future peace of both ; for Septimius no sooner saw her, but he was smitten with an involuntary passion ; and, though he used every effort to suppress desires at once so imprudent and unjust, the emotions of his mind in a short time became so strong, that they brought on a fever, which the physicians judged incurable.

During this illness, Aleander watched him with all the anxiety of fondness, and brought his mistress to join in those amiable offices of friendship. The sagacity of the physicians, by these means, soon discovered that the cause of their patient's disorder was love ; and Aleander being apprised of their discovery, at length extorted a confession from the reluctant dying lover.

It would but delay the narrative to describe the conflict between love and friendship in the breast of Aleander on this occasion ; it is enough to say, that the Athenians were at that time arrived at such refinement in morals, that every virtue was carried to excess. In short, forgetful of his own felicity, he gave up his intended bride, in all her charms, to the young Roman. They were married privately by his connivance, and this unlooked-for change of fortune wrought as unexpected a change in the constitution of the now happy Septimius. In a few days he was perfectly recovered, and set out with his fair partner for Rome. Here, by an exertion of those talents which he was so eminently possessed of, Septimius, in a few years, arrived at the highest dignities of the state, and was constituted the city judge, or praetor.

In the meantime Aleander not only felt the pain of being separated from his friend and his mistress, but a prosecution was also commenced against him by the relations of Hypatia, for having basely given up his bride, as was suggested, for money. His innocence of the crime laid to his charge, and even his eloquence in his own defence, were not able to withstand the influence of a powerful party. He was cast and condemned to pay an enormous fine. However, being unable to raise so large a sum at the time appointed, his possessions were confiscated, he himself was stripped of the habit of freedom, exposed as a slave in the market-place, and sold to the highest bidder.

A merchant of Thrace becoming his purchaser, Aleander, with some other companions of distress, was carried into that region of desolation and sterility. His stated employment was to follow the herds of an imperious master, and his success in hunting was all that was allowed him to supply his precarious subsistence.

Every morning waked him to a renewal of famine or toil, and every change of season served but to aggravate his unsheltered distress. After some years of bondage, however, an opportunity of escaping offered ; he embraced it with ardour ; so that travelling by night, and lodging in caverns by day, to shorten a long story, he at last arrived in Rome. The same day on which Aleander arrived, Septimius sat administering justice in the forum, whither our wanderer came, expecting to be instantly known, and publicly acknowledged, by his former friend. Here he stood the whole day amongst the crowd, watching the eyes of the judge, and expecting to be taken notice of ; but he was so much altered by a long succession of hardships, that he continued unnoted among the rest ; and, in the evening, when he was going up to the praetor's chair, he was brutally repulsed by the attending lictors. The attention of the poor is generally driven from one ungrateful object to another ; for night coming on, he now found himself under a necessity of seeking a place to lie in, and yet knew not where to apply. All emaciated, and in rags as he was, none of the citizens would harbour so much wretchedness ; and sleeping in the streets might be attended with interruption or danger : in short, he was obliged to take up his lodging in one of the tombs without the city, the usual retreat of guilt, poverty, and despair. In this mansion of horror, laying his head upon an inverted urn, he forgot his miseries for a while in sleep ; and found, on his flinty couch, more ease than beds of down can supply to the guilty.

As he continued here, about midnight, two robbers came to make this their retreat ; but happening to disagree about the division of their plunder, one of them stabbed the other to the heart, and left him weltering in blood at the entrance. In these circumstances he was found next morning dead at the mouth of the vault. This naturally inducing a further inquiry, an alarm was spread; the cave was examined; and Aleander being found, was immediately apprehended and accused of robbery and murder. The circumstances against him were strong, and the wretchedness of his appearance confirmed suspicion. Misfortune and he were now so long acquainted, that he at last became regardless of life. He detested a world where he had found only ingratitude, falsehood and cruelty; he was determined to make no defence; and, thus lowering with resolution, he was dragged, bound with cords, before the tribunal of Septimius. As the proofs were positive against him, and he offered nothing in his own vindication, the judge was proceeding to doom him to a most cruel and ignominious death, when the attention of the multitude was soon divided by another object. The robber, who had been really guilty, was apprehended selling his plunder, and, struck with a panic, had confessed his crime. He was brought bound to the same tribunal, and acquitted every other person of any partnership in his guilt. Alcander's innocence therefore appeared, but the sullen rashness of his conduct remained a wonder to the surrounding multitude; but their astonishment was still further increased when they saw their judge start from his tribunal to embrace the supposed criminal: Septimius recollected his friend and former benefactor, and hung upon his neck with tears of pity and of joy. Need the sequel be related? Aleander was acquitted; shared the friendship and honours of the principal citizens of Rome; lived afterwards in happiness and ease; and left it to be engraved on his tomb, That no circumstances are so desperate, which Providence may not relieve.

ESSAY III

ON HAPPINESS OF TEMPER

[Altered from 'Happiness in a great measure dependent on Constitution,' in *The Bee*, No. II]

WHEN I reflect on the unambitious retirement in which I passed the earlier part of my life in the country, I cannot avoid feeling some pain in thinking that those happy days are never to return. In that retreat, all nature seemed capable of affording pleasure; I then made no refinements on happiness, but could be pleased with the most awkward efforts of rustic mirth; thought cross-purposes the highest stretch of human wit; and questions and commands the most rational way of spending the evening. Happy could so charming an illusion still continue! I find that age and knowledge only contribute to sour our dispositions. My present enjoyments may be more refined, but they are infinitely less pleasing. The pleasure the best actor gives, can no way compare to that I have received from a country wag who imitated a Quaker's sermon. The music of the finest singer is dissonance to what I felt when our old dairymaid sung me into tears with 'Johnny Armstrong's Last Good Night ', or ' The Cruelty of Barbara Allen '.

Writers of every age have endeavoured to show that pleasure is in us, and not in the objects offered for our amusement. If the soul be happily disposed, every thing becomes capable of affording entertainment; and distress will almost want a name. Every occurrence passes in review like the figures of a procession; some may be awkward, others ill dressed; but none but a fool is for this enraged with the master of the ceremonies.

I remember to have once seen a slave in a fortification

in Flanders, who appeared no way touched with his situation. He was maimed, deformed, and chained; obliged to toil from the appearance of day till nightfall, and condemned to this for life; yet, with all these circumstances of apparent wretchedness, he sung, would have danced but that he wanted a leg, and appeared the merriest, happiest man of all the garrison. What a practical philosopher was here; a happy constitution supplied philosophy; and, though seemingly destitute of wisdom, he was really wise. No reading or study had contributed to disenchant the fairyland around him. Every thing furnished him with an opportunity of mirth; and, though some thought him, from his insensibility, a fool, he was such an idiot as philosophers should wish to imitate; for all philosophy is only forcing the trade of happiness, when nature seems to deny the means.

They who, like our slave, can place themselves on that side of the world in which everything appears in a pleasing light, will find something in every occurrence to excite their good humour. The most calamitous events, either to themselves or others, can bring no new affliction; the whole world is to them a theatre, on which comedies only are acted. All the bustle of heroism, or the rants of ambition, serve only to heighten the absurdity of the scene, and make the humour more poignant. They feel, in short, as little anguish at their own distress, or the complaints of others, as the undertaker, though dressed in black, feels sorrow at a funeral.

Of all the men I ever read of, the famous Cardinal de Retz possessed this happiness of temper in the highest degree. As he was a man of gallantry, and despised all that wore the pedantic appearance of philosophy, wherever pleasure was to be sold, he was generally foremost to raise the auction. Being an universal admirer of the fair sex, when he found one lady cruel, he generally fell in love with another, from whom he expected a more favourable reception : if she too rejected his addresses, he never thought of retiring into deserts, or pining in hopeless distress. He persuaded himself, that, instead of loving the lady, he only fancied that he had loved her, and so all was well again. When Fortune wore her angriest look, and he at last fell into the power of his most deadly enemy, Cardinal Mazarine (being confined a close prisoner in the castle of Valenciennes) he never attempted to support his distress by wisdom or philosophy, for he pretended to neither. He only laughed at himself and his persecutor, and seemed infinitely pleased at his new situation. In this mansion of distress, though secluded from his friends, though denied all the amusements, and even the conveniences, of life, he still retained his good humour ; laughed at all the little spite of his enemies ; and carried the jest so far, as to be revenged, by writing the life of his jailer.

All that the wisdom of the proud can teach, is to be stubborn or sullen under misfortunes. The cardinal's example will instruct us to be merry in circumstances of the highest affliction. It matters not whether our good humour be construed by others into insensibility, or even idiotism ; it is happiness to ourselves, and none but a fool would measure his satisfaction by what the world thinks of it : for my own part, I never pass by one of our prisons for debt, that I do not envy that felicity which is still going forward among those people, who forget the cares of the world by being shut out from its ambition.

The happiest silly fellow I ever knew, was of the number of those good-natured creatures that are said to do no harm to any but themselves. Whenever he fell into any misery, he usually called it, Seeing Life. If his head was broke by a chairman, or his pocket picked by a sharper, he comforted himself by imitating the Hibernian dialect of the one, or the more fashionable cant of the other. Nothing came amiss to him. His inattention to money matters had incensed his father to such a degree, that all the intercession of friends in his favour was fruitless. The old gentleman was on his death-bed. The whole family, and Dick among the number, gathered around him. ' I leave my second son, Andrew,' said the expiring miser, ' my whole estate, and desire him to be ' frugal.' Andrew, in a sorrowful tone, as is usual on these occasions, prayed Heaven to prolong his life and health to enjoy it himself. ' I recommend Simon, my ' third son, to the care of his elder brother, and leave him ' beside four thousand pounds.' ' Ah ! father,' cried Simon (in great affliction to be sure), ' may Heaven ' give you life and health to enjoy it yourself.' At last, turning to poor Dick, ' As for you, you have always been ' a sad dog ; you'll never come to good ; you'll never be ' rich ; I'll leave you a shilling to buy a halter.' ' Ah ! ' father,' cries Dick, without any emotion, ' may Heaven ' give you life and health to enjoy it yourself.' This was all the trouble the loss of fortune gave this thoughtless imprudent creature. However, the tenderness of an uncle recompensed the neglect of a father ; and my friend is now not only excessively good-humoured, but competently rich.

Yes, let the world cry out at a bankrupt who appears at a ball ; at an author who laughs at the public, which pronounces him a dunce ; at a general who smiles at the reproach of the vulgar, or the lady who keeps her good humour in spite of scandal ; but such is the wisest behaviour that any of us can possibly assume ; it is certainly a better way to oppose calamity by dissipation, than to take up the arms of reason or resolution to oppose it : by the first method, we forget our miseries ;

by the last, we only conceal them from others ; by struggling with misfortunes, we are sure to receive some wounds in the conflict ; but a sure method to come off victorious, is by running away.

ESSAY IV

DESCRIPTION OF VARIOUS CLUBS

[The Busy Body, October 13, 1759]

I REMEMBER to have read in some philosopher (I believe in Tom Brown's works), that, let a man's character, sentiments, or complexion, be what they will, he can find company in London to match them. If he be splenetic, he may every day meet companions on the seats in St. James's Park, with whose groans he may mix his own, and pathetically talk of the weather. If he be passionate, he may vent his rage among the old orators at Slaughter's coffee-house, and damn the nation because it keeps him from starving. If he be phlegmatic, he may sit in silence at the Hum-drum Club in Ivy Lane ; and, if actually mad, he may find very good company in Moorfields, either at Bedlam or the Foundery, ready to cultivate a nearer acquaintance.

But, although such as have a knowledge of the town, may easily class themselves with tempers congenial to their own ; a countryman who comes to live in London, finds nothing more difficult. With regard to myself, none ever tried with more assiduity, or came off with such indifferent success. I spent a whole season in the search, during which time my name has been enrolled in societies, lodges, convocations, and meetings without number. To some I was introduced by a friend, to others invited by an advertisement ; to these I introduced myself, and to those I changed my name to gain admittance. In short, no coquette was ever more solicitous to match her ribbons to her complexion, than I to suit my club to my temper, for I was too obstinate to bring my temper to conform to it.

The first club I entered upon coming to town, was that of the Choice Spirits. The name was entirely suited to my taste ; I was a lover of mirth, good humour, and even sometimes of fun, from my childhood.

As no other passport was requisite but the payment of two shillings at the door, I introduced myself without further ceremony to the members, who were already assembled, and had, for some time, begun upon business. The Grand, with a mallet in his hand, presided at the head of the table. I could not avoid, upon my entrance, making use of all my skill in physiognomy, in order to discover that superiority of genius in men, who had taken a title so superior to the rest of mankind. I expected to see the lines of every face marked with strong thinking ; but, though I had some skill in this science, I could for my life discover nothing but a pert simper, fat, or profound stupidity.

My speculations were soon interrupted by the Grand, who had knocked down Mr. Spriggins for a song. I was, upon this, whispered by one of the company who sat next me, that I should now see something touched off to a nicety, for Mr. Spriggins was going to give us ' Mad Tom ' in all its glory. Mr. Spriggins endeavoured to excuse himself ; for, as he was to act a madman and a king, it was impossible to go through the part properly without a crown and chains. His excuses were overruled by a great majority, and with much vociferation. The president ordered up the jack-chain, and, instead of a crown, our performer covered his brows with an inverted jordan. After he had rattled his chain, and shook his head, to the great delight of the whole company, he began his song. As I have heard few young fellows offer to sing in company, that did not expose themselves, it was no great disappointment to me to find Mr. Spriggins among the number; however, not to seem an odd fish, I rose from my seat in rapture, cried out, 'Bravo! 'Encore!' and slapped the table as loud as any of the rest.

The gentleman who sat next me seemed highly pleased with my taste, and the ardour of my approbation; and whispering, told me that I had suffered an immense loss; for, had I come a few minutes sooner, I might have heard 'Gee-ho-Dobbin' sung in a tip-top manner by the pimple-nosed spirit at the president's right elbow: but he was evaporated before I came.

As I was expressing my uneasiness at this disappointment, I found the attention of the company employed upon a fat figure, who, with a voice more rough than the Staffordshire giant's, was giving us, 'The Softly Sweet, 'in Lydian Measure,' of *Alexander's Feast*. After a short pause of admiration, to this succeeded a Welsh dialogue, with the humours of Teague and Taffy: after that, came on 'Old Jackson', with a story between every stanza: next was sung 'The Dust-cart', and then 'Solomon's Song'. The glass began now to circulate pretty freely; those who were silent when sober, would now be heard in their turn; every man had his song, and he saw no reason why he should not be heard as well as any of the rest: one begged to be heard while he gave 'Death and the Lady' in high taste; another sung to a plate which he kept trundling on the edges; nothing was now heard but singing; voice rose above voice, till the whole became one universal shout, when the landlord came to acquaint the company that the reckoning was drank out. Rabelais calls the moments in which a reckoning is mentioned, the most melancholy of our lives:

never was so much noise so quickly quelled, as by this short but pathetic oration of our landlord : ' Drank out,' was echoed in a tone of discontent round the table : ' Drank out already ! that was very odd ! that so much ' punch could be drank out already: impossible ! ' The landlord, however, seeming resolved not to retreat from his first assurances, the company was dissolved, and a president chosen for the night ensuing.

A friend of mine, to whom I was complaining some time after of the entertainment I have been describing, proposed to bring me to the club that he frequented ; which he fancied would suit the gravity of my temper exactly. ' We have, at the Muzzy Club,' says he, ' no ' riotous mirth, nor awkward ribaldry ; no confusion or ' bawling ; all is conducted with wisdom and decency : ' besides, some of our members are worth forty thousand ' pounds ; men of prudence and foresight every one of ' them : these are the proper acquaintance, and to such ' I will to-night introduce you.' I was charmed at the proposal : to be acquainted with men worth forty thousand pounds, and to talk wisdom the whole night, were offers that threw me into rapture.

At seven o'clock I was accordingly introduced by my friend, not indeed to the company ; for, though I made my best bow, they seemed insensible of my approach, but to the table at which they were sitting. Upon my entering the room, I could not avoid feeling a secret veneration from the solemnity of the scene before me ; the members kept a profound silence, each with a pipe in his mouth, and a pewter pot in his hand, and with faces that might easily be construed into absolute wisdom. Happy society, thought I to myself, where the members think before they speak, deliver nothing rashly, but convey their thoughts to each other pregnant with meaning, and matured by reflection.

In this pleasing speculation I continued a full half-hour, expecting each moment that somebody would begin to open his mouth ; every time the pipe was laid down, I expected it was to speak ; but it was only to spit. At length, resolving to break the charm myself, and overcome their extreme diffidence, for to this I imputed their silence, I rubbed my hands, and, looking as wise as possible, observed that the nights began to grow a little coolish at this time of the year. This, as it was directed to none of the company in particular, none thought himself obliged to answer ; wherefore I continued still to rub my hands and look wise. My next effort was addressed to a gentleman who sat next me ; to whom I òbserved, that the beer was extreme good : my neighbour made no reply, but by a large puff of tobacco-smoke.

I now began to be uneasy in this dumb society, till one of them a little relieved me by observing, that bread had not risen these three weeks : ' Aye,' says another, still keeping the pipe in his mouth, ' that puts me in ' mind of a pleasant story about that—hem—very well'; ' you must know—but before I begin—Sir, my service ' to you—where was I ? '

My next club goes by the name of the Harmonical Society ; probably from that love of order and friendship which every person commends in institutions of this nature. The landlord was himself founder. The money spent is fourpence each ; and they sometimes whip for a double reckoning. To this club few recommendations are requisite, except the introductory fourpence, and my landlord's good word, which, as he gains by it, he never refuses.

We all here talked and behaved as everybody else usually does on his club-night ; we discussed the topic of the day, drank each other's healths, snuffed the candles with our fingers, and filled our pipes from the same plate of tobacco. The company saluted each other in the common manner. Mr. Bellows-mender hoped Mr. Currycomb-maker had not caught cold going home the last club-night; and he returned the compliment, by hoping that young Master Bellows-mender had got well again of the chin-cough. Doctor Twist told us a story of a parliament-man with whom he was intimately acquainted; while the bag-man, at the same time, was telling a better story of a noble lord with whom he could do anything. A gentleman in a black wig and leather breeches, at t'other end of the table, was engaged in a long narrative of the Ghost in Cock Lane; he had read it in the papers of the day, and was telling it to some that sat next him, who could not read. Near him Mr. Dibbins was disputing on the old subject of religion with a Jew pedlar, over the table, while the president vainly knocked down Mr. Leathersides for a song. Besides the combinations of these voices, which I could hear altogether, and which formed an upper part to the concert, there were several others playing under-parts by themselves, and endeavouring to fasten on some luckless neighbour's ear, who was himself bent upon the same design against some other.

We have often heard of the speech of a corporation, and this induced me to transcribe a speech of this club, taken in shorthand, word for word, as it was spoken by every member of the company. It may be necessary to observe, that the man who told of the ghost had the loudest voice, and the longest story to tell, so that his continuing narrative filled every chasm in the conversation.

' So, Sir, d'ye perceive me, the ghost giving three loud raps at the bed-post——Says my lord to .me, My dear Smokeum, you know there is no man upon the face of the yearth for whom I have so high——A damnable false heretical opinion of all sound doctrine and good learning ; for I'll tell it aloud, and spare not that— Silence for a song ; Mr. Leathersides for a song——" As " I was a walking upon the highway, I met a young " damsel "——Then what brings you here ? says the parson to the ghost——Sanconiathan, Manetho, and Berosus——The whole way from Islington turnpike to Dog-house bar—Dam—As for Abel Drugger, Sir, he's damn'd low in it ; my 'prentice boy has more of the gentleman than he——For murder will out one time or another ; and none but a ghost, you know, gentlemen, can——Damme if I don't ; for my friend, whom you know, gentlemen, and who is a parliament-man, a man of consequence, a dear honest creature, to be sure ; we were laughing last night at——Death and damnation upon all his posterity, by simply barely tasting—— Sour grapes, as the fox said once when he could not reach them ; and I'll, I'll tell you a story about that, that will make you burst your sides with laughing : A fox once——Will nobody listen to the song——" As I was " a walking upon the highway, I met a young damsel both " buxom and gay "—No ghost, gentlemen, can be murdered ; nor did I ever hear but of one ghost killed in all my life, and that was stabbed in the belly with a——My blood and soul if I don't——Mr. Bellows- mender, I have the honour of drinking your very good health——Blast me if I do——dam—blood—bugs—fire —whizz—blid—tit—rat—trip '——

Were I to be angry at men for being fools, I could here find ample room for declamation ; but, alas ! I have been a fool myself ; and why should I be angry with them for being something so natural to every child of humanity ?

Fatigued with this society, I was introduced, the

following night, to a club of fashion. On taking my place, I found the conversation sufficiently easy, and tolerably good-natured ; for my lord and Sir Paul were not yet arrived. I now thought myself completely fitted ; and resolving to seek no farther, determined to take up my residence here for the winter ; while my temper began to open insensibly to the cheerfulness I saw diffused on every face in the room : but the delusion soon vanished, when the waiter came to apprise us that his lordship and Sir Paul were just arrived.

From this moment all our felicity was at an end ; our new guests bustled into the room, and took their seats at the head of the table. Adieu now all confidence; every creature strove who should most recommend himself to our members of distinction. Each seemed quite regardless of pleasing any but our new guests ; and, what before wore the appearance of friendship, was now turned into rivalry.

Yet I could not observe that, amidst all this flattery and obsequious attention, our great men took any notice of the rest of the company. Their whole discourse was addressed to each other. Sir Paul told his lordship a long story of Moravia the Jew ; and his lordship gave Sir Paul a very long account of his new method of managing silkworms : he led him, and consequently the rest of the company, through all the stages of feeding, sunning, and hatching ; with an episode on mulberry-trees, a digression upon grass-seeds, and a long parenthesis about his new postilion. In this manner we travelled on, wishing every story to be the last ; but all in vain ;

' Hills over hills, and Alps on Alps arose.'

The last club in which I was enrolled a member, was a society of moral philosophers, as they called themselves, who assembled twice a week, in order to show the absurdity of the present mode of religion, and establish a new one in its stead.

I found the members very warmly disputing when I arrived ; not indeed about religion or ethics, but about who had neglected to lay down his preliminary sixpence upon entering the room. The president swore that he had laid his own down, and so swore all the company.

During this contest, I had an opportunity of observing the laws, and also the members, of the society. The president, who had been, as I was told, lately a bankrupt, was a tall, pale figure, with a long black wig ; the next to him was dressed in a large white wig, and a black cravat ; a third, by the brownness of his complexion, seemed a native of Jamaica ; and a fourth, by his hue, appeared to be a blacksmith. But their rules will give the most just idea of their learning and principles.

I. We, being a laudable society of moral philosophers, intends to dispute twice a week about religion and priest-craft ; leaving behind us old wives' tales, and following good learning and sound sense. And if so be, that any other persons has a mind to be of the society, they shall be entitled so to do, upon paying the sum of three shillings, to be spent by the company in punch.

II. That no member get drunk before nine of the clock, upon pain of forfeiting threepence, to be spent by the company in punch.

III. That, as members are sometimes apt to go away without paying, every person shall pay sixpence upon his entering the room ; and all disputes shall be settled by a majority ; and all fines shall be paid in punch.

IV. That sixpence shall be every night given to the president, in order to buy books of learning for the good of the society : the president has already put himself to a good deal of expense in buying books for the club ;

particularly the works of Tully, Socrates, and Cicero, which he will soon read to the society.

V. All them who brings a new argument against religion, and who, being a philosopher, and a man of learning, as the rest of us is, shall be admitted to the freedom of the society, upon paying sixpence only, to be spent in punch.

VI. Whenever we are to have an extraordinary meeting, it shall be advertised by some outlandish name in the newspapers.

> SAUNDERS MAC WILD, President.
> ANTHONY BLEWIT, Vice-President,
> his X mark.
> WILLIAM TURPIN, Secretary.

ESSAY V

[On the Use of Language. Altered from *The Bee*, No. III]

IT is usually said by grammarians, that the use of language is to express our wants and desires ; but men who know the world, hold, and I think with some show of reason, that he who best knows how to keep his necessities private, is the most likely person to have them redressed ; and that the true use of speech is not so much to express our wants as to conceal them.

When we reflect on the manner in which mankind generally confer their favours, there appears something so attractive in riches, that the large heap generally collects from the smaller ; and the poor find as much pleasure in increasing the enormous mass of the rich, as the miser, who owns it, sees happiness in its increase. Nor is there in this anything repugnant to the laws of morality. Seneca himself allows, that in conferring benefits, the present should always be suited to the dignity of the receiver. Thus the rich receive large presents, and are thanked for accepting them. Men of middling stations are obliged to be content with presents something less ; while the beggar, who may be truly said to want indeed, is well paid if a farthing rewards his warmest solicitations.

Every man who has seen the world, and has had his ups and downs in life, as the expression is, must have frequently experienced the truth of this doctrine ; and must know, that to have much, or to seem to have it, is the only way to have more. Ovid finely compares a man of broken fortune to a falling column ; the lower it sinks, the greater is that weight it is obliged to sustain. Thus, when a man's circumstances are such that he has no occasion to borrow, he finds numbers willing to lend him ; but, should his wants be such that he sues for a trifle, it is two to one whether he may be trusted with the smallest sum. A certain young fellow whom I knew, whenever he had occasion to ask his friend for a guinea, used to prelude his request as if he wanted two hundred ; and talked so familiarly of large sums, that none could ever think he wanted a small one. The same gentleman, whenever he wanted credit for a suit of clothes, always made the proposal in a laced coat ; for he found by experience, that, if he appeared shabby on these occasions, his tailor had taken an oath against trusting ; or, what was every whit as bad, his foreman was out of the way, and would not be at home for some time.

There can be no inducements to reveal our wants, except to find pity, and by this means relief ; but before a poor man opens his mind in such circumstances, he should first consider whether he is contented to lose the esteem of the person he solicits, and whether he is willing to give up friendship to excite compassion. Pity and friendship are passions incompatible with each other ;

and it is impossible that both can reside in any breast for the smallest space, without impairing each other. Friendship is made up of esteem and pleasure ; pity is composed of sorrow and contempt ; the mind may, for some time, fluctuate between them, but it can never entertain both at once.

In fact, pity, though it may often relieve, is but, at best, a short-lived passion, and seldom affords distress more than transitory assistance ; with some it scarce lasts from the first impulse till the hand can be put into the pocket ; with others, it may continue for twice that space ; and on some of extraordinary sensibility, I have seen it operate for half an hour together : but still, last as it may, it generally produces but beggarly effects ; and where, from this motive, we give five farthings, from others we give pounds. Whatever be our feelings from the first impulse of distress, when the same distress solicits a second time, we then feel with diminished sensibility ; and, like the repetition of an echo, every stroke becomes weaker ; till at last our sensations lose all mixture of sorrow, and degenerate into downright contempt.

These speculations bring to my mind the fate of a very good-natured fellow, who is now no more. He was bred in a compting-house, and his father dying just as he was out of his time, left him a handsome fortune and many friends to advise with. The restraint in which my friend had been brought up, had thrown a gloom upon his temper, which some regarded as prudence ; and, from such considerations, he had every day repeated offers of friendship. Such as had money, were ready to offer him their assistance that way ; and they who had daughters, frequently, in the warmth of affection, advised him to marry. My friend, however, was in good circumstances ; he wanted neither money, friends, nor a wife, and therefore modestly declined their proposals.

Some errors, however, in the management of his affairs, and several losses in trade, soon brought him to a different way of thinking ; and he at last considered, that it was his best way to let his friends know that their offers were at length acceptable. His first address was to a scrivener, who had formerly made him frequent offers of money and friendship, at a time when, perhaps, he knew those offers would have been refused. As a man, therefore, confident of not being refused, he requested the use of a hundred guineas for a few days, as he just then had occasion for money. 'And pray, Sir,' replied the scrivener, 'do you want all this money ? ' 'Want 'it, Sir ! ' says the other : 'if I did not want it I should 'not have asked it.' 'I am sorry for that,' says the friend ; 'for those who want money when they borrow, 'will always want money when they should come to 'pay. To say the truth, Sir, money is money now ; 'and I believe it is all sunk in the bottom of the sea, 'for my part ; he that has got a little, is a fool if he does 'not keep what he has got.'

Not quite disconcerted by this refusal, our adventurer was resolved to apply to another, whom he knew was the very best friend he had in the world. The gentleman whom he now addressed, received his proposal with all the affability that could be expected from generous friendship. 'Let me see—you want an hundred guineas ; 'and pray, dear Jack, would not fifty answer ? ' 'If 'you have but fifty to spare, Sir, I must be contented.' 'Fifty to spare ! I do not say that, for I believe I have 'but twenty about me.' 'Then I must borrow the 'other thirty from some other friend.' 'And pray,' replied the friend, 'would it not be the best way to 'borrow the whole money from that other friend, and 'then one note will serve for all, you know ? You 'know, my dear Sir, that you need make no ceremony

'with me at any time ; you know I'm your friend ;
'and when you choose a bit of dinner or so——You,
'Tom, see the gentleman down. You won't forget to
'dine with us now and then. Your very humble servant.'

Distressed, but not discouraged, at this treatment,
he was at last resolved to find that assistance from love,
which he could not have from friendship. A young
lady, a distant relation by the mother's side, had a fortune
in her own hands.; and, as she had already made all
the advances that her sex's modesty would permit,
he made his proposal with confidence. He soon, however,
perceived, that no bankrupt ever found the fair one
kind. She had lately fallen deeply in love with another,
who had more money, and the whole neighbourhood
thought it would be a match.

Every day now began to strip my poor friend of his
former finery ; his clothes flew, piece by piece, to the
pawnbroker's, and he seemed at length equipped in the
genuine livery of misfortune. But still he thought
himself secure from actual necessity ; the numberless
invitations he had received to dine, even after his
losses, were yet unanswered ; he was therefore now
resolved to accept of a dinner, because he wanted one ;
and in this manner he actually lived among his friends
a whole week without being openly affronted. The last
place I saw him in was at a reverend divine's. He had,
as he fancied, just nicked the time of dinner, for he came
in as the cloth was laying. He took a chair without
being desired, and talked for some time without being
attended to. He assured the company, that nothing
procured so good an appetite as a walk in the Park,
where he had been that morning. He went on, and
praised the figure of the damask table-cloth ; talked of
a feast where he had been the day before, but that the
venison was overdone. But all this procured him no

invitation : finding therefore the gentleman of the house insensible to all his fetches, he thought proper, at last, to retire, and mend his appetite by a second walk in the Park.

✓You then, O ye beggars of my acquaintance, whether in rags or lace, whether in Kent Street or the Mall, whether at the Smyrna or St. Giles's, might I be permitted to advise as a friend, never seem to want the favour which you solicit. Apply to every passion but human pity for redress : you may find permanent relief from vanity, from self-interest, or from avarice, but from compassion never. The very eloquence of a poor man is disgusting ; and that mouth which is opened even by wisdom, is seldom expected to close without the horrors of a petition.

✓ To ward off the gripe of Poverty, you must pretend to be a stranger to her, and she will at least use you with ceremony. If you be caught dining upon a half-penny porringer of pease-soup and potatoes, praise the wholesomeness of your frugal repast. You may observe that Dr. Cheyne has prescribed pease-broth for the gravel ; hint that you are not one of those who are always making a deity of your belly. If, again, you are obliged to wear flimsy stuff in the midst of winter, be the first to remark, that stuffs are very much worn at Paris ; or, if there be found some irreparable defects in any part of your equipage, which cannot be concealed by all the arts of sitting cross-legged, coaxing, or darning, say, that neither you nor Samson Gideon were ever very fond of dress. If you be a philosopher, hint that Plato or Seneca are the tailors you choose to employ ; assure the company that man ought to be content with a bare covering, since what now is so much his pride, was formerly his shame. In short, however caught, never give out ; but ascribe to the frugality of your disposition what others might be apt to attribute to the narrowness of your circumstances. To be poor, and to seem poor, is a certain method never to rise : pride in the great is hateful ; in the wise it is ridiculous ; but beggarly pride is a rational vanity which I have been taught to applaud and excuse. √

ESSAY VI

[On Generosity and Justice. Altered from *The Bee*, No. III]

LYSIPPUS is a man whose greatness of soul the whole world admires. His generosity is such, that it prevents a demand, and saves the receiver the trouble and the confusion of a request. His liberality also does not oblige more by its greatness, than by his inimitable grace in giving. Sometimes he even distributes his bounties to strangers, and has been known to do good offices to those who professed themselves his enemies. All the world are unanimous in the praise of his generosity ; there is only one sort of people who complain of his conduct. Lysippus does not pay his debts.

It is no difficult matter to account for a conduct so seemingly incompatible with itself. There is greatness in being generous, and there is only simple justice in his satisfying creditors. Generosity is the part of a soul raised above the vulgar. There is in it something of what we admire in heroes, and praise with a degree of rapture. Justice, on the contrary, is a mere mechanic virtue, only fit for tradesmen, and what is practised by every broker in 'Change Alley.

In paying his debts a man barely does his duty, and it is an action attended with no sort of glory. Should Lysippus satisfy his creditors, who would be at the pains of telling it to the world ? Generosity is a virtue of a very different complexion. It is raised above duty, and, from its elevation, attracts the attention and the praises of us little mortals below.

In this manner do men generally reason upon justice and generosity. The first is despised, though a virtue essential to the good of society ; and the other attracts our esteem, which too frequently proceeds from an impetuosity of temper, rather directed by vanity than reason. Lysippus is told that his banker asks a debt of forty pounds, and that a distressed acquaintance petitions for the same sum. He gives it without hesitating to the latter, for he demands as a favour what the former requires as a debt.

Mankind in general are not sufficiently acquainted with the import of the word Justice : it is commonly believed to consist only in a performance of those duties to which the laws of society can oblige us. This, I allow, is sometimes the import of the word, and in this sense justice is distinguished from equity ; but there is a justice still more extensive, and which can be shown to embrace all the virtues united.

Justice may be defined, that virtue which impels us to give to every person what is his due. In this extended sense of the word, it comprehends the practice of every virtue which reason prescribes, or society should expect. Our duty to our Maker, to each other, and to ourselves, are fully answered, if we give them what we owe them. Thus justice, properly speaking, is the only virtue, and all the rest have their origin in it.

The qualities of candour, fortitude, charity, and generosity, for instance, are not in their own nature virtues ; and, if ever they deserve the title, it is owing only to justice, which impels and directs them. Without such a moderator, candour might become indiscretion, fortitude obstinacy, charity imprudence, and generosity mistaken profusion.

A disinterested action, if it be not conducted by justice, is, at best, indifferent in its nature, and not unfrequently even turns to vice. The expenses of society, of presents, of entertainments, and the other helps to cheerfulness, are actions merely indifferent, when not repugnant to a better method of disposing of our superfluities ; but they become vicious when they obstruct or exhaust our abilities from a more virtuous disposition of our circumstances.

True generosity is a duty as indispensably necessary as those imposed upon us by law. It is a rule imposed upon us by reason, which should be the sovereign law of a rational being. But this generosity does not consist in obeying every impulse of humanity, in following blind passion for our guide, and impairing our circumstances by present benefactions, so as to render us incapable of future ones.

Misers are generally characterized as men without honour, or without humanity, who live only to accumulate, and to this passion sacrifice every other happiness. They have been described as madmen, who, in the midst of abundance, banish every pleasure, and make from imaginary wants real necessities. But few, very few, correspond to this exaggerated picture ; and, perhaps, there is not one in whom all these circumstances are found united. Instead of this, we find the sober and the industrious branded by the vain and the idle with this odious appellation ; men who, by frugality and labour, raise themselves above their equals, and contribute their share of industry to the common stock.

Whatever the vain or the ignorant may say, well were it for society had we more of these characters amongst us In general, these close men are found at last the true benefactors of society. With an avaricious man we seldom lose in our dealings, but too frequently in our commerce with prodigality.

A French priest, whose name was Godinot, went for a long time by the name of the Griper. He refused to relieve the most apparent wretchedness, and, by a skilful management of his vineyard, had the good fortune to acquire immense sums of money. The inhabitants of Rheims, who were his fellow citizens, detested him ; and the populace, who seldom love a miser, wherever he went, followed him with shouts of contempt. He still, however, continued his former simplicity of life, his amazing and unremitted frugality. He had long perceived the wants of the poor in the city, particularly in having no water but what they were obliged to buy at an advanced price ; wherefore, that whole fortune which he had been amassing, he laid out in an aqueduct; by which he did the poor more useful and lasting service, than if he had distributed his whole income in charity every day at his door.

Among men long conversant with books, we too frequently find those misplaced virtues, of which I have been now complaining. We find the studious animated with a strong passion for the great virtues, as they are mistakenly called, and utterly forgetful of the ordinary ones. The declamations of philosophy are generally rather exhausted on those supererogatory duties, than on such as are indispensably necessary. A man, there-fore, who has taken his ideas of mankind from study alone, generally comes into the world with a heart melting at every fictitious distress. Thus he is induced, by misplaced liberality, to put himself into the indigent circumstances of the person he relieves.

I shall conclude this paper with the advice of one of the ancients to a young man whom he saw giving

away all his substance to pretended distress. ' It is
' possible, that the person you relieve may be an honest
' man ; and I know that you, who relieve him, are such.
' You see then, by your generosity, that you rob a man
' who is certainly deserving, to bestow it on one who
' may possibly be a rogue : and, while you are unjust
' in rewarding uncertain merit, you are doubly guilty
' by stripping yourself.'

ESSAY VII

ON THE EDUCATION OF YOUTH

[Altered from *The Bee*, No. VI]

N.B. This treatise was published before Rousseau's
Emilius : if there be a similitude in any one instance, it
is hoped the author of the present essay will not be
deemed a plagiarist.

As few subjects are more interesting to society, so
few have been more frequently written upon, than the
education of youth. Yet it is a little surprising, that it
has been treated almost by all in a declamatory manner.
They have insisted largely on the advantages that
result from it, both to individuals and to society ; and
have expatiated in the praise of what none have ever
been so hardy as to call in question.

Instead of giving us fine but empty harangues upon
this subject, instead of indulging each his particular
and whimsical systems, it had been much better if the
writers on this subject had treated it in a more scientific
manner, repressed all the sallies of imagination, and
given us the result of their observations with didactic
simplicity. Upon this subject, the smallest errors are
of the most dangerous consequence ; and the author

should venture the imputation of stupidity upon a topic, where his slightest deviations may tend to injure posterity. However, such are the whimsical and erroneous productions written upon this subject. Their authors have studied to be uncommon, not to be just ; and, at present, we want a treatise upon education, not to tell us anything new, but to explode the errors which have been introduced by the admirers of novelty. It is in this manner books become numerous ; a desire of novelty produces a book, and other books are required to destroy this production.

The manner in which our youth of London are at present educated, is, some in free-schools in the city, but the far greater number in boarding-schools about town. The parent justly consults the health of his child, and finds an education in the country tends to promote this, much more than a continuance in town. Thus far he is right : if there were a possibility of having even our free-schools kept a little out of town, it would certainly conduce to the health and vigour of, perhaps, the mind as well as the body. It may be thought whimsical, but it is truth ; I have found, by experience, that they who have spent all their lives in cities, contract not only an effeminacy of habit, but even of thinking.

But when I have said that the boarding-schools are preferable to free-schools, as being in the country, this is certainly the only advantage I can allow them, otherwise it is impossible to conceive the ignorance of those who take upon them the important trust of education. Is any man unfit for any of the professions, he finds his last resource in setting up a school. Do any become bankrupts in trade, they still set up a boarding-school, and drive a trade this way, when all others fail : nay, I have been told of butchers and barbers who have turned schoolmasters ; and, more surprising still, made fortunes in their new profession.

Could we think ourselves in a country of civilized people—could it be conceived that we have a regard for posterity, when such persons are permitted to take the charge of the morals, genius, and health of those dear little pledges, who may one day be the guardians of the liberties of Europe, and who may serve as the honour and bulwark of their aged parents ? The care of our children, is it below the state ? Is it fit to indulge the caprice of the ignorant with the disposal of their children in this particular ? For the state to take the charge of all its children, as in Persia or Sparta, might at present be inconvenient ; but surely, with great ease, it might cast an eye to their instructors. Of all professions in society, I do not know a more useful or a more honourable one than a schoolmaster ; at the same time that I do not see any more generally despised, or men whose talents are so ill rewarded.

Were the salaries of schoolmasters to be augmented from a diminution of useless sinecures, how might it turn to the advantage of this people ; a people whom, without flattery, I may, in other respects, term the wisest and greatest upon earth. But while I would reward the deserving, I would dismiss those utterly unqualified for their employment : in short, I would make the business of a schoolmaster every way more respectable, by increasing their salaries, and admitting only men of proper abilities.

It is true, we have already schoolmasters appointed, and they have small salaries ; but where at present there is only one schoolmaster appointed, there should at least be two ; and wherever the salary is at present twenty pounds, it should be augmented to an hundred. Do we give immoderate benefices to our own instructors, and shall we deny even subsistence to those who instruct our children ? Every member of society should be paid in proportion as he is necessary ; and I will be bold enough to say, that schoolmasters in a state are more necessary than clergymen, as children stand in more need of instruction than their parents.

But instead of this, as I have already observed, we send them to board in the country to the most ignorant set of men that can be imagined ; and, lest the ignorance of the master be not sufficient, the child is generally consigned to the usher. This is commonly some poor needy animal, little superior to a footman either in learning or spirit, invited to his place by an advertisement, and kept there merely from his being of a complying disposition, and making the children fond of him. ' You give your child to be educated to a slave,' says a philosopher to a rich man ; ' instead of one slave, ' you will then have two.'

It were well, however, if parents, upon fixing their children in one of these houses, would examine the abilities of the usher, as well as the master ; for, whatever they are told to the contrary, the usher is generally the person most employed in their education. If, then, a gentleman, upon putting out his son to one of these houses, sees the usher disregarded by the master, he may depend upon it, that he is equally disregarded by the boys : the truth is, in spite of all their endeavours to please, they are generally the laughing-stock of the school. Every trick is played upon the usher ; the oddity of his manners, his dress, or his language, are a fund of eternal ridicule ; the master himself, now and then, cannot avoid joining in the laugh ; 'and the poor wretch, eternally resenting this ill usage, seems to live in a state of war with all the family. This is a very proper person, is it not, to give children a relish for learning ? They must esteem learning very much, when they see its professors used with such ceremony. If the usher be despised, the father may be assured his child will never be properly instructed.

But let me suppose, that there are some schools without these inconveniences, where the masters and ushers are men of learning, reputation, and assiduity. If there are to be found such, they cannot be prized in a state sufficiently. A boy will learn more true wisdom in a public school in a year, than by a private education in five. It is not from masters, but from their equals, youth learn a knowledge of the world ; the little tricks they play each other, the punishment that frequently attends the commission, is a just picture of the great world, and all the ways of men are practised in a public school in miniature. It is true, a child is early made acquainted with some vices in a school ; but it is better to know these when a boy, than be first taught them when a man ; for their novelty then may have irresistible charms.

In a public education boys early learn temperance ; and if the parents and friends would give them less money upon their usual visits, it would be much to their advantage ; since it may justly be said, that a great part of their disorders arise from surfeit,—*plus occidit gula quam gladius.* And now I am come to the article of health, it may not be amiss to observe, that Mr. Locke and some others have advised that children should be inured to cold, to fatigue, and hardship, from their youth ; but Mr. Locke was but an indifferent physician. Habit, I grant, has great influence over our constitutions, but we have not precise ideas upon this subject.

We know, that among savages, and even among our peasants, there are found children born with such constitutions, that they cross rivers by swimming, endure cold, thirst, hunger, and want of sleep, to a surprising degree ; that when they happen to fall sick, they are cured without the help of medicine, by nature alone. Such examples are adduced to persuade us to imitate their manner of education, and accustom ourselves betimes to support the same fatigues. But had these gentlemen considered first, how many lives are lost in this ascetic discipline ; had they considered, that these savages and peasants are generally not so long-lived as those who have led a more indolent life ; that the more laborious the life is, the less populous is the country : had they considered that what physicians call the *stamina vitae* by fatigue and labour become rigid, and thus anticipate old age : that the numbers who survive those rude trials, bear no proportion to those who die in the experiment ; had these things been properly considered, they would not have thus extolled an education begun in fatigue and hardships. Peter the Great, willing to inure the children of his seamen to a life of hardship, ordered that they should only drink sea-water, but they unfortunately all died under the trial.

But while I would exclude all unnecessary labours, yet still I would recommend temperance in the highest degree. No luxurious dishes with high seasoning, nothing given children to force an appetite, as little sugared or salted provisions as possible, though ever so pleasing ; but milk, morning and night, should be their constant food. This diet would make them more healthy than any of those slops that are usually cooked by the mistress of a boarding-school ; besides, it corrects any consumptive habits, not infrequently found amongst the children of city parents.

As boys should be educated with temperance, so the first greatest lesson that should be taught them is, to admire frugality. It is by the exercise of this virtue alone, they can ever expect to be useful members of society. It is true, lectures continually repeated upon this subject, may make some boys, when they grow up, run into an extreme, and become misers ; but it were well, had we more misers than we have among us. I know few characters more useful in society ; for a man's having a larger or smaller share of money lying useless by him, no way injures the commonwealth ; since, should every miser now exhaust his stores, this might make gold more plenty, but it would not increase the commodities or pleasures of life ; they would still remain as they are at present : it matters not, therefore, whether men are misers or not, if they be only frugal, laborious, and fill the station they have chosen. If they deny themselves the necessaries of life, society is no way injured by their folly.

Instead, therefore, of romances, which praise young men of spirit, who go through a variety of adventures, and at last conclude a life of dissipation, folly, and extravagance, in riches and matrimony, there should be some men of wit employed to compose books that might equally interest the passions of our youth ; where such an one might be praised for having resisted allure-ments when young, and how he, at last, became Lord Mayor ; how he was married to a lady of great sense, fortune, and beauty : to be as explicit as possible, the old story of Whittington, were his cat left out, might be more serviceable to the tender mind, than either *Tom Jones*, *Joseph Andrews*, or an hundred others, where frugality is the only good quality the hero is not possessed of. Were our schoolmasters, if any of them have sense enough to draw up such a work, thus employed, it would be much more serviceable to their pupils than all the grammars and dictionaries they may publish these ten years.

Children should early be instructed in the arts from which they may afterwards draw the greatest advantages. When the wonders of nature are never exposed to our view, we have no great desire to become acquainted with those parts of learning which pretend to account for the phenomena. One of the ancients complains, that as soon as young men have left school, and are obliged to converse in the world, they fancy themselves transported into a new region. 'Ut cum in forum venerint 'existiment se in alium terrarum orbem delatos.' We should early, therefore, instruct them in the experiments, if I may so express it, of knowledge, and leave to maturer age the accounting for the causes. But, instead of that, when boys begin natural philosophy in colleges, they have not the least curiosity for those parts of the science which are proposed for their instruction ; they have never before seen the phenomena, and consequently have no curiosity to learn the reasons. Might natural philosophy, therefore, be made their pastime at school, by this means it would in college become their amusement.

In several of the machines now in use, there would be ample field both for instruction and amusement ; the different sorts of the phosphorus, the artificial pyrites, magnetism, electricity, the experiments upon the rarefaction and weight of the air, and those upon elastic bodies, might employ their idle hours, and none should be called from play to see such experiments, but such as thought proper. At first then it would be sufficient if the instruments, and the effects of their combination, were only shown ; the causes should be deferred to a maturer age, or to those times when natural curiosity prompts us to discover the wonders of nature. Man is placed in this world as a spectator ; when he is tired of wondering at all the novelties about him, and not till then, does he desire to be made acquainted with the causes that create those wonders.

What I have observed with regard to natural philosophy, I would extend to every other science whatsoever. We should teach them as many of the facts as possible, and defer the causes until they seemed of themselves desirous of knowing them. A mind thus leaving school, stored with all the simple experiences of science, would be the fittest in the world for the college course ; and though such a youth might not appear so bright, or so talkative, as those who had learned the real principles and causes of some of the sciences, yet he would make a wiser man, and would retain a more lasting passion for letters, than he who was early burdened with the disagreeable institution of cause and effect.

In history, such stories alone should be laid before them as might catch the imagination : instead of this, at present, they are too frequently obliged to toil through the four empires, as they are called, where their memories are burdened by a number of disgusting names, that destroy all their future relish for our best historians, who may be termed the truest teachers of wisdom.

Every species of flattery should be carefully avoided ; a boy who happens to say a sprightly thing is generally applauded so much, that he sometimes continues a coxcomb all his life after. He is reputed a wit at fourteen, and becomes a blockhead at twenty. Nurses, footmen, and such, should therefore be driven away as much as possible. I was even going to add, that the mother herself should stifle her pleasure, or her vanity, when little master happens to say a good or a smart thing. Those modest lubberly boys who seem to want spirit, become at length more shining men ; and at school generally go through their business with more ease to themselves, and more satisfaction to their instructors.

There has of late a gentleman appeared, who thinks the study of rhetoric essential to a perfect education. That bold male eloquence, which often, without pleasing, convinces, is generally destroyed by such an institution. Convincing eloquence is infinitely more serviceable to its possessor than the most florid harangue, or the most pathetic tones that can be imagined ; and the man who is thoroughly convinced himself, who understands his subject, and the language he speaks in, will be more apt to silence opposition than he who studies the force of his periods, and fills our ears with sounds, while our minds are destitute of conviction.

It was reckoned the fault of the orators at the decline of the Roman empire, when they had been long instructed by rhetoricians, that their periods were so harmonious, that they could be sung as well as spoken. What a ridiculous figure must one of these gentlemen cut, thus measuring syllables, and weighing words, when he should plead the cause of his client ! Two architects were once candidates for the building a certain temple at Athens : the first harangued the crowd very learnedly upon the different orders of architecture, and showed them in what manner the temple should be built ; the other, who got up after him, only observed, that what his brother had spoken, he could do ; and thus he at once gained his cause.

To teach men to be orators, is little less than to teach them to be poets ; and, for my part, I should have too great a regard for my child, to wish him a manor only in a bookseller's shop.

Another passion which the present age is apt to run into, is to make children learn all things ; the languages, the sciences, music, the exercises, and painting. Thus the child soon becomes a Talker in all, but a Master in none. He thus acquires a superficial fondness for every-

thing, and only shows his ignorance when he attempts
to exhibit his skill.

As I deliver my thoughts without method or con-
nexion, so the reader must not be surprised to find me
once more addressing schoolmasters on the present
method of teaching the learned languages, which is
commonly by literal translations. I would ask such,
if they were to travel a journey, whether those parts of
the road in which they found the greatest difficulties,
would not be the most strongly remembered ? Boys
who, if I may continue the allusion, gallop through one
of the ancients with the assistance of a translation, can
have but a very slight acquaintance either with the
author or his language. It is by the exercise of the
mind alone, that a language is learned ; but a literal
translation, on the opposite page, leaves no exercise for
the memory at all. The boy will not be at the fatigue
of remembering, when his doubts are at once satisfied
by a glance of the eye ; whereas, were every word to be
sought from a dictionary, the learner would attempt to
remember them, to save himself the trouble of looking
out for the future.

To continue in the same pedantic strain, of all the
various grammars now taught in the schools about town,
I would recommend only the old common one ; I have
forgot whether Lilly's, or an emendation of him. The
others may be improvements ; but such improvements
seem, to me, only mere grammatical niceties, no way
influencing the learner, but perhaps loading him with
trifling subtleties, which, at a proper age, he must be
at some pains to forget.

Whatever pains a master may take to make the
learning of the languages agreeable to his pupil, he
may depend upon it, it will be at first extremely unpleasant. The rudiments of every language, therefore,

must be given as a task, not as an amusement. Attempting to deceive children into instruction of this kind, is only deceiving ourselves ; and I know no passion capable of conquering a child's natural laziness, but fear. Solomon has said it before me ; nor is there any more certain, though perhaps more disagreeable truth, than the proverb in verse, too well known to repeat on the present occasion. It is very probable that parents are told of some masters who never use the rod, and consequently are thought the properest instructors for their children ; but, though tenderness is a requisite quality in an instructor, yet there is too often the truest tenderness in well-timed correction.

Some have justly observed, that all passion should be banished on this terrible occasion ; but, I know not how, there is a frailty attending human nature, that few masters are able to keep their temper whilst they correct. I knew a good-natured man, who was sensible of his own weakness in this respect, and consequently had recourse to the following expedient to prevent his passions from being engaged, yet at the same time administer justice with impartiality. Whenever any of his pupils committed a fault, he summoned a jury of his peers, I mean of the boys of his own or the next classes to him : his accusers stood forth ; he had liberty of pleading in his own defence ; and one or two more had the liberty of pleading against him : when found guilty by the panel, he was consigned to the footman, who attended in the house, and had previous orders to punish, but with lenity. By this means the master took off the odium of punishment from himself ; and the footman, between whom and the boys there could not be even the slightest intimacy, was placed in such a light as to be shunned by every boy in the school.

ESSAY VIII

ON THE INSTABILITY OF POPULAR FAVOUR

[Altered from *The Bee*, No. VI]

AN alehouse-keeper, near Islington, who had long lived at the sign of the French King, upon the commencement of the last war pulled down his old sign, and put up that of the Queen of Hungary. Under the influence of her red face and golden sceptre, he continued to sell ale, till she was no longer the favourite of his customers; he changed her, therefore, some time ago, for the King of Prussia, who may probably be changed, in turn, for the next great man that shall be set up for vulgar admiration.

In this manner the great are dealt out, one after the other, to the gazing crowd. When we have sufficiently wondered at one of them, he is taken in, and another exhibited in his room, who seldom holds his station long; for the mob are ever pleased with variety.

I must own I have such an indifferent opinion of the vulgar, that I am ever led to suspect that merit which raises their shout; at least I am certain to find those great and sometimes good men, who find satisfaction in such acclamations, made worse by it; and history has too frequently taught me, that the head which has grown this day giddy with the roar of the million, has the very next been fixed upon a pole.

As Alexander VI was entering a little town in the neighbourhood of Rome, which had been just evacuated by the enemy, he perceived the townsmen busy in the market-place in pulling down from a gibbet a figure which had been designed to represent himself. There were some also knocking down a neighbouring statue of one of the Orsini family, with whom he was at war, in order to put Alexander's effigy in its place. It is possible

a man who knew less of the world, would have condemned the adulation of those bare-faced flatterers ;
but Alexander seemed pleased at their zeal ; and,
turning to Borgia, his son, said with a smile, ' Vides, mi
' fili, quam leve discrimen patibulum inter et statuam.'
' You see, my son, the small difference between a gibbet
' and a statue.' If the great could be taught any lesson,
this might serve to teach them upon how weak a
foundation their glory stands ; for, as popular applause
is excited by what seems like merit, it as quickly
condemns what has only the appearance of guilt.

Popular glory is a perfect coquette ; her lovers must
toil, feel every inquietude, indulge every caprice ; and,
perhaps, at last, be jilted for their pains. True glory,
on the other hand, resembles a woman of sense ; her
admirers must play no tricks ; they feel no great
anxiety, for they are sure, in the end, of being rewarded
in proportion to their merit. When Swift used to appear
in public, he generally had the mob shouting in his
train. ' Pox take these fools,' he would say, ' how
' much joy might all this bawling give my Lord Mayor ! '

We have seen those virtues which have, while living,
retired from the public eye, generally transmitted to
posterity, as the truest objects of admiration and praise.
Perhaps the character of the late Duke of Marlborough
may one day be set up, even above that of his more-
talked-of predecessor ; since an assemblage of all the
mild and amiable virtues is far superior to those
vulgarly called the great ones. I must be pardoned
for this short tribute to the memory of a man, who,
while living, would as much detest to receive anything
that wore the appearance of flattery, as I should to
offer it.

I know not how to turn so trite a subject out of the
beaten road of commonplace, except by illustrating it,

rather by the assistance of my memory than judgement ;
and, instead of making reflections, by telling a story.

A Chinese, who had long studied the works of Confucius, who knew the characters of fourteen thousand
words, and could read a great part of every book that
came in his way, once took it into his head to travel
into Europe, and observe the customs of a people which
he thought not very much inferior even to his own
countrymen.   Upon his arrival at Amsterdam, his
passion for letters naturally led him to a bookseller's
shop ; and, as he could speak a little Dutch, he civilly
asked the bookseller for the works of the immortal
Xixofou.   The bookseller assured him he had never
heard the book mentioned before. ' Alas ! ' cries our
traveller, ' to what purpose, then, has he fasted to death,
' to gain a renown which has never travelled beyond
' the precincts of China ! '

There is scarce a village in Europe, and not one
university, that is not thus furnished with its little
great men.   The head of a petty corporation, who
opposes the designs of a prince who would tyrannically
force his subjects to save their best clothes for Sundays ;
the puny pedant, who finds one undiscovered property
in the polype, or describes an unheeded process in the
skeleton of a mole, and whose mind, like his microscope,
perceives nature only in detail ; the rhymer, who makes
smooth verses, and paints to our imagination, when he
should only speak to our hearts,—all equally fancy
themselves walking forward to immortality, and desire
the crowd behind them to look on.   The crowd takes
them at their word. Patriot, philosopher, and poet, are
shouted in their train. ' Where was there ever so much
' merit seen ; no times so important as our own ; ages,
' yet unborn, shall gaze with wonder and applause ! ' To
such music the important pigmy moves forward, bustling

and swelling, and aptly compared to a puddle in a storm.

I have lived to see generals who once had crowds hallooing after them wherever they went, who were bepraised by newspapers and magazines, those echoes of the voice of the vulgar, and yet they have long sunk into merited obscurity, with scarce even an epitaph left to flatter. A few years ago the herring-fishery employed all Grub Street ; it was the topic in every coffee-house, and the burden of every ballad. We were to drag up oceans of gold from the bottom of the sea ; we were to supply all Europe with herrings upon our own terms. At present, we hear no more of all this. We have fished up very little gold that I can learn ; nor do we furnish the world with herrings, as was expected. Let us wait but a few years longer, and we shall find all our expectations an herring-fishery.

ESSAY IX

SPECIMEN OF A MAGAZINE IN MINIATURE

WE essayists, who are allowed but one subject at a time, are by no means so fortunate as the writers of magazines, who write upon several. If a magaziner be dull upon the Spanish war, he soon has us up again with the Ghost in Cock Lane ; if the reader begins to doze upon that, he is quickly roused by an Eastern tale ; tales prepare us for poetry, and poetry for the meteorological history of the weather. The reader, like the sailor's horse, when he begins to tire, has at least the comfortable refreshment of having the spur changed.

As I see no reason why these should carry off all the rewards of genius, I have some thoughts, for the future, of making my Essays a magazine in miniature : I shall hop from subject to subject ; and, if properly encouraged, I intend in time to adorn my *feuille volante* with pictures, coloured to the perfection. But to begin, in the usual form.

A MODEST ADDRESS TO THE PUBLIC IN BEHALF OF THE INFERNAL MAGAZINE.

THE public has been so often imposed upon by the unperforming promises of others, that it is with the utmost modesty we assure them of our inviolable design to give the very best collection that ever astonished society. The public we honour and regard, and therefore to instruct and entertain them is our highest ambition, with labours calculated as well to the head as the heart. If four extraordinary pages of letterpress be any recommendation of our wit, we may at least boast the honour of vindicating our own abilities. To say more in favour of the INFERNAL MAGAZINE, would be unworthy the Public ; to say less, would be injurious to ourselves. As we have no interested motives for this undertaking, being a society of gentlemen of distinction, we disdain to eat or write like hirelings ; we are all gentlemen, and therefore are resolved to sell our magazine for sixpence merely for our own amusement.

Be careful to ask for the INFERNAL MAGAZINE.

DEDICATION TO THE TRIPOLINE AMBASSADOR.

May it please your Excellency,

As your taste in the fine arts is universally allowed and admired, permit the authors of the INFERNAL MAGAZINE to lay the following sheets humbly at your Excellency's toe ; and, should our labours ever have the happiness of one day adorning the courts of Fez, we doubt not that the influence wherewith we are honoured, shall be ever retained with the most warm ardour, by,

    May it please your excellency,

        Your most devoted humble servants,

           The Authors of the INFERNAL MAGAZINE.

A SPEECH SPOKEN IN THE POLITICAL CLUB AT CATEATON NOT TO DECLARE WAR AGAINST SPAIN.

MY honest friends and brother politicians ; I perceive that the intended war with Spain makes many of you uneasy. Yesterday, as we were told, the stocks rose, and you were glad ; to-day they fall, and you are again miserable. But, my dear friends, what is the rising or the falling of the stocks to us, who have no money ? Let Nathan Ben Funk, the Dutch Jew, be glad or sorry for this ; but, my good Mr. Bellows-mender, what is all this to you or me ? You must mend broken bellows, and I write bad prose, as long as we live, whether we like a Spanish war or not. Believe me, my honest friends, whatever you may talk of liberty and your own reason, both that liberty and reason are conditionally resigned by every poor man in every society ; and, as we are born to work, so others are born to watch over us while we are working. In the name of common sense then, my good friends, let the great keep watch over us, and let us mind our business, and perhaps we may at last get money ourselves, and set beggars to work in our turn. I have a Latin sentence that is worth its weight in gold, and which I shall beg leave to translate for your instruction. An author, called Lilly's Grammar, finely observes, that 'Aes in praesenti perfectum format ;' that is, 'Ready money makes a man perfect.' Let us, then, to become perfect men, get ready money ; and let them that will, spend theirs by going to war with Spain.

Rules for Behaviour drawn up by an Indigent Philosopher.

If you be a rich man, you may enter the room with three loud hems, march deliberately up to the chimney, and turn your back to the fire. If you be a poor man, I would advise you to shrink into the room as fast as you can, and place yourself, as usual, upon the corner of some chair in a corner.

When you are desired to sing in company, I would advise you to refuse. It is a thousand to one but that you torment us with affectation, ignorance of music, or a bad voice. This is a very good rule.

If you be young, and live with an old man, I would advise you not to like gravy ; I was disinherited myself for liking gravy.

Don't laugh much in public ; the spectators that are not as merry as you, will hate you, either because they envy your happiness, or fancy themselves the subject of your mirth.

Rules for raising the Devil. Translated from the Latin of Danaeus de Sortiariis, a Writer contemporary with Calvin, and one of the Reformers of our Church.

The person who desires to raise the Devil, is to sacrifice a dog, a cat, and a hen, all of his own property, to Beelzebub. He is to swear an eternal obedience, and then to receive a mark in some unseen place, either under the eyelid, or in the roof of the mouth, inflicted by the Devil himself. Upon this he has power given him over three spirits ; one for earth, another for air, and a third for the sea. Upon certain times the Devil holds an assembly of magicians, in which each is to give an account of what evil he has done, and what he wishes to do. At this assembly he appears in the shape of an old man, or often like a goat with large horns. They, upon this occasion, renew their vows of obedience ; and then form a grand dance in honour of their false deity. The Devil instructs them in every method of injuring mankind, in gathering poisons, and of riding upon occasion through the air. He shows them the whole method, upon examination, of giving evasive answers ; his spirits have power to assume the form of angels of light, and there is but one method of detecting them ; viz. to ask them, in proper form, What method is the most certain to propagate the faith over all the world ? To this they are not permitted by the Superior Power to make a false reply, nor are they willing to give the true one, wherefore they continue silent, and are thus detected.

ESSAY X

BEAU TIBBS, A CHARACTER

[Altered from Letter LIV in *The Citizen of the World*]

THOUGH naturally pensive, yet I am fond of gay company, and take every opportunity of thus dismissing the mind from duty. From this motive I am often found in the centre of a crowd ; and wherever pleasure is to be sold, am always a purchaser. In those places, without being remarked by any, I join in whatever goes forward, work my passions into a similitude of frivolous earnestness, shout as they shout, and condemn as they happen to disapprove. A mind thus sunk for a while below its natural standard, is qualified for stronger flights ; as those first retire who would spring forward with greater vigour.

Attracted by the serenity of the evening, a friend and I lately went to gaze upon the company in one of the

public walks near the city. Here we sauntered together
for some time, either praising the beauty of such as were
handsome, or the dresses of such as had nothing else
to recommend them. We had gone thus deliberately
forward for some time, when my friend stopping on a
sudden, caught me by the elbow, and led me out of the
public walk; I could perceive, by the quickness of his
pace, and by his frequently looking behind, that he was
attempting to avoid somebody who followed; we now
turned to the right, then to the left; as we went forward,
he still went faster, but in vain; the person whom he
attempted to escape, hunted us through every doubling,
and gained upon us each moment; so that, at last,
we fairly stood still, resolving to face what we could
not avoid.

Our pursuer soon came up, and joined us with all the
familiarity of an old acquaintance. 'My dear Charles,'
cries he, shaking my friend's hand, 'where have you
'been hiding this half a century? Positively I had
'fancied you were gone down to cultivate matrimony
'and your estate in the country.' During the reply,
I had an opportunity of surveying the appearance of our
new companion. His hat was pinched up with peculiar
smartness; his looks were pale, thin, and sharp; round
his neck he wore a broad black ribbon, and in his
bosom a buckle studded with glass; his coat was trimmed
with tarnished twist; he wore by his side a sword with
a black hilt; and his stockings of silk, though newly
washed, were grown yellow by long service. I was so
much engaged with the peculiarity of his dress, that I
attended only to the latter part of my friend's reply,
in which he complimented Mr. Tibbs on the taste of his
clothes, and the bloom in his countenance. 'Psha, psha,
'Charles,' cried the figure, 'no more of that if you love
'me; you know I hate flattery, on my soul I do; and

' yet to be sure an intimacy with the great will improve
' one's appearance, and a course of venison will fatten ;
' and yet, faith, I despise the great as much as you do ;
' but there are a great many damned honest fellows
' among them ; and we must not quarrel with one half
' because the other wants breeding. If they were all
' such as my Lord Mudler, one of the most good-natured
' creatures that ever squeezed a lemon, I should myself
' be among the number of their admirers. I was yester-
' day to dine at the Duchess of Piccadilly's. My lord was
' there. " Ned," says he to me, " Ned," says he, " I'll
' hold gold to silver I can tell where you were poaching
' last night." " Poaching, my lord," says I ; ".faith,
' you have missed already ; for I stayed at home
' and let the girls poach for me." That's my way ;
' I take a fine woman as some animals do their
' prey ; stand still, and swoop, they fall into my
' mouth.'

    ' Ah, Tibbs, thou art a happy fellow,' cried my
companion with looks of infinite pity, ' I hope your
' fortune is as much improved as your understanding
' in such company ? ' ' Improved ! ' replied the other ;
' you shall know,—but let it go no farther,—a great
' secret—five hundred a year to begin with—My lord's
' word of honour for it—His lordship took me down in
' his own chariot yesterday, and we had a *tête-à-tête*
' dinner in the country, where we talked of nothing
' else.' ' I fancy you forgot, sir,' cried I, ' you told us
' but this moment of your dining yesterday in town ! '
' Did I say so ? ' replied he coolly. ' To be sure, if I said
' so it was so.—Dined in town : egad, now I do re-
' member I did dine in town ; but I dined in the country
' too : for you must know, my boys, I eat two dinners.
' By the by, I am grown as nice as the devil in my
' eating. I'll tell you a pleasant affair about that : we

'were a select party of us to dine at Lady Grogram's:
'an affected piece, but let it go no farther ; a secret :
'Well, says I, I'll hold a thousand guineas, and say
'done first, that—But, dear Charles, you are an honest
'creature, lend me half-a-crown for a minute or two,
'or so, just till—But hark'e, ask me for it the next
'time we meet, or it may be twenty to one but I forget
'to pay you.'

When he left us, our conversation naturally turned
upon so extraordinary a character. 'His very dress,'
cries my friend, 'is not less extraordinary than his
'conduct. If you meet him this day, you find him in
'rags ; if the next, in embroidery. With those persons
'of distinction, of whom he talks so familiarly, he has
'scarce a coffee-house acquaintance. However, both for
'the interest of society, and perhaps for his own,
'Heaven has made him poor ; and, while all the world
'perceives his wants, he fancies them concealed from
'every eye. An agreeable companion, because he under-
'stands flattery ; and all must be pleased with the
'first part of his conversation, though all are sure of
'its ending with a demand on their purse. While his
'youth countenances the levity of his conduct, he may
'thus earn a precarious subsistence ; but, when age
'comes on, the gravity of which is incomparable with
'buffoonery, then will he find himself forsaken by all.
'Condemned in the decline of life to hang upon some
'rich family whom he once despised, there to undergo
'all the ingenuity of studied contempt ; to be employed
'only as a spy upon the servants, or a bugbear to
'fright children into duty.'

ESSAY XI

BEAU TIBBS (*continued*)

[Altered from Letter LV of *The Citizen of the World*]

THERE are some acquaintances whom it is no easy matter to shake off. My little beau yesterday overtook me again in one of the public walks, and, slapping me on the shoulder, saluted me with an air of the most perfect familiarity. His dress was the same as usual, except that he had more powder in his hair, wore a dirtier shirt, and had on a pair of temple spectacles, with his hat under his arm.

As I knew him to be a harmless amusing little thing, I could not return his smiles with any degree of severity; so we walked forward on terms of the utmost intimacy, and in a few minutes discussed all the usual topics of a general conversation.

The oddities that marked his character, however, soon began to appear; he bowed to several well-dressed persons, who, by their manner of returning the compliment, appeared perfect strangers. At intervals he drew out a pocket-book, seeming to take memorandums before all the company, with much importance and assiduity. In this manner he led me through the length of the whole Mall, fretting at his absurdities, and fancying myself laughed at as well as he by every spectator.

When we were got to the end of our procession, 'Blast 'me,' cries he, with an air of vivacity, 'I never saw the 'Park so thin in my life before; there's no company at 'all to-day. Not a single face to be seen.' 'No com- 'pany!' interrupted I peevishly; 'no company where 'there is such a crowd! Why, man, there is too much. 'What are the thousands that have been laughing at us 'but company?' 'Lord. my dear,' returned he, with

the utmost good humour, 'you seem immensely
'chagrined; but, blast me, when the world laughs at
'me, I laugh at the world, and so we are even. My
'Lord Trip, Bill Squash the Creolian, and I, sometimes
'make a party at being ridiculous; but I see you are
'grave; so if you are for a fine grave sentimental
'companion, you shall dine with my wife; I must
'insist on 't. I'll introduce you to Mrs. Tibbs, a lady
'of as elegant qualifications as any in nature; she was
'bred, but that's between ourselves, under the inspec-
'tion of the Countess of Shoreditch. A charming body
'of voice! But no more of that, she shall give us a song.
'You shall see my little girl too, Carolina Wilhelmina
'Amelia Tibbs, a sweet pretty creature; I design her
'for my Lord Drumstick's eldest son; but that's in
'friendship, let it go no farther; she's but six years
'old, and yet she walks a minuet, and plays on the
'guitar immensely already. I intend she shall be as
'perfect as possible in every accomplishment. In the
'first place, I'll make her a scholar; I'll teach her
'Greek myself, and I intend to learn that language
'purposely to instruct her; but let that be a secret.'

Thus saying, without waiting for a reply, he took me
by the arm, and hauled me along. We passed through
many dark alleys and winding ways. From some motives
to me unknown, he seemed to have a particular aversion
to every frequented street; but, at last, we got to the
door of a dismal-looking house in the outlets of the town,
where he informed me he chose to reside for the benefit
of the air.

We entered the lower door, which seemed ever to
lie most hospitably open; and began to ascend an old
and creaking staircase; when, as he mounted to show
me the way, he demanded whether I delighted in
prospects; to which answering in the affirmative,

'Then,' says he, 'I shall show you one of the most
'charming out of my windows, for I live at the top of
'the house ; we shall see the ships sailing, and the whole
'country for twenty miles round, tip-top, quite high.
'My Lord Swamp would give ten thousand guineas for
'such a one ; but, as I sometimes pleasantly tell him,
'I always love to keep my prospects at home, that my
'friends may come to see me the oftener.'

By this time we were arrived as high as the stairs
would permit us to ascend, till we came to what he was
facetiously pleased to call the first floor down the
chimney ; and knocking at the door, a voice, with
a Scotch accent, from within, demanded, 'Wha 's there ? '
My conductor answered, that it was him. But this not
satisfying the querist, the voice again repeated the
demand ; to which he answered louder than before ; and
now the door was opened by an old maid-servant, with
cautious reluctance.

When we were got in, he welcomed me to his house
with great ceremony, and turning to the old woman,
asked where her lady was. 'Good troth,' replied she in
the northern dialect, 'she 's washing your twa shirts at
'the next door, because they have taken an oath
'against lending out the tub any longer.' 'My two
'shirts ! ' cries he, in a tone that faltered with confusion,
'what does the idiot mean ? ' 'I ken what I mean well
'enough,' replied the other ; 'she 's washing your twa
'shirts at the next door, because—' 'Fire and fury, no
'more of thy stupid explanations,' cried he ; 'go and
'inform her we have got company. Were that Scotch
'hag,' continued he, turning to me, 'to be for ever in
'my family, she would never learn politeness, nor forget
'that absurd poisonous accent of hers, or testify the
'smallest specimen of breeding or high life ; and yet it
'is very surprising too, as I had her from a Parliament-

man, a friend of mine, from the Highlands, one of the 'politest men in the world ; but that 's a secret.'

We waited some time for Mrs. Tibbs's arrival, during which interval I had a full opportunity of surveying the chamber and all its furniture ; which consisted of four chairs with old wrought bottoms, that he assured me were his wife's embroidery ; a square table that had been once japanned, a cradle in one corner, a lumbering cabinet in the other ; a broken shepherdess, and a Mandarin without a head, were stuck over the chimney ; and round the walls several paltry, unframed pictures, which he observed were all of his own drawing : 'What do 'you think, sir, of that head in the corner, done in the 'manner of Grisoni ? There 's the true keeping in it ; 'it 's my own face ; and, though there happens to be no 'likeness, a countess offered me a hundred for its fellow : 'I refused her, for, hang it, that would be mechanical, 'you know.'

The wife, at last, made her appearance, at once a slattern and a coquette ; much emaciated, but still carrying the remains of beauty. She made twenty apologies for being seen in such an odious dishabille but hoped to be excused, as she had stayed out all night at Vauxhall Gardens with the countess, who was excessively fond of the horns. 'And, indeed, my dear,' added she, turning to her husband, 'his lordship drank your health 'in a bumper.' 'Poor Jack,' cries he, 'a dear good-'natured creature, I know he loves me. But I hope, my 'dear, you have given orders for dinner ; you need 'make no great preparations neither, there are but 'three of us ; something elegant and little will do ; 'a turbot, an ortolan, or a——.' 'Or what do you 'think, my dear,' interrupts the wife, 'of a nice pretty 'bit of ox-cheek, piping hot, and dressed with a little 'of my own sauce ? ' 'The very thing,' replies he ; 'it

'will eat best with some smart bottled beer ; but be sure
'to let 's have the sauce his grace was so fond of. I hate
'your immense loads of meat ; that is country all over ;
'extreme disgusting to those who are in the least
'acquainted with high life.'

By this time my curiosity began to abate, and my
appetite to increase ; the company of fools may at first
make us smile, but at last never fails of rendering us
melancholy. I therefore pretended to recollect a prior
engagement, and, after having shown my respect to the
house, by giving the old servant a piece of money at the
door, I took my leave ; Mr. Tibbs assuring me, that
dinner, if I stayed, would be ready at least in less than
two hours.

ESSAY XII

ON THE IRRESOLUTION OF YOUTH

[Altered from Letter LXI of *The Citizen of the World*]

As it has been observed that few are better qualified
to give others advice, than those who have taken the
least of it themselves ; so in this respect I find myself
perfectly authorized to offer mine ; and must take
leave to throw together a few observations upon that
part of a young man's conduct on his entering into life,
as it is called.

The most usual way among young men who have no
resolution of their own, is first to ask one friend's advice,
and follow it for some time ; then to ask advice of
another, and turn to that ; so of a third ; still unsteady,
always changing. However, every change of this nature
is for the worse ; people may tell you of your being
unfit for some peculiar occupations in life ; but heed
them not ; whatever employment you follow with

perseverance and assiduity, will be found fit for you ; it will be your support in youth, and comfort in age. In learning the useful part of every profession, very moderate abilities will suffice : great abilities are generally obnoxious to the possessors. Life has been compared to a race ; but the allusion still improves, by observing, that the most swift are ever the most apt to stray from the course.

To know one profession only, is enough for one man to know ; and this, whatever the professors may tell you to the contrary, is soon learned. Be contented, therefore, with one good employment ; for if you understand two at a time, people will give you business in neither.

A conjurer and a tailor once happened to converse together. 'Alas !' cries the tailor, 'what an unhappy 'poor creature am I ! If people ever take it into their 'heads to live without clothes, I am undone ; I have 'no other trade to have recourse to.' 'Indeed, friend, 'I pity you sincerely,' replies the conjurer ; 'but, thank 'Heaven, things are not quite so bad with me : for, if 'one trick should fail, I have a hundred tricks more for 'them yet. However, if at any time you are reduced 'to beggary, apply to me, and I will relieve you.' A famine overspread the land ; the tailor made a shift to live, because his customers could not be without clothes ; but the poor conjurer, with all his hundred tricks, could find none that had money to throw away : it was in vain that he promised to eat fire, or to vomit pins ; no single creature would relieve him, till he was at last obliged to beg from the very tailor whose calling he had formerly despised.

There are no obstructions more fatal to fortune than pride and resentment. If you must resent injuries at all, at least suppress your indignation till you become rich, and then show away. The resentment of a poor man is like the efforts of a harmless insect to sting ; it may get him crushed, but cannot defend him. Who values that anger which is consumed only in empty menaces ?

Once upon a time a goose fed its young by a pond-side ; and a goose, in such circumstances, is always extremely proud, and excessive punctilious. If any other animal, without the least design to offend, happened to pass that way, the goose was immediately at it. The pond, she said, was hers, and she would maintain her right in it, and support her honour, while she had a bill to hiss, or a wing to flutter. In this manner she drove away ducks, pigs, and chickens ; nay, even the insidious cat was seen to scamper. A lounging mastiff, however, happened to pass by, and thought it no harm if he should lap a little of the water, as he was thirsty. The guardian goose flew at him like a fury, pecked at him with her beak, and slapped him with her feathers. The dog grew angry, and had twenty times a mind to give her a sly snap ; but suppressing his indignation, because his master was nigh, ' A pox take thee,' cried he, 'for a ' fool ! sure those who have neither strength nor weapons ' to fight, at least should be civil.' So saying, he went forward to the pond, quenched his thirst, in spite of the goose, and followed his master.

Another obstruction to the fortune of youth is, that, while they are willing to take offence from none, they are also equally desirous of giving nobody offence. From hence they endeavour to please all, comply with every request, and attempt to suit themselves to every company ; have no will of their own ; but, like wax, catch every contiguous impression. By thus attempting to give universal satisfaction, they at last find themselves miserably disappointed ; to bring the generality of admirers on our side, it is sufficient to attempt pleasing a very few.

A painter of eminence was once resolved to finish

a piece which should please the whole world. When, therefore, he had drawn a picture, in which his utmost skill was exhausted, it was exposed in the public market-place, with directions at the bottom for every spectator to mark with a brush, that lay by, every limb and feature which seemed erroneous. The spectators came, and, in general, applauded ; but each, willing to show his talent at criticism, stigmatized whatever he thought proper. At evening, when the painter came, he was mortified to find the picture one universal blot ; not a single stroke that had not the marks of disapprobation. Not satisfied with this trial, the next day he was resolved to try them in a different manner ; and exposing his picture as before, desired that every spectator would mark those beauties he approved or admired. The people complied ; and the artist returning, found his picture covered with the marks of beauty ; every stroke that had been yesterday condemned, now received the character of approbation. ' Well,' cries the painter, 'I now find, that the best way to please all the world, ' is to attempt pleasing one half of it.'

ESSAY XIII

ON MAD DOGS

[Altered from Letter LXIX of *The Citizen of the World*]

INDULGENT nature seems to have exempted this island from many of those epidemic evils which are so fatal in other parts of the world. A want of rain for a few days beyond the expected season, in some parts of the globe, spreads famine, desolation, and terror over the whole country ; but, in this fortunate land of Britain, the inhabitant courts health in every breeze, and the husbandman ever sows in joyful expectation.

But, though the nation be exempt from real evils, it is not more happy on this account than others. The people are afflicted, it is true, with neither famine nor pestilence ; but then there is a disorder peculiar to the country, which every season makes strange ravages among them ; it spreads with pestilential rapidity, and infects almost every rank of people ; what is still more strange, the natives have no name for this peculiar malady, though well known to foreign physicians by the appellation of Epidemic Terror.

A season is never known to pass in which the people are not visited by this cruel calamity in one shape or another, seemingly different, though ever the same ; one year it issues from a baker's shop in the shape of a sixpenny loaf ; the next it takes the appearance of a comet with a fiery tail ; the third it threatens like a flat-bottomed boat, and the fourth, it carries consternation in the bite of a mad dog. The people, when once infected, lose their relish for happiness, saunter about with looks of despondence, ask after the calamities of the day, and receive no comfort but in heightening each other's distress. It is insignificant how remote or near, how weak or powerful, the object of terror may be, when once they resolve to fright and be frighted ; the merest trifles sow consternation and dismay ; each proportions his fears, not to the object, but to the dread he discovers in the countenance of others ; for, when once fermentation is begun, it goes on of itself, though the original cause be discontinued which first set it in motion.

· A dread of mad dogs is the epidemic terror which now prevails, and the whole nation is at present actually groaning under the malignity of its influence. The people sally from their houses with that circumspection which is prudent in such as expect a mad dog at every

turning. The physician publishes his prescription, the
beadle prepares his halter, and a few of unusual bravery
arm themselves with boots and buff gloves, in order to
face the enemy if he should offer to attack them. In
short, the whole people stand bravely upon their defence,
and seem, by their present spirit, to show a resolution of
being tamely bit by mad dogs no longer.

Their manner of knowing whether a dog be mad or
no, somewhat resembles the ancient Gothic custom of
trying witches. The old woman suspected was tied
hand and foot, and thrown into the water. If she swam,
then she was instantly carried off to be burnt for a
witch ; if she sunk, then indeed she was acquitted of
the charge, but drowned in the experiment. In the
same manner a crowd gather round a dog suspected of
madness, and they begin by teasing the devoted animal
on every side. If he attempts to stand upon the de-
fensive, and bite, then he is unanimously found guilty,
for ' A mad dog always snaps at everything.' If, on the
contrary, he strives to escape by running away, then he
can expect no compassion, for ' mad dogs always run
' straight forward before them.'

It is pleasant enough for a neutral being like me, who
have no share in those ideal calamities, to mark the
stages of this national disease. The terror at first feebly
enters with a disregarded story of a little dog, that had
gone through a neighbouring village, which was thought
to be mad by several who had seen him. The next account comes, that a mastiff ran through a certain town,
and had bit five geese, which immediately ran mad,
foamed at the bill, and died in great agonies soon after.
Then comes an affecting history of a little boy bit in the
leg, and gone down to be dipped in the salt water. When
the people have sufficiently shuddered at that, they are
next congealed with a frightful account of a man who

was said lately to have died from a bite he had received some years before. This relation only prepares the way for another, still more hideous ; as how the master of a family with seven small children, were all bit by a mad lap-dog ; and how the poor father first perceived the infection by calling for a draught of water, where he saw the lap-dog swimming in the cup.

When epidemic terror is thus once excited, every morning comes loaded with some new disaster ; as in stories of ghosts each loves to hear the account, though it only serves to make him uneasy ; so here each listens with eagerness, and adds to the tidings with new circumstances of peculiar horror. A lady, for instance, in the country, of very weak nerves, has been frighted by the barking of a dog ; and this, alas ! too frequently happens. The story soon is improved and spreads, that a mad dog had frighted a lady of distinction. These circumstances begin to grow terrible before they have reached the neighbouring village ; and there the report is, that a lady of quality was bit by a mad mastiff. This account every moment gathers new strength, and grows more dismal as it approaches the capital ; and, by the time it has arrived in town, the lady is described with wild eyes, foaming mouth, running mad upon all four, barking like a dog, biting her servants, and at last smothered between two beds by the advice of her doctors ; while the mad mastiff is, in the meantime, ranging the whole country over, slavering at the mouth, and seeking whom he may devour.

My landlady, a good-natured woman, but a little credulous, waked me some mornings ago, before the usual hour, with horror and astonishment in her look. She desired me, if I had any regard for my safety, to keep within ; for, a few days ago, so dismal an accident had happened, as to put all the world upon their guard.

A mad dog down in the country, she assured me, had bit a farmer, who soon becoming mad, ran into his own yard, and bit a fine brindled cow : the cow quickly became as mad as the man, began to foam at the mouth, and raising herself up, walked about on her hind legs, sometimes barking like a dog, and sometimes attempting to talk like the farmer. Upon examining the grounds of this story, I found my landlady had it from one neighbour, who had it from another neighbour, who heard it from very good authority.

Were most stories of this nature well examined, it would be found that numbers of such as have been said to suffer were no way injured ; and that of those who have been actually bitten, not one in a hundred was bit by a mad dog. Such accounts in general, therefore, only serve to make the people miserable by false terrors, and sometimes fright the patient into actual frenzy, by creating those very symptoms they pretended to deplore.

But even allowing three or four to die in a season of this terrible death (and four is probably too large a concession), yet still it is not considered, how many are preserved in their health and in their property by this devoted animal's services. The midnight robber is kept at a distance ; the insidious thief is often detected ; the healthful chase repairs many a worn constitution ; and the poor man finds in his dog a willing assistant, eager to lessen his toil, and content with the smallest retribution.

' A dog,' says one of the English poets, ' is an honest ' creature, and I am a friend to dogs.' Of all the beasts that graze the lawn or hunt the forest, a dog is the only animal that, leaving his fellows, attempts to cultivate the friendship of man ; to man he looks in all his necessities, with a speaking eye for assistance ; exerts, for him, all the little service in his power with cheerfulness and pleasure ; for him bears famine and fatigue with patience and resignation ; no injuries can abate his fidelity ; no distress induce him to forsake his benefactor ; studious to please, and fearing to offend, he is still an humble, steadfast dependant ; and in him alone fawning is not flattery. How unkind then to torture this faithful creature, who has left the forest to claim the protection of man ! How ungrateful a return to the trusty animal for all its services !

ESSAY XIV

ON THE INCREASED LOVE OF LIFE WITH AGE

[Altered from Letter LXXIII of *The Citizen of the World*]

AGE, that lessens the enjoyment of life, increases our desire of living. Those dangers which, in the vigour of youth, we had learned to despise, assume new terrors as we grow old. Our caution increasing as our years increase, fear becomes at last the prevailing passion of the mind ; and the small remainder of life is taken up in useless efforts to keep off our end, or provide for a continued existence.

Strange contradiction in our nature, and to which even the wise are liable ! If I should judge of that part of life which lies before me by that which I have already seen, the prospect is hideous. Experience tells me, that my past enjoyments have brought no real felicity ; and sensation assures me, that those I have felt are stronger than those which are yet to come. Yet experience and sensation in vain persuade ; hope, more powerful than either, dresses out the distant prospect in fancied beauty ; some happiness, in long perspective, still beckons me to pursue ; and, like a losing gamester, every new disappointment increases my ardour to continue the game.

Whence then is this increased love of life, which

grows upon us with our years ; whence comes it, that we thus make greater efforts to preserve our existence, at a period when it becomes scarce worth the keeping ? Is it that Nature, attentive to the preservation of mankind, increases our wishes to live, while she lessens our enjoyments ; and, as she robs the senses of every pleasure, equips imagination in the spoils ? Life would be insupportable to an old man, who, loaded with infirmities, feared death no more than when in the vigour of manhood ; the numberless calamities of decaying nature, and the consciousness of surviving every pleasure, would at once induce him, with his own hand, to terminate the scene of misery ; but happily the contempt of death forsakes him at a time when it could only be prejudicial ; and life acquires an imaginary value, in proportion as its real value is no more.

Our attachment to every object around us increases, in general, from the length of our acquaintance with it. ' I would not choose,' says a French philosopher, ' to ' see an old post pulled up with which I had been long ' acquainted.' A mind long habituated to a certain set of objects, insensibly becomes fond of seeing them ; visits them from habit, and parts from them with reluctance : from hence proceeds the avarice of the old in every kind of possession ; they love the world and all that it produces ; they love life and all its advantages ; not because it gives them pleasure, but because they have known it long.

Chinvang the Chaste, ascending the throne of China, commanded that all who were unjustly detained in prison, during the preceding reigns, should be set free. Among the number who came to thank their deliverer on this occasion, there appeared a majestic old man, who, falling at the emperor's feet, addressed him as follows : ' Great father of China, behold a wretch, now eighty-five

' years old, who was shut up in a dungeon at the age of
' twenty-two. I was imprisoned, though a stranger to
' crime, or without being even confronted by my accusers.
' I have now lived in solitude and darkness for more than
' fifty years, and am grown familiar with distress. As
' yet, dazzled with the splendour of that sun to which
' you have restored me, I have been wandering the
' streets to find out some friend that would assist, or
' relieve, or remember me ; but my friends, my family,
' and relations, are all dead, and I am forgotten. Permit
' me then, O Chinvang, to wear out the wretched remains
' of life in my former prison ; the walls of my dungeon
' are to me more pleasing than the most splendid palace :
' I have not long to live, and shall be unhappy except
' I spend the rest of my days where my youth was passed ;
' in that prison from whence you were pleased to release
' me.'

The old man's passion for confinement is similar to
that we all have for life. We are habituated to the
prison, we look round with discontent, are displeased
with the abode, and yet the length of our captivity only
increases our fondness for the cell. The trees we have
planted, the houses we have built, or the posterity we
have begotten, all serve to bind us closer to the earth,
and embitter our parting. Life sues the young like
a new acquaintance ; the companion, as yet unexhausted,
is at once instructive and amusing ; its company pleases ;
yet, for all this, it is but little regarded. To us, who are
declined in years, life appears like an old friend ; its
jests have been anticipated in former conversation ; it
has no new story to make us smile, no new improvement
with which to surprise, yet still we love it ; destitute
of every enjoyment, still we love it ; husband the
wasting treasure with increasing frugality, and feel all
the poignancy of anguish in the fatal separation.

Sir Philip Mordaunt was young, beautiful, sincere, brave, an Englishman. He had a complete fortune of his own, and the love of the king his master, which was equivalent to riches. Life opened all her treasures before him, and promised a long succession of happiness. He came, tasted of the entertainment, but was disgusted even at the beginning. He professed an aversion to living; was tired of walking round the same circle; had tried every enjoyment, and found them all grow weaker at every repetition. ' If life be, in youth, so ' displeasing,' cried he to himself, ' what will it appear ' when age comes on ? if it be at present indifferent, ' sure it will then be execrable.' This thought embittered every reflection ; till, at last, with all the serenity of perverted reason, he ended the debate with a pistol ! Had this self-deluded man been apprised, that existence grows more desirable to us the longer we exist, he would have then faced old age without shrinking ; he would have boldly dared to live ; and served that society by his future assiduity, which he basely injured by his desertion.

ESSAY XV

ON THE PASSION OF WOMEN FOR LEVELLING ALL DISTINCTIONS OF DRESS

[Altered from ' On Dress ' in *The Bee*, No. II]

FOREIGNERS observe that there are no ladies in the world more beautiful, or more ill-dressed, than those of England. Our country-women have been compared to those pictures where the face is the work of a Raphael, but the draperies thrown out by some empty pretender, destitute of taste, and unacquainted with design.

If I were a poet, I might observe, on this occasion,

that so much beauty, set off with all the advantages of dress, would be too powerful an antagonist for the opposite sex ; and therefore it was wisely ordered, that our ladies should want taste, lest their admirers should entirely want reason.

But to confess a truth, I do not find they have a greater aversion to fine clothes than the women of any other country whatsoever. I can't fancy that a shop-keeper's wife in Cheapside has a greater tenderness for the fortune of her husband than a citizen's wife in Paris ; or that Miss in a boarding-school is more an economist in dress than Mademoiselle in a nunnery.

Although Paris may be accounted the soil in which almost every fashion takes its rise, its influence is never so general there as with us. They study there the happy method of uniting grace and fashion, and never excuse a woman for being awkwardly dressed, by saying her clothes are in the mode. A Frenchwoman is a perfect architect in dress ; she never, with Gothic ignorance, mixes the orders ; she never tricks out a squabby Doric shape with Corinthian finery ; or, to speak without metaphor, she conforms to a general fashion only when it happens not to be repugnant to private beauty.

The English ladies, on the contrary, seem to have no other standard of grace but the run of the town. If fashion gives the word, every distinction of beauty, complexion, or stature, ceases. Sweeping trains, Prussian bonnets, and trollopees, as like each other as if cut from the same piece, level all to one standard. The Mall, the gardens, and playhouses, are filled with ladies in uniform ; and their whole appearance shows as little variety or taste as if their clothes were bespoke by the colonel of a marching regiment, or fancied by the artist who dresses the three battalions of guards.

But not only the ladies of every shape and complexion,

but of every age too, are possessed of this unaccountable
passion for levelling all distinction in dress. The lady
of no quality travels fast behind the lady of some quality ;
and a woman of sixty is as gaudy as her granddaughter.
A friend of mine, a good-natured old man, amused me,
the other day, with an account of his journey to the
Mall. It seems, in his walk thither, he, for some time,
followed a lady who, as he thought by her dress, was
a girl of fifteen. It was airy, elegant, and youthful. My
old friend had called up all his poetry on this occasion,
and fancied twenty Cupids prepared for execution in
every folding of her white negligee. He had prepared his
imagination for an angel's face ; but what was his mortification to find that the imaginary goddess was no other
than his cousin Hannah, some years older than himself.

But to give it in his own words, ' After the transports
' of our first salute,' said he, ' were over, I could not avoid
' running my eye over her whole appearance. Her
' gown was of cambric, cut short before, in order to
' discover a high-heeled shoe, which was buckled
' almost at the toe. Her cap consisted of a few bits of
' cambric, and flowers of painted paper stuck on one
' side of her head. Her bosom, that had felt no hand
' but the hand of time these twenty years, rose suing
' to be pressed. I could, indeed, have wished her more
' than a handkerchief of Paris net to shade her beauties ;
' for, as Tasso says of the rose-bud, " Quanto se mostra
' men tanto e piu bella." A female breast is generally
' thought more beautiful as it is more sparingly discovered.

' As my cousin had not put on all this finery for
' nothing, she was at that time sallying out to the Park,
' when I had overtaken her. Perceiving, however, that
' I had on my best wig, she offered, if I would 'squire her
' there, to send home the footman. Though I trembled
' for our reception in public, yet I could not, with any

' civility, refuse ; so, to be as gallant as possible, I took
' her hand in my arm, and thus we marched on together.

' When we made our entry at the Park, two antiquated
' figures, so polite and so tender, soon attracted the eyes
' of the company. As we made our way among crowds
' who were out to show their finery as well as we, where-
' ever we came, I perceived we brought good-humour
' with us. The polite could not forbear smiling, and the
' vulgar burst out into a horse-laugh at our grotesque
' figures. Cousin Hannah, who was perfectly conscious
' of the rectitude of her own appearance, attributed all
' this mirth to the oddity of mine ; while I as cordially
' placed the whole to her account. Thus, from being two
' of the best-natured creatures alive, before we got half-
' way up the Mall, we both began to grow peevish, and,
' like two mice on a string, endeavoured to revenge the
' impertinence of the spectators upon each other. " I am
' amazed, cousin Jeffery," says Miss, " that I can never
' get you to dress like a Christian. I knew we should
' have the eyes of the Park upon us, with your great wig,
' so frizzled, and yet so beggarly, and your monstrous
' muff. I hate those odious muffs." I could have
' patiently borne a criticism on all the rest of my
' equipage ; but, as I had had always a peculiar venera-
' tion for my muff, I could not forbear being piqued
' a little ; and throwing my eyes with a spiteful air
' on her bosom, " I could heartily wish, madam," replied
' I, " that, for your sake, my muff was cut into a tippet."

' As my cousin, by this time, was grown heartily
' ashamed of her gentleman-usher, and as I was never
' very fond of any kind of exhibition myself, it was
' mutually agreed to retire for a while to one of the
' seats, and from that retreat remark on others as freely
' as they had remarked on us.

' When seated we continued silent for some time,

'employed in very different speculations. I regarded
'the whole company, now passing in review before me,
'as drawn out merely for my amusement. For my
'entertainment the beauty had, all that morning, been
'improving her charms; the beau had put on lace, and
'the young doctor a big wig, merely to please me. But
'quite different were the sentiments of cousin Hannah;
'she regarded every well-dressed woman as a victorious
'rival; hated every face that seemed dressed in good
'humour, or wore the appearance of greater happiness
'than her own. I perceived her uneasiness, and at-
'tempted to lessen it, by observing that there was no
'company in the Park to-day. To this she readily
'assented; "and yet," says she, "it is full enough of
'scrubs of one kind or another." My smiling at this
'observation gave her spirits to pursue the bent of her
'inclination, and now she began to exhibit her skill in
'secret history, as she found me disposed to listen.
'"Observe," says she to me, "that old woman in tawdry
'silk, and dressed out beyond the fashion. That is
'Miss Biddy Evergreen. Miss Biddy, it seems, has
'money; and as she considers that money was never
'so scarce as it is now, she seems resolved to keep what
'she has to herself. She is ugly enough, you see; yet,
'I assure you, she has refused several offers, to my own
'knowledge, within this twelvemonth. Let me see;
'three gentlemen from Ireland who study the law, two
'waiting-captains, her doctor, and a Scotch preacher,
'who had like to have carried her off. All her time is
'passed between sickness and finery. Thus she spends
'the whole week in a close chamber, with no other
'company but her monkey, her apothecary, and cat;
'and comes dressed out to the Park every Sunday,
'to show her airs, to get new lovers, to catch a new cold,
'and to make new work for the doctor.

' " There goes Mrs. Roundabout, I mean the fat lady
' in the lutestring trollopee. Between you and I, she is
' but a cutler's wife. See how she's dressed, as fine as
' hands and pins can make her, while her two marriage-
' able daughters, like bunters, in stuff gowns, are now
' taking sixpennyworth of tea at the White Conduit
' House. Odious puss, how she waddles along, with her
' train two yards behind her ! She puts me in mind of
' my Lord Bantam's Indian sheep, which are obliged to
' have their monstrous tails trundled along in a go-cart.
' For all her airs, it goes to her husband's heart to see
' four yards of good lutestring wearing against the
' ground, like one of his knives on a grindstone. To
' speak my mind, cousin Jeffery, I never liked those
' tails ; for, suppose a young fellow should be rude, and
' the lady should offer to step back in the fright, instead
' of retiring, she treads upon her train, and falls fairly
' on her back ; and then you know, cousin,—her clothes
' may be spoiled.

' " Ah ! Miss Mazzard ! I knew we should not miss her
' in the Park ; she in the monstrous Prussian bonnet.
' Miss, though so very fine, was bred a milliner, and
' might have had some custom if she had minded her
' business ; but the girl was fond of finery, and, instead
' of dressing her customers, laid out all her goods in
' adorning herself. Every new gown she put on impaired
' her credit ; she still, however, went on, improving her
' appearance and lessening her little fortune, and is now,
' you see, become a belle and a bankrupt."

' My cousin was proceeding in her remarks, which
' were interrupted by the approach of the very lady
' she had been so freely describing. Miss had perceived
' her at a distance, and approached to salute her. I
' found, by the warmth of the two ladies' protestations,
' that they had been long intimate esteemed friends and

'acquaintance. Both were so pleased at this happy
'rencounter, that they were resolved not to part for the
' day. So we all crossed the Park together, and I saw
' them into a hackney-coach at St. James's.'

ESSAY XVI

ASEM THE MAN-HATER, AN EASTERN TALE

WHERE Tauris lifts its head above the storm, and
presents nothing to the sight of the distant traveller
but a prospect of nodding rocks, falling torrents, and all
the variety of tremendous nature ; on the bleak bosom
of this frightful mountain, secluded from society and
detesting the ways of men, lived Asem the Man-hater.

Asem had spent his youth with men ; had shared in
their amusements ; and had been taught to love his
fellow creatures with the most ardent affection : but
from the tenderness of his disposition, he exhausted all
his fortune in relieving the wants of the distressed. The
petitioner never sued in vain ; the weary traveller never
passed his door ; he only desisted from doing good when
he had no longer the power of relieving.

From a fortune thus spent in benevolence, he expected
a grateful return from those he had formerly relieved ;
and made his application with confidence of redress :
the ungrateful world soon grew weary of his importunity ;
for pity is but a short-lived passion. He soon, therefore,
began to view mankind in a very different light from
that in which he had before beheld them : he perceived
a thousand vices he had never before suspected to exist :
wherever he turned, ingratitude, dissimulation, and
treachery, contributed to increase his detestation of them.
Resolved therefore to continue no longer in a world
which he hated, and which repaid his detestation with

contempt, he retired to this region of sterility, in order to brood over his resentment in solitude, and converse with the only honest heart he knew ; namely, with his own.

A cave was his only shelter from the inclemency of the weather ; fruits gathered with difficulty from the mountain's side, his only food ; and his drink was fetched with danger and toil from the headlong torrent. In this manner he lived, sequestered from society, passing the hours in meditation, and sometimes exulting that he was able to live independently of his fellow creatures.

At the foot of the mountain, an extensive lake displayed its glassy bosom ; reflecting, on its broad surface, the impending horrors of the mountain. To this capacious mirror he would sometimes descend, and, reclining on its steep bank, cast an eager look on the smooth expanse that lay before him. ' How beautiful,' he often cried, ' is Nature ! how lovely, even in her wildest ' scenes ! How finely contrasted is the level plain that ' lies beneath me, with yon awful pile that hides its ' tremendous head in clouds ! But the beauty of these ' scenes is no way comparable with their utility ; from ' hence an hundred rivers are supplied, which distribute ' health and verdure to the various countries through ' which they flow. Every part of the universe is ' beautiful, just, and wise, but man : vile man is a ' solecism in Nature ; the only monster in the creation. ' Tempests and whirlwinds have their use ; but vicious, ' ungrateful man is a blot in the fair page of universal ' beauty. Why was I born of that detested species, ' whose vices are almost a reproach to the wisdom of ' the Divine Creator ! Were men entirely free from vice, ' all would be uniformity, harmony, and order. A world ' of moral rectitude should be the result of a perfectly ' moral agent. Why, why then, O Allah ! must I be ' thus confined in darkness, doubt, and despair ?

Just as he uttered the word despair, he was going to
plunge into the lake beneath him, at once to satisfy his
doubts, and put a period to his anxiety; when he
perceived a most majestic being walking on the surface
of the water, and approaching the bank on which he
stood. So unexpected an object at once checked his
purpose; he stopped, contemplated, and fancied he saw
something awful and divine in his aspect.

'Son of Adam,' cried the Genius, 'stop thy rash
'purpose; the Father of the Faithful has seen thy
'justice, thy integrity, thy miseries, and hath sent me
'to afford and administer relief. Give me thine hand,
'and follow, without trembling, wherever I shall lead;
'in me behold the Genius of Conviction, kept by the
'great Prophet, to turn from their errors those who go
'astray, not from curiosity, but a rectitude of intention.
'Follow me, and be wise.'

Asem immediately descended upon the lake, and his
guide conducted him along the surface of the water;
till, coming near the centre of the lake, they both began
to sink; the waters closed over their heads; they
descended several hundred fathoms, till Asem, just ready
to give up his life as inevitably lost, found himself with
his celestial guide in another world, at the bottom of
the waters, where human foot had never trod before.
His astonishment was beyond description, when he saw
a sun like that he had left, a serene sky over his head,
and blooming verdure under his feet.

'I plainly perceive your amazement,' said the Genius;
'but suspend it for a while. This world was formed by
'Allah, at the request, and under the inspection, of
'our great Prophet, who once entertained the same
'doubts which filled your mind when I found you, and
'from the consequence of which you were so lately
'rescued. The rational inhabitants of this world are

'formed agreeable to your own ideas; they are absolutely
'without vice. In other respects it resembles your
'earth, but differs from it in being wholly inhabited by
'men who never do wrong. If you find this world more
'agreeable than that you so lately left, you have free
'permission to spend the remainder of your days in it;
'but permit me, for some time, to attend you, that
'I may silence your doubts, and make you better
'acquainted with your company and your new habita-
'tion.'

'A world without vice! Rational beings without
'immorality!' cried Asem, in a rapture; 'I thank
'thee, O Allah, who hast at length heard my petitions;
'this, this indeed will produce happiness, ecstasy, and
'ease. O for an immortality, to spend it among men
'who are incapable of ingratitude, injustice, fraud,
'violence, and a thousand other crimes, that render
'society miserable.'

'Cease thine acclamations,' replied the Genius. 'Look
'around thee; reflect on every object and action before
'us, and communicate to me the result of thine observa-
'tions. Lead wherever you think proper, I shall be
'your attendant and instructor.' Asem and his companion travelled on in silence for some time, the former
being entirely lost in astonishment; but, at last,
recovering his former serenity, he could not help observing, that the face of the country bore a near resemblance to that he had left, except that this subterranean
world still seemed to retain its primaeval wildness.

'Here,' cried Asem, 'I perceive animals of prey,
'and others that seem only designed for their sub-
'sistence; it is the very same in the world over our
'heads. But had I been permitted to instruct our
'Prophet, I would have removed this defect, and formed
'no voracious or destructive animals, which only prey

'on the other parts of the creation.' 'Your tenderness
'for inferior animals is, I find, remarkable,' said the
Genius, smiling. 'But, with regard to meaner creatures,
'this world exactly resembles the other; and, indeed,
'for obvious reasons: for the earth can support a more
'considerable number of animals, by their thus becom-
'ing food for each other, than if they had lived entirely
'on the vegetable productions. So that animals of
'different natures thus formed, instead of lessening their
'multitude, subsist in the greatest number possible. But
'let us hasten on to the inhabited country before us, and
'see what that offers for instruction.'

They soon gained the utmost verge of the forest, and
entered the country inhabited by men without vice;
and Asem anticipated in idea the rational delight he
hoped to experience in such an innocent society. But
they had scarce left the confines of the wood, when they
beheld one of the inhabitants flying with hasty steps,
and terror in his countenance, from an army of squirrels
that closely pursued him. 'Heavens!' cried Asem,
'why does he fly? What can he fear from animals so
'contemptible?' He had scarce spoke when he perceived two dogs pursuing another of the human species,
who, with equal terror and haste, attempted to avoid
them. 'This,' cried Asem to his guide, 'is truly
'surprising; nor can I conceive the reason for so
'strange an action.' 'Every species of animals,'
replied the Genius, 'has of late grown very powerful
'in this country; for the inhabitants, at first, thinking
'it unjust to use either fraud or force in destroying them,
'they have insensibly increased, and now frequently
'ravage their harmless frontiers.' 'But they should
'have been destroyed,' cried Asem; 'you see the
'consequence of such neglect.' 'Where is then that
'tenderness you so lately expressed for subordinate

'animals?' replied the Genius smiling: 'you seem to
'have forgot that branch of justice.' 'I must acknow-
'ledge my mistake,' returned Asem; 'I am now
'convinced that we must be guilty of tyranny and
'injustice to the brute creation, if we would enjoy the
'world ourselves. But let us no longer observe the
'duty of man to these irrational creatures, but survey
'their connexions with one another.'

As they walked farther up the country, the more he
was surprised to see no vestiges of handsome houses,
no cities, nor any mark of elegant design. His conductor,
perceiving his surprise, observed, that the inhabitants of
this new world were perfectly content with their ancient
simplicity; each had a house, which, though homely, was
sufficient to lodge his little family; they were too good
to build houses, which could only increase their own
pride, and the envy of the spectator; what they built
was for convenience, and not for show. 'At least,
'then,' said Asem, 'they have neither architects,
'painters, or statuaries, in their society; but these
'are idle arts, and may be spared. However, before
'I spend much more time here, you should have my
'thanks for introducing me into the society of some
'of their wisest men : there is scarce any pleasure to
'me equal to a refined conversation ; there is nothing
'of which I am so enamoured as wisdom.' 'Wisdom!'
replied his instructor, 'how ridiculous ! We have no
'wisdom here, for we have no occasion for it ; true
'wisdom is only a knowledge of our own duty, and the
'duty of others to us ; but of what use is such wisdom
'here ? each intuitively performs what is right in
'himself, and expects the same from others. If by
'wisdom you should mean vain curiosity and empty
'speculation, as such pleasures have their origin in
'vanity, luxury, or avarice, we are too good to pursue

' them.' ' All this may be right,' says Asem ; ' but
' methinks I observe a solitary disposition prevail among
' the people ; each family keeps separately within their
' own precincts, without society, or without intercourse.'
' That, indeed, is true,' replied the other ; ' here is no
' established society ; nor should there be any ; all
' societies are made either through fear or friendship ;
' the people we are among, are too good to fear each
' other ; and there are no motives to private friendship,
' where all are equally meritorious.' ' Well then,' said
the sceptic, ' as I am to spend my time here, if I am
' to have neither the polite arts, nor wisdom, nor friend-
' ship, in such a world, I should be glad, at least, of an
' easy companion, who may tell me his thoughts, and to
' whom I may communicate mine.' ' And to what
' purpose should either do this ? ' says the Genius :
' flattery or curiosity are vicious motives, and never
' allowed of here ; and wisdom is out of the question.'

   ' Still, however,' said Asem, ' the inhabitants must
' be happy ; each is contented with his own possessions,
' nor avariciously endeavours to heap up more than is
' necessary for his own subsistence : each has therefore
' leisure to pity those that stand in need of his com-
' passion.' He had scarce spoken when his ears were
assaulted with the lamentations of a wretch who sat by
the wayside, and, in the most deplorable distress, seemed
gently to murmur at his own misery. Asem immediately
ran to his relief, and found him in the last stage of
a consumption. ' Strange,' cried the son of Adam,
' that men who are free from vice should thus suffer so
' much misery without relief ! ' ' Be not surprised,'
said the wretch who was dying ; ' would it not be the
' utmost injustice for beings, who have only just sufficient
' to support themselves, and are content with a bare
' subsistence, to take it from their own mouths to put

'it into mine ?   They never are possessed of a single
'meal more than is necessary ;   and what is barely
'necessary cannot be dispensed with.'   'They should
'have been supplied with more than is necessary,' cried
Asem ;   'and yet I contradict my own opinion but
'a moment before : all is doubt, perplexity, and con-
'fusion.   Even the want of ingratitude is no virtue here,
'since they never received a favour.   They have, how-
'ever, another excellence, yet behind ;   the love of their
'country is still, I hope, one of their darling virtues.'
'Peace, Asem,' replied the Guardian, with a countenance
not less severe than beautiful, 'nor forfeit all thy
'pretensions to wisdom ;   the same selfish motives by
'which we prefer our own interest to that of others,
'induce us to regard our country preferably to that of
'another.   Nothing less than universal benevolence is
'free from vice, and that you see is practised here.'
'Strange !' cries the disappointed pilgrim, in an agony
of distress ;   'what sort of a world am I now introduced
'to ?   There is scarce a single virtue, but that of temper-
'ance, which they practise ;   and in that they are no
'way superior to the very brute creation.   There is scarce
'an amusement which they enjoy ;   fortitude, liberality,
'friendship, wisdom, conversation, and love of country,
'all are virtues entirely unknown here ;   thus it seems,
'that, to be unacquainted with vice is not to know
'virtue.   Take me, O my Genius, back to that very
'world which I have despised : a world which has
'Allah for its contriver is much more wisely formed
'than that which has been projected by Mahomet.
'Ingratitude, contempt, and hatred, I can now suffer,
'for perhaps I have deserved them.   When I arraigned
'the wisdom of Providence, I only showed my own
'ignorance ;   henceforth let me keep from vice myself,
'and pity it in others.'

He had scarce ended, when the Genius, assuming an air of terrible complacency, called all his thunders around him, and vanished in a whirlwind. Asem, astonished at the terror òf the scene, looked for his imaginary world ; when, casting his eyes around, he perceived himself in the very situation, and in the very place, where he first began to repine and despair ; his right foot had been just advanced to take the fatal plunge, nor had it been yet withdrawn ; so instantly did Providence strike the series of truths just imprinted on his soul. He now departed from the waterside in tranquillity, and, leaving his horrid mansion, travelled to Segestan, his native city ; where he diligently applied himself to commerce, and put in practice that wisdom he had learned in solitude. The frugality of a few years soon produced opulence ; the number of his domestics increased ; his friends came to him from every part of the city ; nor did he receive them with disdain ; and a youth of misery was concluded with an old age of elegance, affluence, and ease.

ESSAY XVII

ON THE ENGLISH CLERGY AND POPULAR PREACHERS

[From *The Ladies' Magazine*]

IT is allowed on all hands, that our English divines receive a more liberal education, and improve that education, by frequent study, more than any others of this reverend profession in Europe. In general, also, it may be observed, that a greater degree of gentility is annexed to the character of a student in England than elsewhere ; by which means our clergy have an opportunity of seeing better company while young, and of sooner wearing off those prejudices young men are apt to imbibe even in the best regulated universities, and which may be justly termed the vulgar errors of the wise.

Yet, with all these advantages, it is very obvious that the clergy are nowhere so little thought of, by the populace, as here ; and, though our divines are foremost, with respect to abilities, yet they are found last in the effects of their ministry ; the vulgar, in general, appearing no way impressed with a sense of religious duty. I am not for whining at the depravity of the times, or for endeavouring to paint a prospect more gloomy than in nature ; but certain it is, no person who has travelled will contradict me, when I aver that the lower orders of mankind, in other countries, testify, on every occasion, the profoundest awe of religion ; while in England they are scarcely awakened into a sense of its duties, even in circumstances of the greatest distress.

This dissolute and fearless conduct foreigners are apt to attribute to climate and constitution ; may not the vulgar, being pretty much neglected in our exhortations from the pulpit, be a conspiring cause ? Our divines seldom stoop to their mean capacities ; and they who want instruction most, find least in our religious assemblies.

Whatever may become of the higher orders of mankind, who are generally possessed of collateral motives to virtue, the vulgar should be particularly regarded, whose behaviour in civil life is totally hinged upon their hopes and fears. Those who constitute the basis of the great fabric of society should be particularly regarded ; for, in policy as in architecture, ruin is most fatal when it begins from the bottom.

Men of real sense and understanding prefer a prudent mediocrity to a precarious popularity ; and, fearing to outdo their duty, leave it half done. Their discourses from the pulpit are generally dry, methodical, and unaffecting ; delivered with the most insipid calmness ; insomuch, that, should the peaceful preacher lift his head over the cushion, which alone he seems to address, he might discover his audience, instead of being awakened to remorse, actually sleeping over his methodical and laboured composition.

This method of preaching is, however, by some called an address to reason, and not to the passions ; this is styled the making of converts from conviction : but such are indifferently acquainted with human nature, who are not sensible, that men seldom reason about their debaucheries till they are committed ; reason is but a weak antagonist when headlong passion dictates ; in all such cases we should arm one passion against another ; it is with the human mind as in nature, from the mixture of two opposites the result is most frequently neutral tranquillity. Those who attempt to reason us out of our follies, begin at the wrong end, since the attempt naturally presupposes us capable of reason ; but to be made capable of this, is one great point of the cure.

There are but few talents requisite to become a popular preacher, for the people are easily pleased if they perceive any endeavours in the orator to please them ; the meanest qualifications will work this effect, if the preacher sincerely sets about it. Perhaps little, indeed very little, more is required, than sincerity and assurance; and a becoming sincerity is always certain of producing a becoming assurance. ' Si vis me fiere, dolendum est ' primum tibi ipsi,' is so trite a quotation, that it almost demands an apology to repeat it ; yet, though all allow the justice of the remark, how few do we find put it in practice ? Our orators, with the most faulty bashfulness, seem impressed rather with an awe of their audience than with a just respect for the truths they are about to deliver;

they, of all professions, seem the most bashful, who have the greatest right to glory in their commission.

The French preachers generally assume all that dignity which becomes men who are ambassadors from Christ; the English divines, like erroneous envoys, seem more solicitous not to offend the court to which they are sent, than to drive home the interests of their employer. The Bishop of Massillon, in the first sermon he ever preached, found the whole audience, upon his getting into the pulpit, in a disposition no way favourable to his intentions; their nods, whispers, or drowsy behaviour, showed him that there was no great profit to be expected from his sowing in a soil so improper; however, he soon changed the disposition of his audience by his manner of beginning: 'If,' says he, 'a cause, the 'most important that could be conceived, were to be 'tried at the bar before qualified judges; if this cause 'interested ourselves in particular; if the eyes of the 'whole kingdom were fixed upon the event; if the most 'eminent counsel were employed on both sides; and if 'we had heard from our infancy of this yet undeter-'mined trial; would you not all sit with due attention, 'and warm expectations, to the pleadings on each side? 'would not all your hopes and fears be hinged upon the 'final decision? And yet, let me tell you, you have 'this moment a cause of much greater importance before 'you; a cause where not one nation, but all the world, 'are spectators; tried not before a fallible tribunal, but 'the awful throne of Heaven, where not your temporal 'and transitory interests are the subject of debate, but 'your eternal happiness or misery, where the cause is still 'undetermined; but, perhaps, the very moment I am 'speaking, may fix the irrevocable decree that shall last 'for ever; and yet, notwithstanding all this, you can 'hardly sit with patience to hear the tidings of your own 'salvation; I plead the cause of Heaven, and yet I am 'scarcely attended to,' &c.

The style, the abruptness of a beginning like this, in the closet would appear absurd: but in the pulpit it is attended with the most lasting impressions : that style, which, in the closet, might justly be called flimsy, seems the true mode of eloquence here. I never read a fine composition, under the title of sermon, that I do not think the author has miscalled his piece ; for the talents to be used in writing well, entirely differ from those of speaking well. The qualifications for speaking, as has been already observed, are easily acquired ; they are accomplishments which may be taken up by every candidate who will be at the pains of stooping. Impressed with a sense of the truths he is about to deliver, a preacher disregards the applause or the contempt of his audience, and he insensibly assumes a just and manly sincerity. With this talent alone we see what crowds are drawn around enthusiasts, even destitute of common sense ; what numbers converted to Christianity. Folly may sometimes set an example for wisdom to practise, and our regular divines may borrow instruction from even Methodists, who go their circuits and preach prizes among the populace. Even Whitfield may be placed as a model to some of our young divines ; let them join to their own good sense his earnest manner of delivery.

It will be perhaps objected, that, by confining the excellences of a preacher to proper assurance, earnestness, and openness of style, I make the qualifications too trifling for estimation : there will be something called oratory brought up on this occasion ; action, attitude, grace, elocution, may be repeated as absolutely necessary to complete the character ; but let us not be deceived ; common sense is seldom swayed by fine tones, musical periods, just attitudes, or the display of a white handkerchief ; oratorial behaviour, except in very able hands indeed, generally sinks into awkward and paltry affectation.

It must be observed, however, that these rules are calculated only for him who would instruct the vulgar, who stand in most need of instruction ; to address philosophers, and to obtain the character of a polite preacher among the polite—a much more useless, though more sought-for character—requires a different method of proceeding. All I shall observe on this head is, to entreat the polemic divine, in his controversy with the Deists, to act rather offensively than to defend ; to push home the grounds of his belief, and the impracticability of theirs, rather than to spend time in solving the objections of every opponent. ' It is ten to one,' says a late writer on the art of war, ' but that the assailant ' who attacks the enemy in his trenches, is always ' victorious.'

Yet, upon the whole, our clergy might employ themselves more to the benefit of society, by declining all controversy, than by exhibiting even the profoundest skill in polemic disputes ; their contests with each other often turn on speculative trifles ; and their disputes with the Deists are almost at an end since they can have no more than victory, and that they are already possessed of, as their antagonists have been driven into a confession of the necessity of revelation, or an open avowal of theism. To continue the dispute longer would only endanger it ; the sceptic is ever expert at puzzling a debate which he finds himself unable to continue ; ' and, like an Olympic boxer, generally fights best when ' undermost.'

ESSAY XVIII

ON THE ADVANTAGES TO·BE DERIVED FROM SENDING A JUDICIOUS TRAVELLER INTO ASIA

[Altered from Letter CVIII of *The Citizen of the World*]

I HAVE frequently been amazed at the ignorance of almost all the European travellers who have penetrated any considerable way eastward into Asia. They have all been influenced either by motives of commerce or piety, and their accounts are such as might reasonably be expected from men of a very narrow or very prejudiced education, the dictates of superstition, or the result of ignorance. Is it not surprising, that, of such a variety of adventurers, not one single philosopher should be found among the number ? For, as to the travels of Gemelli, the learned are long agreed that the whole is but an imposture.

There is scarce any country, how rude or uncultivated soever, where the inhabitants are not possessed of some peculiar secrets, either in nature or art, which might be transplanted with success : thus, for instance, in Siberian Tartary, the natives extract a strong spirit from milk, which is a secret probably unknown to the chemists of Europe. In the most savage parts of India they are possessed of the secret of dyeing vegetable substances scarlet, and likewise that of refining lead into a metal, which, for hardness and colour, is little inferior to silver ; not one of which secrets but would, in Europe, make a man's fortune. The power of the Asiatics in producing winds, or bringing down rain, the Europeans are apt to treat as fabulous, because they have no instances of the like nature among themselves ; but they would have treated the secrets of gunpowder, and the mariner's compass, in the same manner, had they been told the

Chinese used such arts before the invention was common with themselves at home.

Of all the English philosophers, I most reverence Bacon, that great and hardy genius : he it is who, undaunted by the seeming difficulties that oppose, prompts human curiosity to examine every part of nature ; and even exhorts man to try whether he cannot subject the tempest, the thunder, and even earthquakes, to human control. Oh ! had a man of his daring spirit, of his genius, penetration, and learning, travelled to those countries which have been visited only by the superstitious and mercenary, what might not mankind expect ! How would he enlighten the regions to which he travelled ! and what a variety of knowledge and useful improvement would he not bring back in exchange !

There is probably no country so barbarous, that would not disclose all it knew, if it received equivalent information ; and I am apt to think, that a person, who was ready to give more knowledge than he received, would be welcome wherever he came. All his care in travelling should only be to suit his intellectual banquet to the people with whom he conversed : he should not attempt to teach the unlettered Tartar astronomy, nor yet instruct the polite Chinese in the arts of subsistence : he should endeavour to improve the barbarian in the secrets of living comfortably ; and the inhabitant of a more refined country in the speculative pleasures of science. How much more nobly would a philosopher, thus employed, spend his time, than by sitting at home, earnestly intent upon adding one star more to his catalogue, or one monster more to his collection ; or still, if possible, more triflingly sedulous in the incatenation of fleas, or the sculpture of cherry-stones.

I never consider this subject, without being surprised that none of those societies, so laudably established in

England for the promotion of arts and learning, have ever thought of sending one of their members into the most eastern parts of Asia, to make what discoveries he was able. To be convinced of the utility of such an undertaking, let them but read the relations of their own travellers. It will there be found, that they are as often deceived themselves, as they attempt to deceive others. The merchants tell us, perhaps, the price of different commodities, the methods of baling them up, and the properest manner for a European to preserve his health in the country. The missioner, on the other hand, informs us with what pleasure the country to which he was sent embraced Christianity, and the numbers he converted ; what methods he took to keep Lent in a region where there was no fish, or the shifts he made to celebrate the rites of his religion, in places where there was neither bread nor wine : such accounts, with the usual appendage of marriages and funerals, inscriptions, rivers, and mountains, make up the whole of a European traveller's diary ; but as to all the secrets of which the inhabitants are possessed, those are universally attributed to magic ; and when the traveller can give no other account of the wonders he sees performed, he very contentedly ascribes them to the devil.

It was a usual observation of Boyle, the English chemist, that, if every artist would but discover what new observations occurred to him in the exercise of his trade, philosophy would thence gain innumerable improvements. It may be observed, with still greater justice, that, if the useful knowledge of every country, howsoever barbarous, was gleaned by a judicious observer, the advantages would be inestimable. Are there not, even in Europe, many useful inventions, known or practised but in one place ? The instrument, as an example, for cutting down corn in Germany, is much more handy and expeditious, in my opinion, than the sickle used in England. The cheap and expeditious manner of making vinegar, without previous fermentation, is known only in a part of France. If such discoveries therefore remain still to be known at home, what funds of knowledge might not be collected in countries yet unexplored, or only passed through by ignorant travellers in hasty caravans ?

The caution with which foreigners are received in Asia, may be alleged as an objection to such a design. But how readily have several European merchants found admission into regions the most suspicious, under the character of Sanjapins, or northern pilgrims ? To such, not even China itself denies access.

To send out a traveller properly qualified for these purposes, might be an object of national concern ; it would, in some measure, repair the breaches made by ambition ; · and might show that there were still some who boasted a greater name than that of patriots, who professed themselves lovers of men.

The only difficulty would remain in choosing a proper person for so arduous an enterprise. He should be a man of a philosophical turn, one apt to deduce consequences of general utility from particular occurrences, neither swollen with pride, nor hardened by prejudice ; neither wedded to one particular system, nor instructed only in one particular science ; neither wholly a botanist, nor quite an antiquarian : his mind should be tinctured with miscellaneous knowledge, and his manners humanized by an intercourse with men. He should be, in some measure, an enthusiast to the design ; fond of travelling, from a rapid imagination, and an innate love of change ; furnished with a body capable of sustaining every fatigue, and a heart not easily terrified at danger.

ESSAY XIX

A REVERIE AT THE BOAR'S HEAD TAVERN IN EAST-CHEAP

THE improvements we make in mental acquirements, only render us each day more sensible of the defects of our constitution : with this in view, therefore, let us often recur to the amusements of youth ; endeavour to forget age and wisdom, and, as far as innocence goes, be as much a boy as the best of them.

Let idle declaimers mourn over the degeneracy of the age; but, in my opinion, every age is the same. This I am sure of, that man, in every season, is a poor fretful being, with no other means to escape the calamities of the times but by endeavouring to forget them ; for, if he attempts to resist, he is certainly undone. If I feel poverty and pain, I am not so hardy as to quarrel with the executioner, even while under correction : I find myself no way disposed to make fine speeches, while I am making wry faces. In a word, let me drink when the fit is on, to make me insensible ; and drink when it is over, for joy that I feel pain no longer.

The character of old Falstaff, even with all his faults, gives me more consolation than the most studied efforts of wisdom : I here behold an agreeable old fellow, forgetting age, and showing me the way to be young at sixty-five. Sure I am well able to be as merry, though not so comical, as he. Is it not in my power to have, though not so much wit, at least as much vivacity ? Age, care; wisdom, reflection, be gone—I give you to the winds. Let's have t'other bottle : here's to the memory of Shakespeare, Falstaff, and all the merry men of East-cheap.

Such were the reflections that naturally arose while

I sat at the Boar's Head Tavern, still kept at East-
cheap. Here, by a pleasant fire, in the very room where
old Sir John Falstaff cracked his jokes, in the very
chair which was sometimes honoured by Prince Henry,
and sometimes polluted by his immortal merry companions, I sat and ruminated on the follies of youth ;
wished to be young again ; but was resolved to make
the best of life while it lasted, and now and then compared past and present times together. I considered
myself as the only living representative of the old knight,
and transported my imagination back to the times
when the prince and he gave life to the revel, and made
even debauchery not disgusting. The room also conspired to throw my reflections back into antiquity : the
oak floor, the Gothic windows, and the ponderous
chimney-piece, had long withstood the tooth of time :
the watchman had gone twelve : my companions had all
stolen off, and none now remained with me but the
landlord. From him I could have wished to know the
history of a tavern that had such a long succession of
customers. I could not help thinking that an account of
·this kind would be a pleasing contrast of the manners
of different ages ; but my landlord could give me no
information. He continued to doze and sot, and tell
a tedious story, as most other landlords usually do ;
and, though he said nothing, yet was never silent : one
good joke followed another good joke ; and the best
joke of all was generally begun towards the end of
a bottle. I found at last, however, his wine and his
conversation operate by degrees. He insensibly began
to alter his appearance : his cravat seemed quilled into
a ruff, and his breeches swelled out into a fardingale.
I now fancied him changing sexes : and, as my eyes
began to close in slumber, I imagined my fat landlord
actually converted into as fat a landlady. However,

sleep made but few changes in my situation : the tavern,
the apartment and the table, continued as before ;
nothing suffered mutation but my host, who was fairly
altered into a gentlewoman, whom I knew to be Dame
Quickly, mistress of this tavern in the days of Sir John ;
and the liquor we were drinking, seemed converted into
sack and sugar.

  ' My dear Mrs. Quickly,' cried I (for I knew her
perfectly well at first sight), ' I am heartily glad to see
' you. How have you left Falstaff, Pistol, and the rest of
' our friends below stairs ? Brave and hearty, I hope ? '
—' In good sooth,' replied she, ' he did deserve to
' live for ever ; but he maketh foul work on 't where he
' hath flitted. Queen Proserpine and he have quarrelled
' for his attempting a rape upon her divinity ; and
' were it not that she still had bowels of compassion,
' it more than seems probable he might have been now
' sprawling in Tartarus.'

  I now found that spirits still preserve the frailties of
the flesh ; and that, according to the laws of criticism
and dreaming, ghosts have been known to be guilty of
even more than platonic affection : wherefore, as I found
her too much moved on such a topic to proceed, I was
resolved to change the subject ; and desiring she would
pledge me in a bumper, observed, with a sigh, that our
sack was nothing now to what it was in former days :
' Ah, Mrs. Quickly, those were merry times when you
' drew sack for Prince Henry : men were twice as strong,
' and twice as wise, and much braver, and ten thousand
' times more charitable, than now. Those were the
' times ! The Battle of Agincourt was a victory indeed !
' Ever since that we have only been degenerating ; and
' I have lived to see the day when drinking is no longer
' fashionable ; when men wear clean shirts, and women
' show their necks and arms. All are degenerated,

'Mrs. Quickly; and we shall probably, in another
'century, be frittered away into beaux or monkeys. Had
'you been on earth to see what I have seen, it would
'congeal all the blood in your body (your soul, I mean).
'Why, our very nobility now have the intolerable
'arrogance, in spite of what is every day remonstrated
'from the press; our very nobility, I say, have the
'assurance to frequent assemblies, and presume to be as
'merry as the vulgar. See, my very friends have scarce
'manhood enough to sit to it till eleven; and I only am
'left to make a night on 't. Prithee do me the favour
'to console me a little for their absence by the story
'of your own adventures, or the history of the tavern
'where we are now sitting : I fancy the narrative may
'have something singular.'

  ' Observe this apartment,' interrupted my companion ;
'of neat device and excellent workmanship—In this
'room I have lived, child, woman, and ghost, more than
'three hundred years : I am ordered by Pluto to keep
'an annual register of every transaction that passed here ;
'and I have whilom compiled three hundred tomes,
'which eftsoons may be submitted to thy regards.'
'None of your whiloms or eftsoons, Mrs. Quickly, if you
'please,' I replied : 'I know you can talk every whit as
'well as I can ; for, as you have lived here so long, it
'is but natural to suppose you should learn the con-
'versation of the company. Believe me, dame, at best,
'you have neither too much sense nor too much language
'to spare ; so give me both as well as you can : but,
'first, my service to you : old women should water their
'clay a little now and then ; and now to your story.'

  ' The story of my own adventures,' replied the vision,
'is but short and unsatisfactory; for, believe me,
'Mr. Rigmarole, believe me, a woman with a butt of
'sack at her elbow is never long-lived. Sir John's

'death afflicted me to such a degree, that I sincerely
'believe, to drown sorrow, I drank more liquor myself
'than I drew for my customers : my grief was sincere,
'and the sack was excellent. The prior of a neigh-
'bouring convent (for our priors then had as much power
'as a Middlesex justice now), he, I say, it was who gave
'me a licence for keeping a disorderly house, upon
'condition, that I should never make hard bargains with
'the clergy, that he should have a bottle of sack every
'morning, and the liberty of confessing which of my
'girls he thought proper in private every night. I had
'continued, for several years, to pay this tribute ; and
'he, it must be confessed, continued as rigorously to
'exact it. I grew old insensibly ; my customers con-
'tinued, however, to compliment my looks while I was
'by, but I could hear them say I was wearing when my
'back was turned. The prior, however, still was constant,
'and so were half his convent : but one fatal morning
'he missed the usual beverage ; for I had incautiously
'drank over night the last bottle myself. What will you
'have on 't ?—The very next day Doll Tearsheet and
'I were sent to the house of correction, and accused of
'keeping a low bawdy-house. In short, we were so well
'purified there with stripes, mortification, and penance,
'that we were afterwards utterly unfit for worldly
'conversation : though sack would have killed me, had
'I stuck to it, yet I soon died for want of a drop of
'something comfortable, and fairly left my body to the
'care of the beadle.
  ' Such is my own history ; but that of the tavern,
'where I have ever since been stationed, affords greater
'variety. In the history of this, which is one of the
'oldest in London, you may view the different manners,
'pleasures, and follies, of men at different periods. You
'will find mankind neither better nor worse now than

'formerly: the vices of an uncivilized people are
'generally more detestable, though not so frequent, as
'those in polite society. It is the same luxury which
'formerly stuffed your alderman with plum-porridge,
'and now crams him with turtle. It is the same low
'ambition that formerly induced a courtier to give up
'his religion to please his king, and now persuades him
'to give up his conscience to please his minister. It is
'the same vanity that formerly stained our ladies' cheeks
'and necks with woad, and now paints them with
'carmine. Your ancient Briton formerly powdered his
'hair with red earth like brickdust, in order to appear
'frightful: your modern Briton cuts his hair on the
'crown, and plasters it with hog's-lard and flour; and
'this to make him look killing. It is the same vanity,
'the same folly, and the same vice, only appearing
'different, as viewed through the glass of fashion. In
'a word, all mankind are——'

'Sure the woman is dreaming,' interrupted I. 'None
'of your reflections, Mrs. Quickly, if you love me; they
'only give me the spleen. Tell me your history at once.
'I love stories, but hate reasoning.'

'If you please then, sir,' returned my companion, 'I'll
'read you an abstract which I made of the three hundred
'volumes I mentioned just now.'

'My body was no sooner laid in the dust, than the
'prior and several of his convent came to purify the
'tavern from the pollutions with which they said I had
'filled it. Masses were said in every room, relics were
'exposed upon every piece of furniture, and the whole
'house washed with a deluge of holy-water. My
'habitation was soon converted into a monastery;
'instead of customers now applying for sack and sugar,
'my rooms were crowded with images, relics, saints,
'whores, and friars. Instead of being a scene of occa-

'sional debauchery, it was now filled with continual
' lewdness. The prior led the, fashion, and the whole
' convent imitated his pious example. Matrons came
' hither to confess their sins,, and to commit new. Virgins
' came hither who seldom went virgins away. Nor was
' this a convent peculiarly wicked ; every convent at
' that period was equally fond of pleasure, and gave
' a boundless loose to appetite. The laws allowed it ;
' each priest had a right to a favourite companion, and
' a .power of discarding her as often as he pleased. The
' laity grumbled, quarrelled with their wives and
' daughters, hated their confessors, and maintained them
' in opulence and ease. These, these were happy times,
' Mr. Rigmarole ; these were times of piety, bravery,
' and simplicity ! '—' Not so very happy, neither, good
' madam ; pretty much like the present ; those that
' labour starve, and those that do nothing wear fine
' clothes and live in luxury.'

' In this manner the fathers lived, for some years,
' without molestation ; they transgressed, confessed
' themselves . to each other, and were forgiven. One
' evening, however, our prior keeping a lady of distinction
' somewhat too long at confession, her husband unex-
' pectedly came upon them, and testified all the indigna-
' tion which was natural upon such an occasion. The
' prior assured the gentleman that it was the devil who
' had put it into his heart ; and the lady was very
' certain, that she was under the influence of magic, or
' she could never have behaved in so unfaithful a manner.
' The husband, however, was not to be put off by such
' evasions, but summoned both before the tribunal of
' justice. His proofs were flagrant, and he expected
' large damages. Such, indeed, he had a right to expect,
' were the tribunals of those days constituted in the same
' manner as they are now. The cause of the priest was to

' be tried before an assembly of priests ; and a layman
' was to expect redress only from their impartiality and
' candour. What plea then do you think the prior made
' to obviate this accusation ? He denied the fact, and
' challenged the plaintiff to try the merits of their cause
' by single combat. It was a little hard, you may be
' sure, upon the poor gentleman, not only to be made
' a cuckold, but to be obliged to fight a duel into the
' bargain ; yet such was the justice of the times. The
' prior threw down his glove, and the injured husband
' was obliged to take it up, in token of his accepting the
' challenge. Upon this the priest supplied his champion,
' for it was not lawful for the clergy to fight ; and the
' defendant and plaintiff, according to custom, were put
' in prison ; both ordered to fast and pray, every method
' being previously used to induce both to a confession of
' the truth. After a month's imprisonment, the hair of
' each was cut, the bodies anointed with oil, the field of
' battle appointed and guarded by soldiers, while his
' majesty presided over the whole in person. Both the
' champions were sworn not to seek victory either by
' fraud or magic. They prayed and confessed upon their
' knees ; and after these ceremonies, the rest was left
' to the courage and conduct of the combatants. As the
' champion whom the prior had pitched upon, had
' fought six or eight times upon similar occasions, it was
' no way extraordinary to . find him victorious in the
' present combat. In short, the husband was dis-
' comfited ; he was taken from the field of battle,
' stripped to his shirt, and, after one of his legs was
' cut off, as justice ordained in such cases, he was
' hanged as a terror to future offenders. These, these
' were the times, Mr. Rigmarole ; you see how much
' more just, and wise, and valiant, our ancestors were
' than us.'—'I rather fancy, madam, that the times

' then were pretty much like our own ; where a multi-
'plicity of laws give a judge as much power as a want
' of law ; since he is ever sure to find among the number
' some to countenance his partiality.'

 ' Our convent, victorious over their enemies, now gave
' a loose to every demonstration of joy. The lady
' became a nun, the prior was made a bishop, and three
' Wickliffites were burned in the illuminations and fire-
' works that were made on the present occasion. Our
' convent now began to enjoy a very high degree of
' reputation. There was not one in London that had
' the character of hating heretics so much as ours. Ladies
' of the first distinction chose from our convent their
' confessors ; in short, it flourished, and might have
' flourished to this hour, but for a fatal accident which
' terminated in its overthrow. The lady, whom the prior
' had placed in a nunnery, and whom he continued to
' visit for some time with great punctuality, began at
' last to perceive that she was quite forsaken. Secluded
' from conversation, as usual, she now entertained the
' visions of a devotee ; found herself strangely disturbed ;
' but hesitated in determining, whether she was possessed
' by an angel or a demon. She was not long in suspense ;
' for upon vomiting a large quantity of crooked pins, and
' finding the palms of her hands turned outwards, she
' quickly concluded that she was possessed by the devil.
' She soon lost entirely the use of speech ; and, when she
' seemed to speak, everybody that was present perceived
' that her voice was not her own, but that of the devil
' within her. In short, she was bewitched ; and all the
' difficulty lay in determining who it could be that
' bewitched her. The nuns and the monks all demanded
' the magician's name, but the devil made no reply ; for
' he knew they had no authority to ask questions. By
' the rules of witchcraft, when an evil spirit has taken

'possession, he may refuse to answer any questions
'asked him, unless they are put by a bishop, and to
'these he is obliged to reply.   A bishop, therefore, was
'sent for, and now the whole secret came out : the devil
'reluctantly owned that he was a servant of the prior ;
'that, by his command, he resided in his present habita-
'tion ; and that, without his command, he was resolved
'to keep in possession. The bishop was an able exorcist ;
'he drove the devil out by force of mystical arms ; the
'prior was arraigned for witchcraft ; the witnesses were
'strong and numerous against him, not less than fourteen
'persons being by who heard the devil talk Latin. There
'was no resisting such a cloud of witnesses ; the prior
'was condemned ; and he who had assisted at so many
'burnings, was burned himself in turn.   These were
'times, Mr. Rigmarole ; the people of those times were
'not infidels, as now, but sincere believers ! '—' Equally
'faulty with ourselves ; they believed what the devil
'was pleased to tell them ; and we seem resolved, at
'last, to believe neither God nor devil.'

'After such a stain upon the convent, it was not to be
'supposed it could subsist any longer ; the fathers were
'ordered to decamp, and the house was once again
'converted into a tavern. The king conferred it on one
'of his cast-off mistresses ; she was constituted landlady
'by royal authority ; and as the tavern was in the
'neighbourhood of the court, and the mistress a very
'polite woman, it began to have more business than ever,
'and sometimes took not less than four shillings a day.

'But perhaps you are desirous of knowing what were
'the peculiar qualifications of women of fashion at that
'period ; and in a description of the present landlady,
'you will have a tolerable idea of all the rest. This lady
'was the daughter of a nobleman, and received such an
'education in the country as became her quality,

' beauty, and great expectations. She could make
' shifts and hose for herself and all the servants of the
' family, when she was twelve years old. She knew the
' names of the four and twenty letters, so that it was
' impossible to bewitch her ; and this was a greater
' piece of learning than any lady in the whole country
' could prétend to. She was always up early, and saw
' breakfast served in the great hall by six o'clock. At
' this scene of festivity she generally improved good
' humour, by telling her dreams, relating stories of
' spirits, several of which she herself had seen, and one
' of which she was reported to have killed with a black-
' hafted knife. From hence she usually went to make
' pastry in the larder, and here she was followed by her
' sweethearts, who were much helped on in conversation
' by struggling with her for kisses. About ten, Miss
' generally went to play at hot-cockles and blindman's
' buff in the parlour ; and when the young folks (for
' they seldom played at hot-cockles when grown old)
' were tired of such amusements, the gentlemen enter-
' tained Miss with the history of their greyhounds,
' bear-baitings, and victories at cudgel-playing. If the
' weather was fine, they ran at the ring, shot at butts,
' while Miss held in her hand a ribbon, with which she
' adorned the conqueror. Her mental qualifications were
' exactly fitted to her external accomplishments. Before
' she was fifteen, she could tell the story of Jack the
' Giant Killer, could name every mountain that was
' inhabited by fairies, knew a witch at first sight, and
' could repeat four Latin prayers without a prompter.
' Her dress was perfectly fashionable ; her arms and her
' hair were completely covered ; a monstrous ruff was
' put round her neck ; so that her head seemed like that
' of John the Baptist placed in a charger. In short,
' when completely equipped, her appearance was so very

'modest, that she discovered little more than her nose.
'These were the times, Mr. Rigmarole; when every
'lady that had a good nose might set up for a beauty;
'when every woman that could tell stories might be
'cried up for a wit.'—'I am as much displeased at those
'dresses which conceal too much, as at those which
'discover too much : I am equally an enemy to a female
'dunce or a female pedant.'

'You may be sure that Miss chose a husband with
'qualifications resembling her own ; she pitched upon
'a courtier, equally remarkable for hunting and drinking,
'who had given several proofs of his great virility among
'the daughters of his tenants and domestics. They fell
'in love at first sight (for such was the gallantry of the
'times), were married, came to court, and Madam
'appeared with superior qualifications. The king was
'struck with her beauty. All property was at the king's
'command ; the husband was obliged to resign all
'pretensions in his wife to the sovereign whom God had
'anointed, to commit adultery where he thought proper.
'The king loved her for some time ; but at length,
'repenting of his misdeeds, and instigated by his father-
'confessor, from a principle of conscience, removed her
'from his levee to the bar of this tavern, and took a new
'mistress in her stead. Let it not surprise you to
'behold the mistress of a king degraded to so humble an
'office. As the ladies had no mental accomplishments,
'a good face was enough to raise them to the royal
'couch ; and she who was this day a royal mistress,
'might the next, when her beauty palled upon enjoy-
'ment, be doomed to infamy and want.

'Under the care of this lady, the tavern grew into
'great reputation ; the courtiers had not yet learned to
'game, but they paid it off by drinking : drunkenness is
'ever the vice of a barbarous, and gaming of a luxurious,

' age. They had not such frequent entertainments as
' the moderns have, but were more expensive and more
' luxurious in those they had. All their fooleries were
' more elaborate, and more admired by the great and
' the vulgar than now. A courtier has been known to
' spend his whole fortune at a single feast, a king to
' mortgage his dominions to furnish out the frippery of
' a tournament. There were certain days appointed for
' riot and debauchery, and to be sober at such times was
' reputed a crime. Kings themselves set the example ;
' and I have seen monarchs in this room drunk before
' the entertainment was half concluded. These were the
' times, sir, when kings kept mistresses, and got drunk in
' public ; they were too plain and simple in those happy
' times to hide their vices, and act the hypocrite, as now.'
—' Lord ! Mrs. Quickly,' interrupting her, ' I expected
' to have heard a story, and here you are going to tell
' me I know not what of times and vices ; prithee let
' me entreat thee once more to waive reflections, and
' give thy history without deviation.'

' No lady upon earth,' continued my visionary correspondent, ' knew how to put off her damaged wine or
' women with more art than she. When these grew
' flat, or those paltry, it was but changing the names ;
' the wine became excellent, and the girls agreeable. She
' was also possessed of the engaging leer, the chuck
' under the chin, winked at a *double entendre*, could
' nick the opportunity of calling for something comfort-
' able, and perfectly understood the discreet moments
' when to withdraw. The gallants of those times pretty
' much resembled the bloods of ours ; they were fond
' of pleasure, but quite ignorant of the art of refining
' upon it : thus a court-bawd of those times resembled
' the common low-lived harridan of a modern bagnio.
' Witness, ye powers of debauchery, how often I have

'been present at the various appearances of drunkenness,
'riot, guilt, and brutality ! A tavern is a true picture of
'human infirmity ; in history we find only one side of the
'age exhibited to our view; but in the accounts of a tavern
'we see every age equally absurd and equally vicious.'

'Upon this lady's decease the tavern was successively
'occupied by adventurers, bullies, pimps, and gamesters.
'Towards the conclusion of the reign of Henry VII gaming
'was more universally practised in England than even
'now. Kings themselves have been known to play off,
'at Primero, not only all the money and jewels they
'could part with, but the very images in churches. The
'last Henry played away, in this very room, not only
'the four great bells of St. Paul's Cathedral, but the fine
'image of St. Paul, which stood upon the top of the
'spire, to Sir Miles Partridge, who took them down the
'next day, and sold them by auction. Have you then
'any cause to regret being born in the times you now
'live? or do you still believe that human nature continues
'to run on declining every age ? If we observe the
'actions of the busy part of mankind, your ancestors
'will be found infinitely more gross, servile, and even
'dishonest, than you. If, forsaking history, we only
'trace them in their hours of amusement and dissipation,
'we shall find them more sensual, more entirely
'devoted to pleasure, and infinitely more selfish.

'The last hostess of note I find upon record, was
'Jane Rouse. She was born among the lower ranks
'of the people ; and, by frugality and extreme com-
'plaisance, contrived to acquire a moderate fortune :
'this she might have enjoyed for many years, had she
'not unfortunately quarrelled with one of her neighbours,
'a woman who was in high repute for sanctity through
'the whole parish. In the times of which I speak, two
'women seldom quarrelled, that one did not accuse the

'other of witchcraft, and she who first contrived to
'vomit crooked pins was sure to come off victorious.
'The scandal of a modern tea-table differs widely from
'the scandal of former times : the fascination of a lady's
'eyes, at present, is regarded as a compliment ; but if
'a lady, formerly, should be accused of having witchcraft
'in her eyes, it were much better, both for her soul and
'body, that she had no eyes at all.

'In short, Jane Rouse was accused of witchcraft ; and,
'though she made the best defence she could, it was all
'to no purpose ; she was taken from her own bar to
'the bar of the Old Bailey, condemned, and executed
'accordingly. These were times, indeed ! when even
'women could not scold in safety.

'Since her time the tavern underwent several revolu-
'tions, according to the spirit of the times, or the dis-
'position of the reigning monarch. It was this day
'a brothel, and the next a conventicle for enthusiasts.
'It was one year noted for harbouring Whigs, and the
'next infamous for a retreat to Tories. Some years ago
'it was in high vogue, but at present it seems declining.
'This only may be remarked in general, that whenever
'taverns flourish most, the times are then most ex-
'travagant and luxurious.'——'Lord ! Mrs. Quickly,'
interrupted I, 'you have really deceived me ; I expected
'a romance, and here you have been this half-hour
'giving me only a description of the spirit of the times :
'if you have nothing but tedious remarks to com-
'municate, seek some other hearer ; I am determined
'to hearken only to stories.'

I had scarce concluded, when my eyes and ears
seemed opened to my landlord, who had been all this
while giving me an account of the repairs he had made
in the house, and was now got into the story of the
cracked glass in the dining-room.

ESSAY XX

ON QUACK DOCTORS

[Altered from Letters XXIV and LXVIII of *The Citizen of the World*]

WHATEVER may be the merits of the English in other sciences, they seem peculiarly excellent in the art of healing. There is scarcely a disorder incident to humanity, against which our advertising doctors are not possessed with a most infallible antidote. The professors of other arts confess the inevitable intricacy of things ; talk with doubt, and decide with hesitation ; but doubting is entirely unknown in medicine ; the advertising professors here delight in cases of difficulty : be the disorder never so desperate or radical, you will find numbers in every street, who, by levelling a pill at the part affected, promise a certain cure, without loss of time, knowledge of a bedfellow, or hindrance of business.

When I consider the assiduity of this profession, their benevolence amazes me. They not only, in general, give their medicines for half value, but use the most persuasive remonstrances to induce the sick to come and be cured. Sure there must be something strangely obstinate in an English patient, who refuses so much health upon such easy terms ! Does he take a pride in being bloated with a dropsy ? Does he find pleasure in the alternations of an intermittent fever ? or feel as much satisfaction in nursing up his gout, as he found pleasure in acquiring it ? He must, otherwise he would never reject such repeated assurances of instant relief. What can be more convincing than the manner in which the sick are invited to be well ? The doctor first begs the most earnest attention of the public to what he is going to propose ; he solemnly affirms the pill was never found to want success; he produces a list of those who have been rescued from the grave by taking it. Yet, notwithstanding all this, there are many here who now and then think proper to be sick. Only sick! did I say? There are some who even think proper to die. Yes, by the head of Confucius, they die; though they might have purchased the health-restoring specific for half a crown at every corner.

I can never enough admire the sagacity of this country for the encouragement given to the professors of this art. With what indulgence does she foster up those of her own growth, and kindly cherish those that come from abroad! Like a skilful gardener, she invites them from every foreign climate to herself. Here every great exotic strikes root as soon as imported, and feels the genial beam of favour; while the mighty metropolis, like one vast munificent dunghill, receives them indiscriminately to her breast, and supplies each with more than native nourishment.

In other countries, the physician pretends to cure disorders in the lump: the same doctor who combats the gout in the toe, shall pretend to prescribe for a pain in the head; and he who at one time cures a consumption, shall at another give drugs for a dropsy. How absurd and ridiculous! This is being a mere jack of all trades. Is the animal machine less complicated than a brass pin? Not less than ten different hands are required to make a brass pin; and shall the body be set right by one single operator?

The English are sensible of the force of this reasoning; they have therefore one doctor for the eyes, another for the toes; they have their sciatica doctors, and inoculating doctors; they have one doctor who is modestly content with securing them from bug-bites, and five hundred who prescribe for the bite of mad dogs.

But as nothing pleases curiosity more than anecdotes of the great, however minute or trifling, I must present you, inadequate as my abilities are to the subject, with an account of one or two of those personages who lead in this honourable profession.

The first upon the list of glory is Doctor Richard Rock. This great man is short of stature, is fat, and waddles as he walks. He always wears a white three-tailed wig nicely combed, and frizzled upon each cheek. Sometimes he carries a cane, but a hat never; it is indeed very remarkable that this extraordinary personage should never wear a hat, but so it is; a hat he never wears. He is usually drawn, at the top of his own bills, sitting in his arm-chair, holding a little bottle between his finger and thumb, and surrounded with rotten teeth, nippers, pills, packets, and gallipots. No man can promise fairer or better than he; for, as he observes, 'Be your disorder never so far gone, be under no un= 'easiness, make yourself quite easy, I can cure you.'

The next in fame, though by some reckoned of equal pretensions, is Doctor Timothy Franks, living in the Old Bailey. As Rock is remarkably squab, his great rival Franks is remarkably tall. He was born in the year of the Christian era 1692, and is, while I now write, exactly sixty-eight years, three months and four days old. Age, however, has no ways impaired his usual health and vivacity; I am told he generally walks with his breast open. This gentleman, who is of a mixed reputation, is particularly remarkable for a becoming assurance, which carries him gently through life; for, except Doctor Rock, none are more blessed with the advantage of face than Doctor Franks.

And yet the great have their foibles as well as the little. I am almost ashamed to mention it—let the foibles of the great rest in peace—yet I must impart the whole. These two great men are actually now at variance ; like mere men, mere common mortals. Rock advises the world to beware of bog-trotting quacks ; Franks retorts the wit and the sarcasm, by fixing on his rival the odious appellation of Dumpling Dick. He calls the serious Doctor Rock, Dumplin Dick ! What profanation ! Dumplin Dick ! What a pity, that the learned, who were born mutually to assist in enlightening the world, should thus differ among themselves, and make even the profession ridiculous ! Sure the world is wide enough, at least, for two great personages to figure in ; men of science should leave controversy to the little world below them ; and then we might see Rock and Franks walking together, hand in hand, smiling, onward to immortality.

ESSAY XXI

ADVENTURES OF A STROLLING PLAYER

I AM fond of amusement, in whatever company it is to be found ; and wit, though dressed in rags, is ever pleasing to me. I went some days ago to take a walk in St. James's Park, about the hour in which company leave it to go to dinner. There were but few in the walks, and those who stayed, seemed by their looks rather more willing to forget that they had an appetite than gain one. I sat down on one of the benches, at the other end of which was seated a man in very shabby clothes.

We continued to groan, to hem, and to cough, as usual upon such occasions ; and, at last, ventured upon conversation. ‘I beg pardon, sir,’ cried I, ‘but I think ‘I have seen you before; your face is familiar to me.’ ‘Yes, sir,’ replied he, ‘I have a good familiar face, as 'my friends tell me. I am as well known in every town 'in England as the dromedary, or live crocodile. You 'must understand, sir, that I have been these sixteen years 'Merry Andrew to a puppet-show; last Bartholomew Fair 'my master and I quarrelled, beat each other, and parted; 'he to sell his puppets to the pincushion-makers in 'Rosemary Lane, and I to starve in St. James's Park.'

'I am sorry, sir, that a person of your appearance 'should labour under any difficulties.' 'O, sir,' returned he, 'my appearance is very much at your service; but 'though I cannot boast of eating much, yet there are 'few that are merrier: if I had twenty thousand a year, 'I should be very merry; and, thank the fates, though 'not worth a groat, I am very merry still. If I have 'three-pence in my pocket, I never refuse to be my 'three halfpence; and if I have no money, I never 'scorn to be treated by any that are kind enough to 'pay my reckoning. What think you, sir, of a steak 'and a tankard? You shall treat me now, and I will 'treat you again when I find you in the Park in love 'with eating, and without money to pay for a dinner.'

As I never refuse a small expense for the sake of a merry companion, we instantly adjourned to a neighbouring alehouse, and in a few moments had a frothing tankard and a smoking steak spread on the table before us. It is impossible to express how much the sight of such good cheer improved my companion's vivacity. 'I like this dinner, sir,' says he, 'for three reasons: 'first, because I am naturally fond of beef; secondly, 'because I am hungry; and, thirdly and lastly, because 'I get it for nothing: no meat eats so sweet as that for 'which we do not pay.'

He therefore now fell to, and his appetite seemed to correspond with his inclination. After dinner was over, he observed that the steak was tough; 'and yet, sir,'

returns he, 'bad as it was, it seemed a rump-steak to
'me. Oh, the delights of poverty and a good appetite!
'We beggars are the very foundlings of Nature; the
'rich she treats like an arrant stepmother; they are
'pleased with nothing : cut a steak from what part you
'will, and it is insupportably tough; dress it up with
'pickles,—even pickles cannot procure them an appetite.
'But the whole creation is filled with good things for
'the beggar; Calvert's butt out-tastes champagne, and
'Sedgeley's home-brewed excels tokay. Joy, joy, my
'blood! though our estates lie nowhere, we have fortunes
'wherever we go. If an inundation sweeps away half
'the grounds of Cornwall, I am content; I have no
'lands there : if the stocks sink, that gives me no
'uneasiness; I am no Jew.' The fellow's vivacity,
joined to his poverty, I own, raised my curiosity to
know something of his life and circumstances; and I
entreated that he would indulge my desire.—'That I will,
'sir,' said he, 'and welcome; only let us drink to prevent
'our sleeping; let us have another tankard while we
'are awake; let us have another tankard; for, ah, how
'charming a tankard looks when full!

'You must know, then, that I am very well descended;
'my ancestors have made some noise in the world; for
'my mother cried oysters, and my father beat a drum:
'I am told we have even had some trumpeters in our
'family. Many a nobleman cannot show so respectful
'a genealogy : but that is neither here nor there. As
'I was their only child, my father designed to breed me
'up to his own employment, which was that of drummer
'to a puppet-show. Thus the whole employment of my
'younger years was that of interpreter to Punch and
'King Solomon in all his glory. But, though my father
'was very fond of instructing me in beating all the
'marches and points of war, I made no very great

'progress, because I naturally had no ear for music ;
'so, at the age of fifteen, I went and listed for a soldier.
'As I had ever hated beating a drum, so I soon found
'that I disliked carrying a musket also ; neither the
'one trade nor the other was to my taste, for I was
'by nature fond of being a gentleman : besides, I was
'obliged to obey my captain ; he has his will, I have
'mine, and you have yours : now I very reasonably
'concluded, that it was much more comfortable for
'a man to obey his own will than another's.

'The life of a soldier soon therefore gave me the
'spleen. I asked leave to quit the service ; but, as
'I was tall and strong, my captain thanked me for my
'kind intention, and said, because he had a regard for
'me, we should not part. I wrote to my father a very
'dismal penitent letter, and desired that he would
'raise money to pay for my discharge ; but the good
'man was as fond of drinking as I was (Sir, my service to
'you),—and those who are fond of drinking never pay for
'other people's discharges : in short, he never answered
'my letter. What could be done ? If I have not money,
'said I to myself, to pay for my discharge, I must
'find an equivalent some other way ; and that must be
'by running away. I deserted, and that answered my
'purpose every bit as well as if I had bought my
'discharge.

'Well, I was now fairly rid of my military employ-
'ment ; I sold my soldier's clothes, bought worse, and,
'in order not to be overtaken, took the most unfre-
'quented roads possible. One evening, as I was entering
'a village, I perceived a man, whom I afterwards found
'to be the curate of the parish, thrown from his horse
'in a miry road, and almost smothered in the mud.
'He desired my assistance ; I gave it, and drew him out
'with some difficulty. He thanked me for my trouble,

'and was going off; but I followed him home, for I
'loved always to have a man thank me at his own door.
'The curate asked an hundred questions; as, whose son
'I was; from whence I came; and whether I would
'be faithful? I answered him greatly to his satisfaction,
'and gave myself one of the best characters in the
'world for sobriety (Sir, I have the honour of drinking
'your health), discretion, and fidelity. To make a long
'story short, he wanted a servant, and hired me. With
'him I lived but two months; we did not much like
'each other; I was fond of eating, and he gave me
'but little to eat: I loved a pretty girl, and the old
'woman, my fellow servant, was ill-natured and ugly.
'As they endeavoured to starve me between them,
'I made a pious resolution to prevent their committing
'murder: I stole the eggs as soon as they were laid;
'I emptied every unfinished bottle that I could lay my
'hands on; whatever eatable came in my way was
'sure to disappear: in short, they found I would not
'do; so I was discharged one morning, and paid three
'shillings and sixpence for two months' wages.

'While my money was getting ready, I employed
'myself in making preparations for my departure;
'two hens were hatching in an out-house; I went and
'habitually took the eggs; and, not to separate the
'parents from the children, I lodged hens and all in my
'knapsack. After this piece of frugality, I returned to
'receive my money, and, with my knapsack on my back,
'and a staff in my hand, I bid adieu, with tears in my eyes,
'to my old benefactor. I had not gone far from the
'house when I heard behind me the cry of " Stop
'thief! " but this only increased my dispatch; it would
'have been foolish to stop, as I knew the voice could
'not be levelled at me. But hold, I think I passed those
'two months at the curate's without drinking. Come,

'the times are dry, and may this be my poison if ever
'I spent two more pious, stupid months in all my life.

'Well, after travelling some days, whom should I
'light upon but a company of strolling players. The
'moment I saw them at a distance my heart warmed to
'them; I had a sort of natural love for everything of the
'vagabond order: they were employed in settling their
'baggage, which had been overturned in a narrow way;
'I offered my assistance, which they accepted; and we
'soon became so well acquainted, that they took me as
'a servant. This was a paradise to me; they sung,
'danced, drank, eat, and travelled, all at the same time.
'By the blood of the Mirabels, I thought I had never
'lived till then; I grew as merry as a grig, and laughed
'at every word that was spoken. They liked me as
'much as I liked them; I was a very good figure, as
'you see; and, though I was poor, I was not modest.

'I love a straggling life above all things in the world;
'sometimes good, sometimes bad; to be warm to-day,
'and cold to-morrow; to eat when one can get it, and
'drink when (the tankard is out) it stands before me.
'We arrived that evening at Tenderden, and took a
'large room at the Greyhound, where we resolved to
'exhibit *Romeo and Juliet*, with the funeral procession,
'the grave, and the garden scene. Romeo was to be
'performed by a gentleman from the Theatre Royal in
'Drury Lane; Juliet by a lady who had never appeared
'on any stage before; and I was to snuff the candles:
'all excellent in our way. We had figures enough, but
'the difficulty was to dress them. The same coat that
'served Romeo, turned with the blue lining outwards,
'served for his friend Mercutio: a large piece of crape
'sufficed at once for Juliet's petticoat and pall: a pestle
'and mortar, from a neighbouring apothecary's, answered
'all the purposes of a bell; and our landlord's own

'family, wrapped in white sheets, served to fill up the
'procession. In short, there were but three figures
'among us that might be said to be dressed with any
'propriety : I mean the nurse, the starved apothecary,
'and myself. Our performance gave universal satis-
'faction : the whole audience were enchanted with our
'powers, and Tenderden is a town of taste.

'There is one rule by which a strolling player may be
'ever secure of success ; that is, in our theatrical way of
'expressing it, to make a great deal of the character.
'To speak and act as in common life, is not playing, nor
'is it what people come to see : natural speaking, like
'sweet wine, runs glibly over the palate, and scarce
'leaves any taste behind it ; but being high in a part
'resembles vinegar, which grates upon the taste, and
'one feels it while he is drinking. To please in town or
'country, the way is, to cry, wring, cringe into attitudes,
'mark the emphasis, slap the pockets, and labour like
'one in the falling sickness : that is the way to work
'for applause ; that is the way to gain it.

'As we received much reputation for our skill on this
'first exhibition, it was but natural for me to ascribe
'part of the success to myself : I snuffed the candles,
'and let me tell you, that without a candle-snuffer
'the piece would lose half its embellishments. In this
'manner we continued a fortnight, and drew tolerable
'houses ; but the evening before our intended departure,
'we gave out our very best piece, in which all our
'strength was to be exerted. We had great expectations
'from this, and even doubled our prices, when behold
'one of the principal actors fell ill of a violent fever.
'This was a stroke like thunder to our little company :
'they were resolved to go, in a body, to scold the man
'for falling sick at so inconvenient a time, and that too
'of a disorder that threatened to be expensive ; I seized

'.the moment, and offered to act the part myself in his
' stead. The case was desperate ; they accepted my
' offer ; and I accordingly sat down, with the part in
' my hand and a tankard before me (Sir, your health),
' and studied the character, which was to be rehearsed
' the next day, and played soon after.

  ' I found my memory excessively helped by drinking :
' I learned my part with astonishing rapidity, and bid
' adieu to snuffing candles ever after. I found that
' Nature had designed me for more noble employments,
' and I was resolved to take her when in the humour.
' We got together in order to rehearse; and I informed my
' companions, masters now no longer, of the surprising
' change I felt within me. " Let the sick man," said
' I, " be under no uneasiness to get well again ; I'll fill
' his place to universal satisfaction : he may even die
' if he thinks proper ; I'll engage that he shall never
' be missed." I rehearsed before them, strutted, ranted,
' and received applause. They soon gave out that a new
' actor of eminence was to appear, and immediately all
' the genteel places were bespoke. Before I ascended
' the stage, however, I concluded within myself, that, as
' I brought money to the house, I ought to have my
' share in the profits. " Gentlemen," said I, addressing
' our company, " I don't pretend to direct you ; far be
' it from me to treat you with so much ingratitude : you
' have published my name in the bills with the utmost
' good nature ; and, as affairs stand, cannot act without
' me ; so, gentlemen, to show you my gratitude, I expect
' to be paid for my acting as much as any of you, other-
' wise I declare off ; I'll brandish my snuffers, and clip
' candles as usual." This was a very disagreeable proposal,
' but they found that it was impossible to refuse it ; it
' was irresistible, it was adamant : they consented, and
' I went on in King Bajazet : my frowning brows

'bound with a stocking stuffed into a turban, while on
'my captiv'd arms I brandished a jack-chain. Nature
'seemed to have fitted me for the part ; I was tall, and
'had a loud voice ; my very entrance excited universal
'applause ; I looked round on the audience with a smile,
'and made a most low and graceful bow, for that is the
'rule among us. As it was a very passionate part,
'I invigorated my spirits with three full glasses (the
'tankard is almost out) of brandy. By Allah ! it is
'almost inconceivable how I went through it ; Tamer-
'lane was but a fool to me ; though he was sometimes
'loud enough too, yet I was still louder than he : but
'then, besides, I had attitudes in abundance : in general
'I kept my arms folded up thus upon the pit of my
'stomach ; it is the way at Drury Lane, and has always
'a fine effect. The tankard would sink to the bottom
'before I could get through the whole of my merits :
'in short, I came off like a prodigy ; and such was my
'success, that I could ravish the laurels even from a
'sirloin of beef. The principal gentlemen and ladies of
'the town came to me, after the play was over, to
'compliment me upon my success : one praised my
'voice, another my person. " Upon my word," says the
'squire's lady, " he will make one of the finest actors
'in Europe ; I say it, and I think I am something of
'a judge."——Praise in the beginning is agreeable
'enough, and we receive it as a favour ; but when it
'comes in great quantities, we regard it only as a debt,
'which nothing but our merit could extort : instead of
'thanking them, I internally applauded myself. We
'were desired to give our piece a second time ; we
'obeyed, and I was applauded even more than before.
  'At last we left the town, in order to be at a horse-
'race at some distance from thence. I shall never
'think of Tenderden without tears of gratitude and

'respect. The ladies and gentlemen there, take my word
'for it, are very good judges of plays and actors. Come,
'let us drink their healths, if you please, sir. We quitted
'the town, I say ; and there was a wide difference
'between my coming in and going out : I entered the
'town a candle-snuffer, and I quitted it an hero !——
'Such is the world ; little to-day, and great to-morrow.
'I could say a great deal more upon that subject ;
'something truly sublime, upon the ups and downs of
'fortune ; but it would give us both the spleen, and so
'I shall pass it over.

   'The races were ended before we arrived at the next
'town, which was no small disappointment to our
'company ; however, we were resolved to take all we
'could get. I played capital characters there too, and
'came off with my usual brilliancy. I sincerely believe
'I should have been the first actor of Europe, had my
'growing merit been properly cultivated ; but there
'came an unkindly frost, which nipped me in the bud,
'and levelled me once more down to the common
'standard of humanity. I played Sir Harry Wildair ;
'all the country ladies were charmed : if I but drew
'out my snuff-box, the whole house was in a roar of
'rapture ; when I exercised my cudgel, I thought they
'would have fallen into convulsions.

   'There was here a lady who had received an education
'of nine months in London ; and this gave her pre-
'tensions to taste, which rendered her the indisputable
'mistress of the ceremonies wherever she came. She
'was informed of my merits ; everybody praised me ;
'yet she refused at first going to see me perform : she
'could not conceive, she said, anything but stuff from
'a stroller ; talked something in praise of Garrick, and
'amazed the ladies with her skill in enunciations, tones,
'and cadences : she was at last, however, prevailed upon

' to go ; and it was privately intimated to me what
' a judge was to be present at my next exhibition :
' however, no way intimidated, I came on in Sir Harry,
' one hand stuck in my' breeches, and the other in my
' bosom, as usual at Drury Lane ; but, instead of looking
' at me, I perceived the whole audience had their eyes
' turned upon the lady who had been nine months in
' London ; from her they expected the decision which
' was to secure the general's truncheon in my hand,
' or sink me down into a theatrical letter-carrier. I
' opened my snuff-box, took snuff ; the lady was
' solemn, and so were the rest ; I broke my cudgel on
' Alderman Smuggler's back ; still gloomy, melancholy
' all : the lady groaned and shrugged her shoulders ;
' I attempted, by laughing myself, to excite at least
' a smile ; but the devil a cheek could I perceive wrinkled
' into sympathy : I found it would not do ; all my
' good humour now became forced ; my laughter was
' converted into hysteric grinning ; and, while I pre-
' tended spirits, my eye showed the agony of my heart :
' in short, the lady came with an intention to be dis-
' pleased, and displeased she was ; my fame expired ;
' I am here, and (the tankard is no more !) '

ESSAY XXII

RULES ENJOINED TO BE OBSERVED AT A RUSSIAN ASSEMBLY

[From *The Ladies' Magazine*]

WHEN Catharina Alexowna was made Empress of
Russia, the women were in an actual state of bondage,
but she undertook to introduce mixed assemblies, as in
other parts of Europe : she altered the women's dress
by substituting the fashions of England ; instead of
furs, she brought in the use of taffeta and damask ; and

cornets and commodes instead of caps of sable. The women now found themselves no longer shut up in separate apartments, but saw company, visited each other, and were present at every entertainment.

But as the laws to this effect were directed to a savage people, it is amusing enough, the manner in which the ordinances ran. Assemblies were quite unknown among them; the Czarina was satisfied with introducing them, for she found it impossible to render them polite. An ordinance was therefore published according to their notions of breeding; which, as it is a curiosity, and has never been before printed, that we know of, we shall give our readers.

'I. The person at whose house the assembly is to 'be kept, shall signify the same by hanging out a bill, 'or by giving some other public notice, by way of 'advertisement, to persons of both sexes.

'II. The assembly shall not be open sooner than four 'or five o'clock in the afternoon, nor continue longer 'than ten at night.

'III. The master of the house shall not be obliged to 'meet his guests, or conduct them out, or keep them 'company; but, though he is exempt from all this, he 'is to find them chairs, candles, liquors, and all other 'necessaries that company may ask for: he is likewise 'to provide them with cards, dice, and every necessary 'for gaming.

'IV. There shall be no fixed hour for coming or going 'away; it is enough for a person to appear in the assembly.

'V. Every one shall be free to sit, walk, or game, 'as he pleases; nor shall any one go about to hinder 'him, or take exceptions at what he does, upon pain of 'emptying the great eagle (a pint-bowl full of brandy): 'it shall likewise be sufficient, at entering or retiring, to 'salute the company.

'VI. Persons of distinction, noblemen, superior
'officers, merchants, and tradesmen of note, head-
'workmen, especially carpenters, and persons employed
'in chancery, are to have liberty to enter the assemblies;
'as likewise their wives and children.

'VII. A particular place shall be assigned the foot-
'men, except those of the house, that there may be room
'enough in the apartments designed for the assembly.

'VIII. No ladies are to get drunk upon any pretence
'whatsoever, nor shall gentlemen be drunk before nine.

'IX. Ladies who play at forfeitures, questions and
'commands, &c. shall not be riotous : no gentleman
'shall attempt to force a kiss, and no person shall offer
'to strike a woman in the assembly, under pain of
'future exclusion.'

Such are the statutes upon this occasion, which, in
their very appearance, carry an air of ridicule and
satire. But politeness must enter every country by
degrees ; and these rules resemble the breeding of a
clown, awkward but sincere.

ESSAY XXIII

THE GENIUS OF LOVE, AN EASTERN APOLOGUE

[Altered from Letter CXIV of *The Citizen of the World*]

THE formalities, delays, and disappointments, that
precede a treaty of marriage here, are usually as numerous
as those previous to a treaty of peace. The laws of this
country are finely calculated to promote all commerce
but the commerce between the sexes. Their encouragements for propagating hemp, madder, and tobacco, are
indeed admirable ! Marriages are the only commodity
that meets with discouragement.

Yet, from the vernal softness of the air, the verdure of

the fields, the transparency of the streams, and the beauty of the women, I know few countries more proper to invite to courtship. Here Love might sport among painted lawns and warbling groves, and revel amidst gales, wafting at once both fragrance and harmony. Yet it seems he has forsaken the island; and, when a couple are now to be married, mutual love, or an union of minds, is the last and most trifling consideration. If their goods and chattels can be brought to unite, their sympathetic souls are ever ready to guarantee the treaty. The gentleman's mortgaged lawn becomes enamoured of the lady's marriageable grove; the match is struck up, and both parties are piously in love—according to act of parliament.

Thus they who have fortune, are possessed at least of something that is lovely; but I actually pity those who have none. I am told there was a time, when ladies, with no other merit but youth, virtue, and beauty, had a chance for husbands, at least among our clergymen and officers. The blush and innocence of sixteen was said to have a powerful influence over these two professions. But of late, all the little traffic of blushing, ogling, dimpling, and smiling, has been forbidden by an act in that case wisely made and provided. A lady's whole cargo of smiles, sighs, and whispers, is declared utterly contraband, till she arrives in the warm latitude of twenty-two, where commodities of this nature are too often found to decay. She is then permitted to dimple and smile, when the dimples begin to forsake her; and, when perhaps grown ugly, is charitably entrusted with an unlimited use of her charms. Her lovers, however, by this time, have forsaken her; the captain has changed for another mistress; the priest himself leaves her in solitude, to bewail her virginity, and she dies even without benefit of clergy.

Thus you find the Europeans discouraging Love with
as much earnestness as the rudest savage of Sofala. The
Genius is surely now no more. In every region there
seem enemies in arms to oppress him. Avarice in Europe,
jealousy in Persia, ceremony in China, poverty among
the Tartars, and lust in Circassia, are all prepared to
oppose his power. The Genius is certainly banished from
earth, though once adored under such a variety of forms.
He is nowhere to be found ; and all that the ladies of
each country can produce, are but a few trifling relics,
as instances of his former residence and favour.

‘The Genius of Love,’ says the Eastern Apologue,
‘ had long resided in the happy plains of Abra, where
‘ every breeze was health, and every sound produced
‘ tranquillity. His temple at first was crowded, but
‘ every age lessened the number of his votaries, or
‘ cooled their devotion. Perceiving therefore his altars
‘ at length quite deserted, he was resolved to remove to
‘ some more propitious region ; and he apprised the fair
‘ sex of every country, where he could hope for a proper
‘ reception, to assert their right to his presence among
‘ them.’ In return to this proclamation, embassies were
‘ sent from the ladies of every part of the world to
‘ invite him, and to display the superiority of their
‘ claims.

‘ ‘And, first, the beauties of China appeared. No
‘ country could compare with them for modesty, either
‘ of look, dress, or behaviour ; their eyes were never
‘ lifted from the ground ; their robes, of the most
‘ beautiful silk, hid their hands, bosom, and neck, while
‘ their faces only were left uncovered. They indulged
‘ no airs that might express loose desire, and they
‘ seemed to study only the graces of inanimate beauty.
‘ Their black teeth and plucked eyebrows were, however,
‘ alleged by the Genius against them, but he set them

'entirely aside when he came to examine their little
'feet.

'The beauties of Circassia next made their appearance.
'They advanced hand in hand, singing the most im-
'modest airs, and leading up a dance in the most
'luxurious attitudes. Their dress was but half a cover-
'ing ; the neck, the left breast, and all the limbs, were
'exposed to view ; which, after some time, seemed
'rather to satiate than inflame desire. The lily and the
'rose contended in forming their complexions ; and
'a soft sleepiness of eye added irresistible poignance to
'their charms : but their beauties were obtruded, not
'offered, to their admirers ; they seemed to give rather
'than receive courtship ; and the Genius of Love
'dismissed them as unworthy his regard, since they
'exchanged the duties of love, and made themselves not
'the pursued, but the pursuing sex.

'The kingdom of Kashmire next produced its charm-
'ing deputies. This happy region seemed peculiarly
'sequestered by nature for his abode. Shady mountains
'fenced it on one side from the scorching sun, and
'sea-borne breezes on the other gave peculiar luxuriance
'to the air. Their complexions were of a bright yellow,
'that appeared almost transparent, while the crimson
'tulip seemed to blossom on their cheeks. Their features
'and limbs were delicate beyond the statuary's power to
'express ; and their teeth whiter than their own ivory.
'He was almost persuaded to reside among them, when
'unfortunately one of the ladies talked of appointing
'his seraglio.

'In this procession the naked inhabitants of Southern
'America would not be left behind ; their charms were
'found to surpass whatever the warmest imagination
'could conceive ; and served to show, that beauty
'could be perfect, even with the seeming disadvantage

‘ of a brown complexion. But their savage education
‘ rendered them utterly unqualified to make the proper
‘ use of their power, and they were rejected as being
‘ incapable of uniting mental with sensual satisfaction.
‘ In this manner the deputies of other kingdoms had
‘ their suits rejected : the black beauties of Benin, and
‘ the tawny daughters of Borneo ; the women of Wida
‘ with scarred faces, and the hideous virgins of Caffraria ;
‘ the squab ladies of Lapland, three feet high, and the
‘ giant fair ones of Patagonia.

   ‘ The beauties of Europe at last appeared : grace in
their steps, and sensibility smiling in every eye. It was
‘ the universal opinion, while they were approaching,
‘ that they would prevail ; and the Genius seemed to
‘ lend them his most favourable attention. They opened
‘ their pretensions with the utmost modesty ; but
‘ unfortunately, as their orator proceeded, she happened
‘ to let fall the words, “ House in town,” “ Settlement,”
‘ and “ Pin-money.” These seemingly harmless terms
‘ had instantly a surprising effect : the Genius, with
‘ ungovernable rage, burst from amidst the circle ; and,
‘ waving his youthful pinions, left this earth, and flew
‘ back to those ethereal mansions from whence he
‘ descended.

   ‘ The whole assembly was struck with amazement ;
‘ they now justly apprehended that female power would
‘ be no more, since Love had forsaken them. They
‘ continued some time thus in a state of torpid despair ;
‘ when it was proposed by one of the number, that, since
‘ the real Genius of Love had left them, in order to
‘ continue their power, they should set up an idol in
‘ his stead ; and that the ladies of every country should
‘ furnish him with what each liked best. This proposal
‘ was instantly relished and agreed to. An idol of gold
‘ was formed by uniting the capricious gifts of all the

' assembly, though no way resembling the departed
' Genius. The ladies of China furnished the monster with
' wings; those of Kashmire supplied him with horns;
' the dames of Europe clapped a purse into his hand;
' and the virgins of Congo furnished him with a tail.
' Since that time, all the vows addressed to Love are in
' reality paid to the idol; while, as in other false
' religions, the adoration seems most fervent, where the
' heart is least sincere.' √

ESSAY XXIV
THE DISTRESSES OF A COMMON SOLDIER

[Altered from Letter CXIX of *The Citizen of the World*]

No observation is more common, and at the same time
more true, than that one half of the world are ignorant
how the other half lives. The misfortunes of the great
are held up to engage our attention ; are enlarged upon
in tones of declamation ; and the world is called upon to
gaze at the noble sufferers : the great, under the pressure
of calamity, are conscious of several others sympathizing
with their distress ; and have, at once, the comfort of
admiration and pity.

There is nothing magnanimous in bearing misfortunes
with fortitude, when the whole world is looking on : men
in such circumstances will act bravely even from motives
of vanity ; but he who, in the vale of obscurity, can
brave adversity ; who, without friends to encourage;
acquaintances to pity, or even without hope to alleviate
his misfortunes, can behave with tranquillity and
indifference, is truly great : whether peasant or courtier,
he deserves admiration, and should be held up for our
imitation and respect.

While the slightest inconveniences of the great are

magnified into calamities ; while tragedy mouths out their sufferings in all the strains of eloquence, the miseries of the poor are entirely disregarded ; and yet some of the lower ranks of people undergo more real hardships in one day, than those of a more exalted station suffer in their whole lives. It is inconceivable what difficulties the meanest of our common sailors and soldiers endure without murmuring or regret ; without passionately declaiming against Providence, or calling their fellows to be gazers on their intrepidity. Every day is to them a day of misery, and yet they entertain their hard fate without repining.

With what indignation do I hear an Ovid, a Cicero, or a Rabutin, complain of their misfortunes and hardships, whose greatest calamity was that of being unable to visit a certain spot of earth, to which they had foolishly attached an idea of happiness. Their distresses were pleasures, compared to what many of the adventuring poor every day endure without murmuring. They ate, drank, and slept ; they had slaves to attend them, and were sure of subsistence for life : while many of their fellow creatures are obliged to wander without a friend to comfort or assist them, and even without shelter from the severity of the season.

I have been led into these reflections from accidentally meeting, some days ago, a poor fellow, whom I knew when a boy, dressed in a sailor's jacket, and begging at one of the outlets of the town, with a wooden leg. I knew him to have been honest and industrious when in the country, and was curious to learn what had reduced him to his present situation. Wherefore, after giving him what I thought proper, I desired to know the history of his life and misfortunes, and the manner in which he was reduced to his present distress. The disabled soldier, for such he was, though dressed in a sailor's habit, scratching his head, and leaning on his crutch, put himself into an attitude to comply with my request, and gave me his history as follows :

'As for my misfortunes, master, I can't pretend to
'have gone through any more than other folks ; for,
'except the loss of my limb, and my being obliged to
'beg, I don't know any reason, thank Heaven, that
'I have to complain ; there is Bill Tibbs, of our regiment,
'he has lost both his legs, and an eye to boot ; but,
'thank Heaven, it is not so bad with me yet.

'I was born in Shropshire ; my father was a labourer,
'and died when I was five years old ; so I was put upon
'the parish. As he had been a wandering sort of a man,
'the parishioners were not able to tell to what parish
'I belonged, or where I was born, so they sent me to
'another parish, and that parish sent me to a third.
'I thought in my heart, they kept sending me about so
'long, that they would not let me be born in any parish
'at all ; but, at last, however, they fixed me. I had
'some disposition to be a scholar, and was resolved, at
'least, to know my letters ; but the master of the
'workhouse put me to business as soon as I was able
'to handle a mallet ; and here I lived an easy kind of
'a life for five years. I only wrought ten hours in the
'day, and had my meat and drink provided for my
'labour. It is true, I was not suffered to stir out of the
'house, for fear, as they said, I should run away ; but
'what of that, I had the liberty of the whole house, and
'the yard before the door, and that was enough for
'me. I was then bound out to a farmer, where I was
'up both early and late ; but I ate and drank well, and
'liked my business well enough, till he died, when I was
'obliged to provide for myself ; so I was resolved to go
'seek my fortune.

'In this manner I went from town to town, worked

'when I could get employment, and starved when
'I could get none; when happening one day to go
'through a field belonging to a justice of peace, I spied
'a hare crossing the path just before me; and I believe
'the devil put it in my head to fling my stick at it.—
'Well, what will you have on 't? I killed the hare, and
'was bringing it away, when the justice himself met me:
'he called me a poacher and a villain; and collaring
'me, desired I would give an account of myself: I fell
'upon my knees, begged his worship's pardon, and
'began to give a full account of all that I knew of my
'breed, seed, and generation; but though I gave
'a very true account, the justice said I could give no
'account; so I was indicted at sessions, found guilty
'of being poor, and sent up to London to Newgate,
'in order to be transported as a vagabond.

   'People may say this and that of being in jail; but,
'for my part, I found Newgate as agreeable a place as
'ever I was in in all my life. I had my bellyful to eat
'and drink, and did no work at all. This kind of life
'was too good to last for ever; so I was taken out of
'prison, after five months, put on board a ship, and
'sent off, with two hundred more, to the plantations.
'We had but an indifferent passage, for, being all
'confined in the hold, more than a hundred of our
'people died for want of sweet air; and those that
'remained were sickly enough, God knows. When we
'came ashore, we were sold to the planters, and I was
'bound for seven years more. As I was no scholar,
'for I did not know my letters, I was obliged to work
'among the negroes; and I served out my time, as in
'duty bound to do.

   'When my time was expired, I worked my passage
'home, and glad I was to see Old England again, because
'I loved my country. I was afraid, however, that I should

' be indicted for a vagabond once more, so did not
' much care to go down into the country, but kept about
' the town, and did little jobs when I could get them.

' I was very happy in this manner for some time, till
' one evening, coming home from work, two men knocked
' me down, and then desired me to stand. They belonged
' to a press-gang : I was carried before the justice, and,
' as I could give no account of myself, I had my choice
' left, whether to go on board a man-of-war, or list for
' a soldier. I chose the latter ; and, in this post of
' a gentleman, I served two campaigns in Flanders, was
' at the battles of Val and Fontenoy, and received but
' one wound, through the breast here ; but the doctor
' of our regiment soon made me well again.

' When the peace came on I was discharged ; and
' as I could not work, because my wound was sometimes
' troublesome, I listed for a landman in the East India
' Company's service. I here fought the French in six
' pitched battles ; and I verily believe, that if I could
' read or write, our captain would have made me a
' corporal. But it was not my good fortune to have any
' promotion, for I soon fell sick, and so got leave to
' return home again with forty pounds in my pocket.
' This was at the beginning of the present war, and
' I hoped to be set on shore, and to have the pleasure of
' spending my money ; but the Government wanted
' men, and so I was pressed for a sailor before ever
' I could set foot on shore.

' The boatswain found me, as he said, an obstinate
' fellow : he swore he knew that I understood my business
' well, but that I shammed Abraham, to be idle ; but
' God knows, I knew nothing of sea-business, and he
' beat me without considering what he was about. I had
' still, however, my forty pounds, and that was some
' comfort to me under every beating ; and the money

' I might have had to this day, but that our ship was
' taken by the French, and so I lost all.

. ' Our crew was carried into Brest, and many of them
' died, because they were not used to live in a jail ; but,
' for my part, it was nothing to me, for I was seasoned.
' One night, as. I was sleeping on the bed of boards,
' with a warm blanket about me, for ·I always loved to
' lie well, I was awakened by the boatswain, who had
·' a dark lantern in his hand ; "Jack," says he to me,
' " will you knock out the French sentries' brains ? "
' " I don't care," says I, striving to keep myself awake,
' " if I lend a hand." "Then follow me," says he, "and
' I hope we shall do business." So up I got, and tied my
' blanket, which was all the clothes I had, about my
' middle, and went with him to fight the Frenchmen.
' I hate the French because they are all slaves, and
' wear wooden shoes.

' Though we had no arms, one Englishman is able to
' beat five French at any time ; so we went down to
' the door, where both the sentries were posted, and
' rushing upon them, seized their arms in a moment,
' and knocked them down. From thence, nine of us
' ran together to the quay, and, seizing the first boat
' we met, got out of the harbour and put to sea. We
' had not been here three days before we were taken
' up by the *Dorset* privateer, who were glad of so many
' good hands ; and we consented to run our chance.
' However, we had not as much luck as we expected. In
' three days we fell in with the *Pompadour* privateer,
' of forty guns, while we had but twenty-three ; so to
' it we went, yard-arm and yard-arm. The fight lasted
' for three hours, and I verily believe we should have
' taken the Frenchman, had we but had some more men
' left behind ; but, unfortunately, we lost all our men
' just as we were going to get the victory.

'I was once more in the power of the French, and
'I believe it would have gone hard with me had I been
'brought back to Brest; but, by good fortune, we were
'retaken by the *Viper*. I had almost forgot to tell you,
'that, in that engagement, I was wounded in two places:
'I lost four fingers of the left hand, and my leg was
'shot off. If I had had the good fortune to have lost
'my leg and use of my hand on board a king's ship,
'and not aboard a privateer, I should have been entitled
'to clothing and maintenance during the rest of my life;
'but that was not my chance: one man is born with
'a silver spoon in his mouth, and another with a wooden
'ladle. However, blessed be God, I enjoy good health,
'and will for ever love liberty and Old England. Liberty,
'property, and Old England, for ever, huzza!'

Thus saying, he limped off, leaving me in admiration
at his intrepidity and content; nor could I avoid
acknowledging, that an habitual acquaintance with
misery serves better than philosophy to teach us to
despise it.

ESSAY XXV

SUPPOSED TO BE WRITTEN BY THE ORDINARY OF NEWGATE

MAN is a most frail being, incapable of directing his
steps, unacquainted with what is to happen in this life;
and perhaps no man is a more manifest instance of the
truth of this maxim, than Mr. The. Cibber, just now
gone out of the world. Such a variety of turns of
fortune, yet such a persevering uniformity of conduct,
appears in all that happened in his short span, that the
whole may be looked upon as one regular confusion:
every action of his life was matter of wonder and surprise,
and his death was an astonishment.

This gentleman was born of creditable parents, who gave him a very good education, and a great deal of good learning, so that he could read and write before he was sixteen. However, he early discovered an inclination to follow lewd courses ; he refused to take the advice of his parents, and pursued the bent of his inclination ; he played at cards on Sundays ; called himself a gentleman ; fell out with his mother and laundress ; and, even in these early days, his father was frequently heard to observe, that young The.—would be hanged.

As he advanced in years, he grew more fond of pleasure ; would eat an ortolan for dinner, though he begged the guinea that bought it ; and was once known to give three pounds for a plate of green peas, which he had collected overnight as charity for a friend in distress : he ran into debt with everybody that would trust him, and none could build a sconce better than he ; so that at last his creditors swore, with one accord, that The.—would be hanged.

But, as getting into debt by a man who had no visible means but impudence for subsistence, is a thing that every reader is not acquainted with, I must explain that point a little, and that to his satisfaction.

There are three ways of getting into debt ; first, by pushing a face ; as thus : ' You, Mr. Lutestring, send ' me home six yards of that paduasoy, dammee ; —but, ' harkee, don't think I ever intend to pay you for it, ' dammee.' At this, the mercer laughs heartily ; cuts off the paduasoy, and sends it home ; nor is he, till too late, surprised to find the gentleman had said nothing but truth, and kept his word.

The second method of running into debt is called fineering ; which is getting goods made up in such a fashion as to be unfit for every other purchaser ; and if the tradesman refuses to give them upon credit, then threaten to leave them upon his hands.

But the third and best method is called, ' Being the ' good customer.' The gentleman first buys some trifle, and pays for it in ready money : he comes a few days after with nothing about him but bank bills, and buys, we will suppose, a sixpenny tweezer-case ; the bills are too great to be changed, so he promises to return punctually the day after and pay for what he has bought. In this promise he is punctual, and this is repeated for eight or ten times, till his face is well known, and he has got, at last, the character of a good customer. By this means he gets credit for something considerable, and then never pays for it.

In all this, the young man who is the unhappy subject of our present reflections was very expert ; and could face, fineer, and bring custom to a shop with any man in England : none of his companions could exceed him in this ; and his very companions at last said that The.—would be hanged.

As he grew old, he grew never the better ; he loved ortolans and green peas as before ; he drank gravy-soup when he could get it, and always thought his oysters tasted best when he got them for nothing ; or, which was just the same, when he bought them upon tick : thus the old man kept up the vices of the youth, and what he wanted in power, he made up by inclination ; so that all the world thought that old The.—would be hanged.

And now, reader, I have brought him to his last scene ; a scene where, perhaps, my duty should have obliged me to assist. You expect, perhaps, his dying words, and the tender farewell he took of his wife and children ; you expect an account of his coffin and white gloves, his pious ejaculations, and the papers he left

behind him. In this I cannot indulge your curiosity;
for, oh ! the mysteries of fate, The.——was drown'd !

' Reader,' as Hervey saith, ' pause and ponder ; and
' ponder and pause ; who knows what thy own end may
' be ! '

ESSAY XXVI[1]

*The following was written at the time of the last Coronation,
and supposed to come from a Common Council-man.*

Sir,

I have the honour of being a Common Council-
man, and am greatly pleased with a paragraph from
Southampton in yours of yesterday. There we learn,
that the mayor and aldermen of that loyal borough, had
the particular satisfaction of celebrating the royal nuptials
by a magnificent turtle feast. By this means the gentlemen had the pleasure of filling their bellies, and showing
their loyalty together. I must confess, it would give me
some pleasure to see some such method of testifying our
loyalty practised in this metropolis, of which I am an
unworthy member, instead of presenting His Majesty
(God bless him) on every occasion with our formal
addresses, we might thus sit comfortably down to dinner,
and wish him prosperity in a sirloin of beef ; upon our
army levelling the walls of a town, or besieging a fortification, we might at our city feast imitate our brave troops,
and demolish the walls of venison pasty, or besiege the
shell of a turtle, with as great a certainty of success.

At present, however, we have got into a sort of dry,
unsocial manner of drawing up addresses upon every
occasion ; and though I have attended upon six
cavalcades, and two foot processions in a single year,
yet I came away as lean and hungry as if I had been

---

[1] First inserted in second edition.

a juryman at the Old Bailey. For my part, Mr. Printer, I don't see what is got by these processions and addresses, except an appetite, and that, thank Heaven, we have all in a pretty good degree without ever leaving our own houses for it. It is true, our gowns of mazarine blue, edged with fur, cut a pretty figure enough, parading it through the streets, and so my wife tells me. In fact, I generally bow to all my acquaintance, when thus in full dress ; but alas, as the proverb has it, fine clothes never fill the belly.

But even though all this bustling, parading, and powdering through the streets be agreeable enough to many of us ; yet I would have my brethren consider whether the frequent repetition of it be so very agreeable to our betters above. To be introduced to Court, to see the Queen, to kiss hands, to smile upon lords, to ogle the ladies, and all the other fine things there, may, I grant, be a perfect show to us that view it but seldom ; but it may be a troublesome business enough to those who are to settle such ceremonies as these every day. To use an instance adapted to all our apprehensions; suppose my family and I should go to Bartholomew Fair. Very well, going to Bartholomew Fair, the whole sight is perfect rapture to us, who are only spectators once and away ; but I am of opinion, that the wire-walker and fire-eater find no such great sport in all this ; I am of opinion, they had as lief remain behind the curtain, at their own pastimes, drinking beer, eating shrimps, and smoking tobacco.

Besides, what can we tell His Majesty in all we say on these occasions, but what he knows perfectly well already ? I believe if I were to reckon up, I could not find above five hundred disaffected in the whole kingdom, and here are we every day telling His Majesty how loyal we are. Suppose the addresses of a people for instance

should run thus. 'May it please your M——y, we are
' many of us worth a hundred thousand pounds ; and
' are possessed of several other inestimable advantages.
' For the preservation of this money and those advantages
' we are chiefly indebted to your M——y. We are
' therefore once more assembled to assure your M——y
' of our fidelity. This, it is true, we have lately assured
' your M——y five or six times, but we are willing once
' more to repeat what can't be doubted, and to kiss your
' royal hand, and the Queen's hand, and thus sincerely
' to convince you, that we shall never do anything to
' deprive you of one loyal subject, or any one of ourselves
' of one hundred thousand pounds.' Should we not upon
reading such an address, think that people a little silly,
who thus made such unmeaning professions ?——Excuse
me, Mr. Printer, no man upon earth has a more profound
respect for the abilities of the aldermen and the Common
Council than I ; but I could wish they would not take
up a monarch's time in these good-natured trifles, who
I am told seldom spends a moment in vain.

The example set by the City of London will probably
be followed by every other community in the British
Empire. Thus we shall have a new set of addresses from
every little borough with but four freemen and a burgess ;
day after day shall we see them come up with hearts
filled with gratitude, laying the vows of a loyal people
at the foot of the throne. Death! Mr. Printer, they'll
hardly leave our courtiers time to scheme a single
project for beating the French ; and our enemies may
gain upon us, while we are thus employed in telling our
governor how much we intend to keep them under.

But a people by too frequent a use of addresses may
by this means come at last to defeat the very purpose
for which they are designed. If we are thus exclaiming
in raptures upon every occasion, we deprive ourselves

of the powers of flattery when there may be a real
necessity. A boy three weeks ago swimming across the
Thames, was every minute crying out, for his amusement, ' I've got the cramp, I've got the cramp ; ' the
boatmen pushed off once or twice, and they found it was
fun ; he soon after cried out in earnest, but nobody
believed him, and so he sunk to the bottom.

In short, sir, I am quite displeased with any unnecessary cavalcade whatever. I hope we shall soon have
occasion to triumph, and then I shall be ready myself
either to eat at a turtle feast, or to shout at a bonfire ;
and will lend either my faggot at the fire, or flourish
my hat at every loyal health that may be proposed.

I am,
Sir, &c.

ESSAY XXVII [1]

TO THE PRINTER

SIR,

I am the same Common Council-man who troubled
you some days ago. To whom can I complain but to
you ? for you have many a dismal correspondent ; in this
time of joy my wife does not choose to hear me, because
she says I'm always melancholy when she's in spirits.
I have been to see the Coronation, and a fine sight it was,
as I am told. To those who had the pleasure of being
near spectators, the diamonds, I am told, were as thick
as Bristol stones in a show-glass ; the ladies and gentlemen walked all along, one foot before another, and threw
their eyes about them, on this side and that, perfectly
like clock-work. Oh ! Mr. Printer, it had been a fine
sight indeed, if there was but a little more eating.

---

[1] First inserted in second edition.

Instead of that, there we sat, penned up in our scaffoldings, like sheep upon a market-day in Smithfield; but the devil a thing could I get to eat (God pardon me for swearing) except the fragments of a plum-cake, that was all squeezed into crumbs in my wife's pocket, as she came through the crowd.

You must know, sir, that in order to do the thing genteelly, and that all my family might be amused at the same time, my wife, my daughter, and I, took two guinea places for the Coronation, and I gave my two eldest boys (who, by the by, are twins, fine children) eighteenpence apiece to go to Sudrick Fair, to see the court of the Black King of Morocco, which will serve to please children well enough.

That we might have good places on the scaffolding, my wife insisted upon going at seven o'clock the evening before the Coronation, for she said she would not lose a full prospect for the world. This resolution I own shocked me. 'Grizzle,' said I to her, 'Grizzle, my dear, 'consider that you are but weakly, always ailing, and 'will never bear sitting out all night upon the scaffold. 'You remember what a cold you caught the last fast-'day, by rising but half an hour before your time to go 'to church, and how I was scolded as the cause of it. 'Beside, my dear, our daughter Anna Amelia Wilhelmina 'Carolina, will look like a perfect fright, if she sits up, 'and you know the girl's face is something at her time 'of life, considering her fortune is but small.' 'Mr. 'Grogan,' replied my wife, 'Mr. Grogan, this is always 'the case, when you find me in spirits; I don't want to 'go, not I; nor I don't care whether I go at all, it is 'seldom that I am in spirits, but this is always the case.' In short, Mr. Printer, what will you have on 't? to the Coronation we went.

What difficulties we had in getting a coach, how we

were shoved about in the mob, how I had my pocket picked of the last new almanac, and my steel tobacco-box; how my daughter lost half an eyebrow and her laced shoe in a gutter; my wife's lamentation upon this, with the adventures of the crumbled plum cake, and broken brandy-bottle, what need I relate all these; we suffered this and ten times more before we got to our places.

At last, however, we were seated. My wife is certainly a heart of oak; I thought sitting up in the damp night air would have killed her; I have known her for two months take possession of our easy-chair, mobbed up in flannel nightcaps, and trembling at a breath of air; but she now bore the night as merrily as if she had sat up at a christening. My daughter and she did not seem to value it of a farthing. She told me two or three stories that she knows will always make me laugh, and my daughter sung me the Noontide air, towards one o'clock in the morning. However, with all their endeavours I was as cold and as dismal as ever I remember. If this be the pleasures of a coronation, cried I to myself, I had rather see the court of King Solomon in all his glory at my ease in Bartholomew Fair.

Towards morning sleep began to come fast upon me; and the sun rising and warming the air, still inclined me to rest a little. You must know, sir, that I am naturally of a sleepy constitution; I have often sat up at table with my eyes open, and have been asleep all the while. What will you have on 't? just about eight o'clock in the morning I fell fast asleep. I fell into the most pleasing dream in the world. I shall never forget it; I dreamed that I was at my Lord Mayor's feast, and had scaled the crust of a venison pasty. I kept eating and eating, in my sleep, and thought I could never have enough. After some time, the pasty methought was taken away, and the dessert was brought in its room. Thought I to myself, if I have not got enough of the venison, I am resolved to make it up by the largest snap at the sweet-meats. Accordingly, I grasped a whole pyramid ; the rest of the guests seeing me with so much, one gave me a snap, and the other gave me a snap, I was pulled this way by my neighbour on the right hand, and that by my neighbour on the left, but still kept my ground without flinching, and continued eating and pocketing as fast as I could. I never was so pulled and hauled in my whole life. At length, however, going to smell to a lobster that lay before me, methought it caught me with its claws fast by the nose. The pain I felt upon this occasion is inexpressible ; in fact it broke my dream ; when, awaking, I found my wife and daughter applying a smelling-bottle to my nose ; and telling me it was time to go home, they assured me every means had been tried to awake me, while the procession was going forward, but that I still continued to sleep till the whole ceremony was over. Mr. Printer, this is a hard case, and as I read your most ingenious work, it will be some comfort, when I see this inserted, to find that——I write for it too.

I am,

Sir,

Your distressed,

Humble Servant,

L. GROGAN.

EIGHT ESSAYS
FIRST COLLECTED IN THE
POSTHUMOUS EDITION OF 1798

NATIONAL CONCORD

I TAKE the liberty to communicate to the public a few loose thoughts upon a subject which, though often handled, has not yet, in my opinion, been fully discussed,—I mean national concord, or unanimity, which in this kingdom has been generally considered as a bare possibility, that existed nowhere but in speculation. Such a union is perhaps neither to be expected nor wished for in a country whose liberty depends rather upon the genius of the people than upon any precautions which they have taken in a constitutional way for the guard and preservation of this inestimable blessing.

There is a very honest gentleman with whom I have been acquainted these thirty years, during which there has not been one speech uttered against the ministry in parliament, nor a struggle at an election for a burgess to serve in the.House of Commons, nor a pamphlet published in opposition to any measure of the administration, nor even a private censure passed in his hearing upon the misconduct of any person concerned in public affairs, but he is immediately alarmed, and loudly exclaims against such factious doings, in order to set the people by the ears together at such a delicate juncture. 'At any other time,' says he, 'such opposition might not be improper, and I don't question the facts that are alleged ; but at this crisis, sir, to inflame the nation !—the man deserves to be punished as a traitor to his country.' In a word, according to this gentleman's opinion, the nation has been in a violent crisis at any time these thirty years ; and were it possible for him to live another century, he would never find any period at which a man might with safety impugn the infallibility of a minister.

The case is no more than this : my honest friend has invested his whole fortune in the stocks, on Government security, and trembles at every whiff of popular discontent. Were every British subject of the same tame and timid disposition, Magna Charta (to use the coarse phrase of Oliver Cromwell) would be no more regarded by an ambitious prince than Magna F—ta, and the liberties of England expire without a groan. Opposition, when restrained within due bounds, is the salubrious gale that ventilates the opinions of the people, which might otherwise stagnate into the most abject submission. It may be said to purify the atmosphere of politics ; to dispel the gross vapours raised by the influence of ministerial artifice and corruption, until the constitution, like a mighty rock, stands full disclosed to the view of every individual who dwells within the shade of its protection. Even when this gale blows with augmented violence, it generally tends to the advantage of the commonwealth : it awakes the apprehension, and consequently arouses all the faculties of the pilot at the helm, who redoubles his vigilance and caution, exerts his utmost skill, and, becoming acquainted with the nature of the navigation, in a little time learns to suit his canvas to the roughness of the sea and the trim of the vessel. Without these intervening storms of opposition to exercise his faculties, he would become enervate, negligent, and presumptuous ; and in the wantonness of his power, trusting to some deceitful calm, perhaps hazard a step that would wreck the constitution. Yet there is a measure in all things. A moderate frost will fertilize the glebe with nitrous particles, and destroy the eggs of pernicious insects that prey upon the fancy of the year : but if this frost increases in severity and duration, it will chill the seeds, and even freeze up the roots of vegetables ; it will check the bloom, nip the buds, and blast all the promise of the spring. The vernal breeze that drives the frogs before it, that brushes the cobwebs from the boughs, that fans the air, and fosters vegetation, if augmented to a tempest, will strip the leaves, overthrow the tree, and desolate the garden. The auspicious gale before which the trim vessel ploughs the bosom of the sea, while the mariners are kept alert in duty and in spirits, if converted to a hurricane, overwhelms the crew with terror and confusion. The sails are rent, the cordage cracked, the masts give way; the master eyes the havoc with mute despair, and the vessel founders in the storm. Opposition, when confined within its proper channel, sweeps away those beds of soil and banks of sand which corruptive power had gathered ; but when it overflows its banks, and deluges the plain, its course is marked by ruin and devastation.

The opposition necessary in a free state, like that of Great Britain, is not at all incompatible with that national concord which ought to unite the people on all emergencies in which the general safety is at stake. It is the jealousy of patriotism, not the rancour of party —the warmth of candour, not the virulence of hate— a transient dispute among friends, not an implacable feud that admits of no reconciliation. The history of all ages teems with the fatal effects of internal discord ; and were history and tradition annihilated, common sense would plainly point out the mischiefs that must arise from want of harmony and national union. Every schoolboy can have recourse to the fable of the rods, which, when united in a bundle, no strength could bend, but when separated into single twigs, a child could break with ease.

FEMALE WARRIORS

I HAVE spent the greater part of my life in making observations on men and things, and in projecting schemes for the advantage of my country ; and though my labours have met with an ungrateful return, I will still persist in my endeavours for its service, like that venerable, unshaken, and neglected patriot, Mr. Jacob Henriquez, who, though of the Hebrew nation, hath exhibited a shining example of Christian fortitude and perseverance. And here my conscience urges me to confess, that the hint upon which the following proposals are built was taken from an advertisement of the said patriot Henriquez, in which he gives the public to understand, that Heaven had indulged him with 'seven blessed daughters.' Blessed they are, no doubt, on account of their own and their father's virtues ; but more blessed may they be, if the scheme I offer should be adopted by the legislature.

The proportion which the number of females born in these kingdoms bears to the male children is, I think, supposed to be as thirteen to fourteen ; but as women are not so subject as the other sex to accidents and intemperance, in numbering adults we shall find the balance on the female side. If, in calculating the numbers of the people, we take in the multitudes that emigrate to the plantations, from whence they never return ; those that die at sea, and make their exit at Tyburn ; together with the consumption of the present war, by sea and land, in the Atlantic, Mediterranean, in the German and Indian Oceans, in Old France, New France, North America, the Leeward Islands, Germany, Africa, and Asia, we may fairly state the loss of men during the war at one hundred thousand. If this be the case, there must be a superplus of the other sex, amounting to the same number, and this superplus will consist of women able to bear arms ; as I take it for granted, that all those who are fit to bear children are likewise fit to bear arms. Now, as we have seen the nation governed by old women, I hope to make it appear, that it may be defended by young women : and surely this scheme will not be rejected as unnecessary at such a juncture [1762], when our armies, in the four quarters of the globe, are in want of recruits ; when we find ourselves entangled in a new war with Spain, on the eve of a rupture in Italy, and, indeed, in a fair way of being obliged to make head against all the great potentates of Europe.

But, before I unfold my design, it may be necessary to obviate, from experience, as well as argument, the objections which may be made to the delicate frame and tender disposition of the female sex, 'rendering them incapable of the toils, and insuperably averse to the horrors, of war. All the world has heard of the nation of Amazons, who inhabited the banks of the river Thermodoon in Cappadocia, who expelled their men by force of arms, defended themselves by their own prowess, managed the reins of government, prosecuted the operations in war, and held the other sex in the utmost contempt. We are informed by Homer that Penthesilea, queen of the Amazons, acted as auxiliary to Priam, and fell, valiantly fighting in his cause, before the walls of Troy. Quintus Curtius tells us, that Thalestris brought one hundred armed Amazons in a present to Alexander the Great. Diodorus Siculus expressly says there was a nation of female warriors in Africa, who fought against the Lybian Hercules. We read in the voyages of Columbus, that one of the Caribbee Islands was possessed by a tribe of female warriors, who kept all the neighbouring Indians in awe ; but we

need not go further than our own age and country to
prove, that the spirit and constitution of the fair sex
are equal to the dangers and fatigues of war.   Every
novice who has read the authentic and important
History of the Pirates is well acquainted with the exploits
of two heroines, called Mary Read and Anne Bonny.
I myself have had the honour to drink with Anne
Cassier, *alias* Mother Wade, who had distinguished herself among the Buccaneers of America, and in her old
age kept a punch-house, in Port-Royal of Jamaica.
I have likewise conversed with Moll Davis, who had
served as a dragoon in all Queen Anne's wars, and was
admitted on the pension of Chelsea.   The late war with
Spain, and even the present, hath produced instances of
females enlisting both in the land and sea service, and
behaving with remarkable bravery in the disguise of
the other sex.   And who has not heard of the celebrated
Jenny Cameron, and some other enterprising ladies of
North Britain, who attended a certain Adventurer in all
his expeditions, and headed their respective clans in
a military character ?   That strength of body is often
equal to the courage of mind implanted in the fair sex
will not be denied by those who have seen the water-
women of Plymouth ;   the female drudges of Ireland,
Wales, and Scotland ;   the fishwomen of Billingsgate ;
the weeders, podders, and hoppers, who swarm in the
fields ;   and the bunters who swagger in the streets of
London ;   not to mention the indefatigable trulls who
follow the camp, and keep up with the line of march,
though loaded with bantlings and other baggage.

There is scarcely a street in this metropolis without
one or more viragos, who discipline their husbands and
domineer over the whole neighbourhood.   Many months
are not elapsed since I was witness to a pitched battle
between two athletic females, who fought with equal

skill and fury until one of them gave out, after having sustained seven falls on the hard stones. They were both stripped to the under petticoat ; their breasts were carefully swathed with handkerchiefs ; and as no vestiges of features were to be seen in either when I came up, I imagined the combatants were of the other sex, until a bystander assured me of the contrary, giving me to understand, that the conqueror had lain-in about five weeks of twin-bastards, begot by her second, who was an Irish chairman. When I see the avenues of the Strand beset every night with troops of fierce Amazons, who, with dreadful imprecations, stop, and beat, and plunder passengers, I cannot help wishing that such martial talents were converted to the benefit of the public ; and that those who were so loaded with temporal fire, and so little afraid of eternal fire, should, instead of ruining the souls and bodies of their fellow citizens, be put in a way of turning their destructive qualities against the enemies of the nation.

Having thus demonstrated that the fair sex are not deficient in strength and resolution, I would humbly propose, that as there is an excess on their side in quantity to the amount of one hundred thousand, part of that number may be employed in recruiting the army, as well as in raising thirty new Amazonian regiments, to be commanded by females, and serve in regimentals adapted to their sex. The Amazons of old appeared with the left breast bare, an open jacket, and trousers that descended no farther than the knee ; the right breast was destroyed, that it might not impede them in bending the bow, or darting the javelin: but there is no occasion for this cruel excision in the present discipline, as we have seen instances of women who handle the musket, without finding any inconvenience from that protuberance.

As the sex love gaiety, they may be clothed in vests of pink satin, and open drawers of the same, with buskins on their feet and legs, their hair tied behind, and floating on their shoulders, and their hats adorned with white feathers : they may be armed with light carbines and long bayonets, without the encumbrance of swords or shoulder-belts. I make no doubt but many young ladies of figure and fashion will undertake to raise companies at their own expense, provided they like their colonels ; but I must insist upon it, if this scheme should be embraced, that Mr. Henriquez's seven blessed daughters may be provided with commissions, as the project is in some measure owing to the hints of that venerable patriot. I, moreover, give it as my opinion, that Mrs. Kitty Fisher shall have the command of a battalion, and the nomination of her own officers, provided she will warrant them all sound, and be content to wear proper badges of distinction.

A female brigade, properly disciplined and accoutred, would not, I am persuaded, be afraid to charge a numerous body of the enemy, over whom they would have a manifest advantage ; for if the barbarous Scythians were ashamed to fight with the Amazons who invaded them, surely the French, who pique themselves on their sensibility and devotion to the fair sex, would not act upon the offensive against a band of female warriors, arrayed in all the charms of youth and beauty.

NATIONAL PREJUDICES

As I am one of that sauntering tribe of mortals who spend the greatest part of their time in taverns, coffee-houses, and other places of public resort, I have thereby an opportunity of observing an infinite variety of characters, which to a person of a contemplative turn is a much higher entertainment than a view of all the curiosities of art or nature. In one of these my late rambles I accidentally fell into the company of half a dozen gentlemen, who were engaged in a warm dispute about some political affair, the decision of which, as they were equally divided in their sentiments, they thought proper to refer to me, which naturally drew me in for a share of the conversation.

Amongst a multiplicity of other topics, we took occasion to talk of the different characters of the several nations of Europe; when one of the gentlemen, cocking his hat, and assuming such an air of importance as if he had possessed all the merit of the English nation in his own person, declared that the Dutch were a parcel of avaricious wretches; the French a set of flattering sycophants; that the Germans were drunken sots, and beastly gluttons; and the Spaniards proud, haughty, and surly tyrants; but that in bravery, generosity, clemency, and in every other virtue, the English excelled all the other world.

This very learned and judicious remark was received with a general smile of approbation by all the company —all, I mean, but your humble servant, who, endeavouring to keep my gravity as well as I could, and reclining my head upon my arm, continued for some time in a posture of affected thoughtfulness, as if I had been musing on something else, and did not seem to attend to the subject of conversation; hoping by this means to avoid the disagreeable necessity of explaining myself, and thereby depriving the gentleman of his imaginary happiness.

But my pseudo-patriot had no mind to let me escape so easily. Not satisfied that his opinion should pass without contradiction, he was determined to have it ratified by the suffrage of every one in the company;

for which purpose, addressing himself to me with an air of inexpressible confidence, he asked me if I was not of the same way of thinking. As I am never forward in giving my opinion, especially when I have reason to believe that it will not be agreeable ; so, when I am obliged to give it, I always hold it for a maxim to speak my real sentiments. I therefore told him that, for my own part, I should not have ventured to talk in such a peremptory strain unless I had made the tour of Europe, and examined the manners of these several nations with great care and accuracy : that perhaps a more impartial judge would not scruple to affirm, that the Dutch were more frugal and industrious, the French more temperate and polite, the Germans more hardy and patient of labour and fatigue, and the Spaniards more staid and sedate, than the English ; who, though undoubtedly brave and generous, were at the same time rash, headstrong, and impetuous ; too apt to be elated with prosperity, and to despond in adversity.

I could easily perceive, that all the company began to regard me with a jealous eye before I had finished my answer, which I had no sooner done, than the patriotic gentleman observed, with a contemptuous sneer, that he was greatly surprised how some people could have the conscience to live in a country which they did not love, and to enjoy the protection of a government to which in their hearts they were inveterate enemies. Finding that by this modest declaration of my sentiments I had forfeited the good opinion of my companions, and given them occasion to call my political principles in question, and well knowing that it was in vain to argue with men who were so very full of themselves, I threw down my reckoning and retired to my own lodgings, reflecting on the absurd and ridiculous nature of national prejudice and prepossession.

Among all the famous sayings of antiquity, there is none that does greater honour to the author, or affords greater pleasure to the reader (at least if he be a person of a generous and benevolent heart), than that of the philosopher who, being asked what countryman he was, replied, that he was ' a citizen of the world.' How few are there to be found in modern times who can say the same, or whose conduct is consistent with such a pro-- fession ! We are now become so much Englishmen, Frenchmen, Dutchmen, Spaniards, or Germans, that we are no longer citizens of the world ; so much the natives of one particular spot, or members of one petty society, that we no longer consider ourselves as the general inhabitants of the globe, or members of that grand society which comprehends the whole human kind.

Did these prejudices prevail only among the meanest and lowest of the people, perhaps they might be excused, as they have few, if any, opportunities of correcting them by reading, travelling, or conversing with foreigners: but the misfortune is, that they infect the minds, and influence the conduct, even of our gentlemen ; of those, I mean, who have every title to this appellation but an exemption from prejudice, which, however, in my opinion, ought to be regarded as the characteristical mark of a gentleman ; for let a man's birth be ever so high, his station ever so exalted, or his fortune ever so large, yet if he is not free from national and all other prejudices, I should make bold to tell him, that he had a low and vulgar mind, and had no just claim to the character of a gentleman. And, in fact, you will always find that those are most apt to boast of national merit, who have little or no merit of their own to depend on; than which, to be sure, nothing is more natural: the slender vine twists around the sturdy oak, for no other reason in the world but because it has not strength sufficient to support itself.

Should it be alleged in defence of national prejudice, that it is the natural and necessary growth of love to our country, and that therefore the former cannot be destroyed without hurting the latter, I answer that this is a gross fallacy and delusion. That it is the growth of love to our country, I will allow ; but that it is the natural and necessary growth of it, I absolutely deny. Superstition and enthusiasm, too, are the growth of religion ; but who ever took it in his head to affirm, that they are the necessary growth of this noble principle ? They are, if you will, the bastard sprouts of this heavenly plant, but not its natural and genuine branches, and may safely enough be lopt off, without doing any harm to the parent stock : nay, perhaps, till once they are lopped off, this goodly tree can never flourish in perfect health and vigour.

Is it not very possible that I may love my own country, without hating the natives of other countries ? that I may exert the most heroic bravery, the most undaunted resolution, in defending its laws and liberty, without despising all the rest of the world as cowards and poltroons ? Most certainly it is ; and if it were not—But why need I suppose what is absolutely impossible ?—But if it were not, I must own I should prefer the title of the ancient philosopher, viz. a citizen of the world, to that of an Englishman, a Frenchman, an European, or to any other appellation whatever.

SCHOOLS OF MUSIC

A school, in the polite arts, properly signifies that succession of artists which has learned the principles of the art from some eminent master, either by hearing his lessons or studying his works, and consequently who imitate his manner either through design or from habit.

Musicians seem agreed in making only three principal schools in music ; namely, the school of Pergolese in Italy, of Lully in France, and of Handel in England ; though some are for making Rameau the founder of a new school, different from those of the former, as he is the inventor of beauties peculiarly his own.

Without all doubt Pergolese's music deserves the first rank ; though excelling neither in variety of movements, number of parts, nor unexpected flights, yet he is universally allowed to be the musical Raphael of Italy. This great master's principal art consisted in knowing how to excite our passions by sounds which seem frequently opposite to the passion they would express : by slow solemn sounds he is sometimes known to throw us into all the rage of battle ; and even by faster movements he excites melancholy in every heart that sounds are capable of affecting. This is a talent which seems born with the artist. We are unable to tell why such sounds affect us : they seem no way imitative of the passion they would express, but operate upon us by an inexpressible sympathy ; the original of which is as inscrutable as the secret springs of life itself. To this excellence he adds another, in which he is superior to every other artist of the profession,—the happy transitions from one passion to another. No dramatic poet better knows to prepare his incidents than he ; the audience are pleased in those intervals of passion with the delicate, the simple harmony, if I may so express it, in which the parts are all thrown into fugues, or often are barely unison. His melodies also, where no passion is expressed, give equal pleasure from this delicate simplicity ; and I need only instance that song in the *Serva Padrona* which begins ' Lo conosco a quegl' occelli,' as one of the finest instances of excellence in the duo.

The Italian artists in general have followed his manner

yet seem fond of embellishing the delicate simplicity of the original. Their style in music seems somewhat to resemble that of Seneca in writing, where there are some beautiful starts of thought ; but the whole is filled with studied elegance and unaffecting affectation.

Lully, in France, first attempted the improvement of their music, which in general resembled that of our old solemn chants in churches. It is worthy of remark, in general, that the music of every country is solemn in proportion as the inhabitants are merry ; or, in other words, the merriest sprightliest nations are remarked for having the slowest music ; and those whose character it is to be melancholy are pleased with the most brisk and airy movements. Thus, in France, Poland, Ireland, and Switzerland, the national music is slow, melancholy, and solemn ; in Italy, England, Spain, and Germany, it is faster, proportionably as the people are grave. Lully only changed a bad manner, which he found, for a bad one of his own. His drowsy pieces are played still to the most sprightly audience that can be conceived ; and even though Rameau, who is at once a musician and a philosopher, has shown, both by precept and example, what improvements French music may still admit of, yet his countrymen seem little convinced by his reasonings ; and the Pont-Neuf taste, as it is called, still prevails in their best performances.

The English school was first planned by Purcell : he attempted to unite the Italian manner that prevailed in his time with the ancient Celtic carol and the Scotch ballad, which probably had also its origin in Italy; for some of the best Scotch ballads,—'The Broom of Cowdenknows,' for instance,—are still ascribed to David Rizzio. But be that as it will, his manner was something peculiar to the English ; and he might have continued as head of the English school, had not his merits been entirely eclipsed by Handel. Handel, though originally a German, yet adopted the English manner : he had long laboured to please by Italian composition, but without success ; and though his English oratorios are accounted inimitable, yet his Italian operas are fallen into oblivion. Pergolese excelled in passionate simplicity : Lully was remarkable for creating a new species of music, where all is elegant, but nothing passionate or sublime. Handel's true characteristic is sublimity ; he has employed all the variety of sounds and parts in all his pieces : the performances of the rest may be pleasing, though executed by few performers ; his require the full band. The attention is awakened, the soul is roused up at his pieces ; but distinct passion is seldom expressed. In this particular he has seldom found success ; he has been obliged, in order to express passion, to imitate words by sounds, which, though it gives the pleasure which imitation always produces, yet it fails of exciting those lasting affections which it is in the power of sounds to produce. In a word, no man ever understood harmony so well as he ; but in melody he has been exceeded by several.

CAROLAN, THE IRISH BARD

THERE can be perhaps no greater entertainment than to compare the rude Celtic simplicity with modern refinement. Books, however, seem incapable of furnishing the parallel ; and to be acquainted with the ancient manners of our own ancestors, we should endeavour to look for their remains in those countries, which, being in some measure retired from an intercourse with other nations, are still untinctured with foreign refinement, language, or breeding.

The Irish will satisfy curiosity in this respect preferably to all other nations I have seen. They in several parts of that country, still adhere to their ancient language, dress, furniture, and superstitions; several customs among them still speak their original; and in some respects, Caesar's description of the ancient Britons is applicable to these.

Their bards, in particular, are still held in great veneration among them; those traditional heralds are invited to every funeral, in order to fill up the intervals of the howl with their songs and harps. In these they rehearse the actions of the ancestors of the deceased, bewail the bondage of their country under the English government, and generally conclude with advising the young men and maidens to make the best use of their time; for they will soon, for all their present bloom, be stretched under the table, like the dead body before them.

Of all the bards this country ever produced, the last and the greatest was CAROLAN THE BLIND. He was at once a poet, a musician, a composer, and sung his own verses to his harp. The original natives never mention his name without rapture; both his poetry and music they have by heart; and even some of the English themselves, who have been transplanted there, find his music extremely pleasing. A song beginning, 'O'Rourke's noble fare will ne'er be forgot,' translated by Dean Swift, is of his composition; which, though perhaps by this means the best known of his pieces, is yet by no means the most deserving. His songs, in general, may be compared to those of Pindar, as they have frequently the same flights of imagination, and are composed (I don't say written, for he could not write) merely to flatter some man of fortune upon some excellence of the same kind. In these one man is praised for the excellence of his stable, as in Pindar, another for his hospitality, a third for the beauty of his wife and children, and a fourth for the antiquity of his family. Whenever any of the original natives of distinction were assembled at feasting or revelling, Carolan was generally there, where he was always ready with his harp to celebrate their praises. He seemed by nature formed for his profession ; for as he was born blind, so also he was possessed of a most astonishing memory, and a facetious turn of thinking, which gave his entertainers infinite satisfaction. Being once at the house of an Irish nobleman, where there was a musician present, who was eminent in the profession, Carolan immediately challenged him to a trial of skill. To carry the jest forward, his lordship persuaded the musician to accept the challenge, and he accordingly played over on his fiddle the fifth concerto of Vivaldi. Carolan, immediately taking his harp, played over the whole piece after him, without missing a note, though he had never heard it before ; which produced some surprise : but their astonishment increased, when he assured them he could make a concerto in the same taste himself, which he instantly composed, and that with such spirit and elegance, that it may compare (for we have it still) with the finest compositions of Italy.

His death was not more remarkable than his life. Homer was never more fond of a glass than he ; he would drink whole pints of usquebaugh, and, as he used to think, without any ill consequence. His intemperance, however, in this respect, at length brought on an incurable disorder, and when just at the point of death, he called for a cup of his beloved liquor. Those who were standing round him, surprised at the demand, endeavoured to persuade him to the contrary ; but he persisted, and when the bowl was brought him, attempted

to drink, but could not ; wherefore, giving away the
bowl, he observed, with a smile, that it would be hard
if two such friends as he and the cup should part at
least without kissing ; and then expired.

ON THE TENANTS OF THE LEASOWES

OF all men who form gay illusions of distant happiness, perhaps a poet is the most sanguine. Such is the
ardour of his hopes, that they often are equal to actual
enjoyment ; and he feels more in expectance than actual
fruition. I have often regarded a character of this kind
with some degree of envy. A man possessed of such
warm imagination commands all nature, and arrogates
possessions of which the owner has a blunter relish.
While life continues, the alluring prospect lies before
him ; he travels in the pursuit with confidence, and
resigns it only with his last breath.

It is this happy confidence which gives life its true
relish, and keeps up our spirits amidst every distress
and disappointment. How much less would be done,
if a man knew how little he can do ! How wretched
a creature would he be if he saw the end as well as the
beginning of his projects ! He would have nothing left
but to sit down in torpid despair, and exchange employment for actual calamity.

I was led into this train of thinking upon lately
visiting the beautiful gardens of the late Mr. Shenstone,
who was himself a poet, and possessed of that warm
imagination which made him ever foremost in the pursuit of flying happiness. Could he but have foreseen
the end of all his schemes, for whom he was improving,
and what changes his designs were to undergo, he
would have scarcely amused his innocent life with what,

for several years, employed him in a most harmless manner, and abridged his scanty fortune. As the progress of this Improvement is a true picture of sublunary vicissitude, I could not help calling up my imagination, which, while I walked pensively along, suggested the following Reverie.

As I was turning my back upon a beautiful piece of water, enlivened with cascades and rock-work, and entering a dark walk, by which ran a prattling brook, the Genius of the place appeared before me, but more resembling the God of Time, than him more peculiarly appointed to the care of gardens. Instead of shears he bore a scythe ; and he appeared rather with the implements of husbandry than those of a modern gardener. Having remembered this place in its pristine beauty, I could not help condoling with him on its present ruinous situation. I spoke to him of the many alterations which had been made, and all for the worse ; of the many shades which had been taken away, of the bowers that were destroyed by neglect, and the hedgerows that were spoiled by clipping. The Genius, with a sigh, received my condolement, and assured me that he was equally a martyr to ignorance and taste, to refinement and rusticity. Seeing me desirous of knowing farther, he went on :

'You see, in the place before you, the paternal 'inheritance of a poet; and, to a man content with little, 'fully sufficient for his subsistence : but a strong imagina- 'tion, and a long acquaintance with the rich, are dangerous 'foes to contentment. Our poet, instead of sitting down 'to enjoy life, resolved to prepare for its future enjoy- 'ment, and set about converting a place of profit into 'a scene of pleasure. This he at first supposed could be 'accomplished at a small expense; and he was willing 'for a while to stint his income, to have an opportunity

'of displaying his taste. The Improvement in this manner
'went forward; one beauty attained led him to wish for
'some other; but he still hoped that every emendation
'would be the last. It was now therefore found, that
'the Improvement exceeded the subsidy—that the place
'was grown too large and too fine for the inhabitant.
'But that pride which was once exhibited could not
'retire; the garden was made for the owner, and though
'it was become unfit for him, he could not willingly
'resign it to another. Thus the first idea, of its beauties
'contributing to the happiness of his life, was found
'unfaithful; so that, instead of looking within for
'satisfaction, he began to think of having recourse to
'the praises of those who came to visit his Improve-
'ment.

'In consequence of this hope, which now took posses-
'sion of his mind, the gardens were opened to the visits
'of every stranger; and the country flocked round to
'walk, to criticize, to admire, and to do mischief. He
'soon found that the admirers of his taste left by no
'means such strong marks of their applause, as the
'envious did of their malignity. All the windows of his
'temples and the walls of his retreats were impressed
'with the characters of profaneness, ignorance, and
'obscenity; his hedges were broken, his statues and
'urns defaced, and his lawns worn bare. It was now,
'therefore, necessary to shut up the gardens once more,
'and to deprive the public of that happiness which had
'before ceased to be his own.

'In this situation the poet continued for a time, in
'the character of a jealous lover, fond of the beauty he
'keeps, but unable to supply the extravagance of every
'demand. The garden by this time was completely
'grown and finished; the marks of art were covered up
'by the luxuriance of nature; the winding walks were

'grown dark; the brook assumed a natural sylvage;
'and the rocks were covered with moss. Nothing now
'remained but to enjoy the beauties of the place, when
'the poor poet died, and his garden was obliged to be
'sold for the benefit of those who had contributed to its
'embellishment.

'The beauties of the place had now for some time
'been celebrated as well in prose as in verse; and all
'men of taste wished for so envied a spot, where every
'turn was marked with the poet's pencil, and every
'walk awakened genius and meditation. The first pur-
'chaser was one Mr. Truepenny, a button-maker, who
'was possessed of three thousand pounds, and was willing
'also to be possessed of taste and genius.

'As the poet's ideas were for the natural wildness of
'the landscape, the button-maker's were for the more
'regular productions of art. He conceived, perhaps, that
'as it is a beauty in a button to be of a regular pattern,
'so the same regularity ought to obtain in a landscape.
'Be this as it will, he employed the shears to some pur-
'pose; he clipped up the hedges, cut down the gloomy
'walks, made vistas upon the stables and hog-sties, and
'showed his friends that a man of taste should always
'be doing.

'The next candidate for taste and genius was a captain
'of a ship, who bought the garden because the former
'possessor could find nothing more to mend: but un-
'fortunately he had taste too. His great passion lay in
'building, in making Chinese temples and cage-work
'summer-houses. As the place before had an appearance
'of retirement and inspired meditation, he gave it a more
'peopled air; every turning presented a cottage, or ice-
'house, or a temple; the Improvement was converted
'into a little city, and it only wanted inhabitants to give
'it the air of a village in the East Indies.

' In this manner, in less than ten years, the Improve-
' ment has gone through the hands of as many proprietors,
' who were all willing to have taste, and to show their
' taste too. As the place had received its best finishing
' from the hand of the first possessor, so every innovator
' only lent a hand to do mischief. Those parts which
' were obscure, have been enlightened ; those walks
' which led naturally, have been twisted into serpentine
' windings. The colour of the flowers of the field is not
' more various than the variety of tastes that have been
' employed here, and all in direct contradiction to the
' original aim of the first improver. Could the original
' possessor but revive, with what a sorrowful heart would
' he look upon his favourite spot again ! He would
' scarcely recollect a Dryad or a Wood-nymph of his
' former acquaintance, and might perhaps find himself
' as much a stranger in his own plantation as in the
' deserts of Siberia.'

SENTIMENTAL COMEDY

THE theatre, like all other amusements, has its
fashions and its prejudices ; and when satiated with
its excellence, mankind begin to mistake change for
improvement. For some years tragedy was the reigning
entertainment ; but of late it has entirely given way to
comedy, and our best efforts are now exerted in these
lighter kinds of composition. The pompous train, the
swelling phrase, and the unnatural rant are displaced
for that natural portrait of human folly and frailty, of
which all are judges, because all have sat for the
picture.

But as in describing nature it is presented with
a double face, either of mirth or sadness, our modern

writers find themselves at a loss which chiefly to copy from ; and it is now debated, whether the exhibition of human distress is likely to afford the mind more entertainment than that of human absurdity ?

Comedy is defined by Aristotle to be a picture of the frailties of the lower part of mankind, to distinguish it from tragedy, which is an exhibition of the misfortunes of the great. When comedy, therefore, ascends to pro- duce the characters of princes or generals upon the stage, it is out of its walk, since low life and middle life are entirely its object. The principal question therefore is, whether, in describing low or middle life, an exhibition of its follies be not preferable to a detail of its calamities ? Or, in other words, which deserves the preference,— the weeping sentimental comedy so much in fashion at present [1773], or the laughing and even low comedy which seems to have been last exhibited by Vanbrugh and Cibber ?

If we apply to authorities, all the great masters in the dramatic art have but one opinion. Their rule is, that as tragedy displays the calamities of the great, so comedy should excite our laughter by ridiculously exhibiting the follies of the lower -part of mankind. Boileau, one of the best modern critics, asserts that comedy will not admit of tragic distress :

> Le comique, ennemi des soupirs et des pleurs,
> N'admet point dans ses vers de tragiques douleurs.

Nor is this rule without the strongest foundation in nature, as the distresses of the mean by no means affect us so strongly as the calamities of the great. When tragedy exhibits to us some great man fallen from his height, and struggling with want and adversity, we feel his situation in the same manner as we suppose he himself must feel, and our pity is increased in proportion to the height from whence he fell. On the contrary, we do not so strongly

sympathize with one born in humbler circumstances,
and encountering accidental distress; so that while we
melt for Belisarius, we scarce give halfpence to the
beggar who accosts us in the street. The one has our
pity; the other our contempt. Distress, therefore, is
the proper object of tragedy, since the great excite our
pity by their fall; but not equally so of comedy, since
the actors employed in it are originally so mean, that
they sink but little by their fall.

Since the first origin of the stage, tragedy and comedy
have run in distinct channels, and never till of late
encroached upon the provinces of each other. Terence,
who seems to have made the nearest approaches, always
judiciously stops short before he comes to the downright
pathetic; and yet he is even reproached by Caesar for
wanting the *vis comica*. All the other comic writers of
antiquity aim only at rendering folly or vice ridiculous,
but never exalt their characters into buskined pomp,
or make what Voltaire humorously calls *a tradesman's
tragedy*.

Yet notwithstanding this weight of authority, and
the universal practice of former ages, a new species of
dramatic composition has been introduced, under the
name of sentimental comedy, in which the virtues of
private life are exhibited, rather than the vices exposed;
and the distresses rather than the faults of mankind
make our interest in the piece. These comedies have
had of late great success, perhaps from their novelty,
and also from their flattering every man in his favourite
foible. In these plays almost all the characters are
good, and exceedingly generous; they are lavish enough
of their tin money on the stage; and though they want
humour, have abundance of sentiment and feeling. If
they happen to have faults or foibles, the spectator is
taught, not only to pardon, but to applaud them, in

consideration of the goodness of their hearts ; so that folly, instead of being ridiculed, is commended, and the comedy aims at touching our passions without the power of being truly pathetic. In this manner we are likely to lose one great source of entertainment on the stage ; for while the comic poet is invading the province of the tragic-muse, he leaves her lovely sister quite neglected. Of this, however, he is no way solicitous, as he measures his fame by his profits.

But it will be said that the theatre is formed to amuse mankind, and that it matters little, if this end be answered, by what means it is obtained. If mankind find delight in weeping at comedy, it would be cruel to abridge them in that or any other innocent pleasure. If those pieces are denied the name of comedies, yet call them by any other name, and if they are delightful, they are good. Their success, it will be said, is a mark of their merit, and it is only abridging our happiness to deny us an inlet to amusement.

These objections, however, are rather specious than solid. It is true that amusement is a great object of the theatre, and it will be allowed that these sentimental pieces do often amuse us ; but the question is, whether the true comedy would not amuse us more? The question is, whether a character supported throughout a piece with its ridicule still attending, would not give us more delight than this species of bastard tragedy, which only is applauded because it is new?

A friend of mine, who was sitting unmoved at one of these sentimental pieces, was asked how he could be so indifferent? 'Why, truly,' says he, ' as the hero is but a ' tradesman, it is indifferent to me whether he be turned ' out of his counting-house on Fish-street Hill, since he ' will still have enough left to open shop in St. Giles's.'

The other objection is as ill-grounded ; for though

we should give these pieces another name, it will not mend their efficacy. It will continue a kind of mulish production, with all the defects of its opposite parents, and marked with sterility. If we are permitted to make comedy weep, we have an equal right to make tragedy laugh, and to set down in blank verse the jests and repartees of all the attendants in a funeral procession.

But there is one argument in favour of sentimental comedy, which will keep it on the stage, in spite of all that can be said against it. It is, of all others, the most easily written. Those abilities that can hammer out a novel are fully sufficient for the production of a sentimental comedy. It is only sufficient to raise the characters a little; to deck out the hero with a riband, or give the heroine a title; then to put an insipid dialogue, without character or humour, into their mouths, give them mighty good hearts, very fine clothes, furnish a new set of scenes, make a pathetic scene or two, with a sprinkling of tender melancholy conversation through the whole, and there is no doubt but all the ladies will cry, and all the gentlemen applaud.

Humour at present seems to be departing from the stage, and it will soon happen that our comic players will have nothing left for it but a fine coat and a song. It depends upon the audience whether they will actually drive those poor merry creatures from the stage, or sit at a play as gloomy as at the tabernacle. It is not easy to recover an art when once lost; and it will be but a just punishment, that when, by our being too fastidious, we have banished humour from the stage, we should ourselves be deprived of the art of laughing.

SCOTCH MARRIAGES

As I see you are fond of gallantry, and seem willing to set young people together as soon as you can, I cannot help lending my assistance to your endeavours, as I am greatly concerned in the attempt. You must know, sir, that I am landlady of one of the most noted inns on the road to Scotland, and have seldom less than eight or ten couples a week, who go down rapturous lovers, and return man and wife.

If there be in this world an agreeable situation, it must be that in which a young couple find themselves, when just let loose from confinement, and whirling off to the land of promise. When the post-chaise is driving off, and the blinds are drawn up, sure nothing can equal it. And yet, I do not know how, what with the fears of being pursued, or the wishes for greater happiness, not one of my customers but seems gloomy and out of temper. The gentlemen are all sullen, and the ladies discontented.

But if it be so going down, how is it with them coming back? Having been for a fortnight together, they are then mighty good company to be sure. It is then that the young lady's indiscretion stares her in the face, and the gentleman himself finds that much is to be done before the money comes in.

For my own part, sir, I was married in the usual way; all my friends were at the wedding; I was conducted with great ceremony from the table to the bed; and I do not find that it any ways diminished my happiness with my husband, while, poor man! he continued with me. For my part, I am entirely for doing things in the old family way; I hate your new-fashioned manners, and never loved an outlandish marriage in my life.

As I have had numbers call at my house, you may be sure I was not idle in inquiring who they were, and how they did in the world after they left me. I cannot say that I ever heard much good come of them : and of a history of twenty-five that I noted down in my ledger, I do not know a single couple that would not have been full as happy if they had gone the plain way to work, and asked the consent of their parents. To convince you of it, I will mention the names of a few, and refer the rest to some fitter opportunity.

Imprimis, Miss Jenny Hastings went down to Scotland with a tailor, who, to be sure, for a tailor, was a very agreeable sort of man. But, I do not know how, he did not take proper measure of the young lady's disposition they quarrelled at my house on their return ; so she left him for a cornet of dragoons, and he went back to his shop-board.

Miss Rachel Runfort went off with a grenadier. They spent all their money going down ; so that he carried her down in a post-chaise, and coming back, she helped to carry his knapsack.

Miss Racket went down with her lover in their own phaeton ; but upon their return, being very fond of driving, she would be every now and then for holding the whip. This bred a dispute ; and before they were a fortnight together, she felt that he could exercise the whip on somebody else besides the horses.

Miss Meekly, though all compliance to the will of her lover, could never reconcile him to the change of his situation. It seems he married her supposing she had a large fortune ; but being deceived in his expectations, they parted ; and they now keep separate garrets in Rosemary Lane.

The next couple of whom I have any account actually lived together in great harmony and uncloying kindness for no less than a month ; but the lady, who was a little in years, having parted with her fortune to her dearest life, he left her to make love to that better part of her which he valued more.

The next pair consisted of an Irish fortune-hunter and one of the prettiest, modestest ladies that ever my eyes beheld. As he was a well-looking gentleman, all dressed in lace, and as she seemed very fond of him, I thought they were blest for life. Yet I was quickly mistaken. The lady was no better than a common woman of the town, and he was no better than a sharper ; so they agreed upon a mutual divorce : he now dresses at the York Ball, and she is in keeping by the member for our borough in Parliament.

In this manner we see that all those marriages, in which there is interest on one side, and disobedience on the other, are not likely to promise a long harvest of delights. If our fortune-hunting gentlemen would but speak out, the young lady, instead of a lover, would often find a sneaking rogue, that only wanted the lady's purse, and not her heart. For my own part, I never saw anything but design and falsehood in every one of them ; and my blood has boiled in my veins when I saw a young fellow of twenty kneeling at the feet of a twenty-thousand pounder, professing his passion, while he was taking aim at her money. I do not deny but there may be love in a Scotch marriage, but it is generally all on one side.

Of all the sincere admirers I ever knew, a man of my acquaintance, who however did not run away with his mistress to Scotland, was the most so. An old excise-man of our town, who, as you may guess, was not very rich, had a daughter who, as you shall see, was not very handsome. It was the opinion of everybody that this young woman would not soon be married, as she wanted two main articles, beauty and fortune. But, for all this, a very well-looking man, that happened to be travelling those parts, came and asked the exciseman for his daughter in marriage. The exciseman, willing to deal openly by him, asked if he had seen the girl ; ' for,' says he, ' she is humpbacked.'—' Very ' well,' cried the stranger, 'that will do for me.'—'Aye,' says the exciseman, ' but my daughter is as brown as ' a berry.'—' So much the better,' cried the stranger ; ' such skins wear well.'—' But she is bandy-legged,' says the exciseman.—'No matter,' cries the other ; ' her petticoats will hide that defect.'—' But then she is ' very poor, and wants an eye.'—' Your description ' delights me,' cries the stranger : ' I have been long ' looking out for one of her make ; for I keep an ex- ' hibition of wild beasts, and intend to show her off ' for a chimpanzee.'

THE

L I F E

O F

RICHARD NASH, Efq;

LATE

Mafter of the Ceremonies at BATH.

Extracted principally from

His O R I G I N A L P A P E R S.

——————*Non ego paucis*
Offendar Maculis.—— HOR.

THE SECOND EDITION.

L O N D O N:

Printed for J. NEWBERY, in St. Paul's Church-
yard; W. FREDERICK, at Bath; and
G. FAULKENER, in Dublin.
M DCC LXII.

TO

THE RIGHT WORSHIPFUL,

THE MAYOR,

RECORDER,

ALDERMEN,

AND

COMMON COUNCIL,

OF THE

CITY OF BATH;

THIS VOLUME

IS HUMBLY INSCRIBED

BY THEIR

MOST OBEDIENT HUMBLE SERVANT,

THE EDITOR.

PREFACE

THE following memoir is neither calculated to inflame the reader's passions with descriptions of gallantry, nor to gratify his malevolence with details of scandal. The amours of coxcombs, and the pursuits of debauchees, are as destitute of novelty to attract us, as they are of variety to entertain, they still present us but the same picture, a picture we have seen a thousand times repeated. The life of Mr. Nash is incapable of supplying any entertainment of this nature to a prurient curiosity. Though it was passed in the very midst of debauchery, he practised but few of those vices he was often obliged to assent to. Though he lived where gallantry was the capital pursuit, he was never known to favour it by his example, and what authority he had was set to oppose it. Instead therefore of a romantic history, filled with warm pictures and fanciful adventures, the reader of the following account must rest satisfied with a genuine and candid recital compiled from the papers he left behind, and others equally authentic ; a recital neither written with a spirit of satire nor panegyric, and with scarce any other art than that of arranging the materials in their natural order.

But though little art has been used, it is hoped that some entertainment may be collected from the life of a person so much talked of, and yet so little known, as

Mr. Nash. The history of a man, who for more than fifty years presided over the pleasures of a polite kingdom, and whose life, though without anything to surprise, was ever marked with singularity, deserves the attention of the present age ; the pains he took in pursuing pleasure, and the solemnity he assumed in adjusting trifles, may one day claim the smile of posterity. At least such a history is well enough calculated to supply a vacant hour with innocent amusement, however it may fail to open the heart, or improve the understanding.

Yet his life, how trifling soever it may appear to the inattentive, was not without its real advantages to the public. He was the first who diffused a desire of society, and an easiness of address, among a whole people who were formerly censured by foreigners for a reservedness of behaviour and an awkward timidity in their first approaches. He first taught a familiar intercourse among strangers at Bath and Tunbridge, which still subsists among them. That ease and open access first acquired there, our gentry brought back to the metropolis, and thus the whole kingdom by degrees became more refined by lessons originally derived from him.

Had it been my design to have made this history more pleasing at the expense of truth, it had been easily performed ; but I chose to describe the man as he was, not such as imagination could have helped in completing his picture ; he will be found to be a weak man, governing weaker subjects, and may be considered as resembling a monarch of Cappadocia, whom Cicero somewhere calls, *the little king of a little people.*

But while I have been careful in describing the monarch, his dominions have claimed no small share of my attention ; I have given an·exact account of the rise, regulation, and nature of the amusements of the city of Bath, how far Mr. Nash contributed to establish and refine them, and what pleasure a stranger may expect there upon his arrival. Such anecdotes as are at once true and worth preserving are produced in their order, and some stories are added, which, though commonly known, more necessarily belong to this history than to the places from whence they have been extracted. But it is needless to point out the pains that have been taken, or the entertainment that may be expected from the perusal of this performance. It is but an indifferent way to gain the reader's esteem, to be my own panegyrist, nor is this preface so much designed to lead him to beauties, as to demand pardon for defects.

ADVERTISEMENT

We have the permission of George Scott, Esq. (who kindly undertook to settle the affairs of Mr. Nash, for the benefit of his family and creditors) to assure the public, that all the papers found in the custody of Mr. Nash, which any ways respected his life, and were thought interesting to the public, were communicated to the Editor of this volume ; so that the reader will, at least, have the satisfaction of perusing an account that is genuine, and not the work of imagination, as biographical writings too frequently are.

THE
LIFE OF RICHARD NASH, Esq.

HISTORY owes its excellence more to the writer's manner than the materials of which it is composed. The intrigues of courts, or the devastation of armies, are regarded by the remote spectator with as little attention as the squabbles of a village, or the fate of a malefactor, that fall under his own observation. The great and the little, as they have the same senses, and the same affections, generally present the same picture to the hand of the draughtsman ; and whether the hero or the clown be the subject of the memoir, it is only man that appears with all his native minuteness about him ; for nothing very great was ever yet formed from the little materials of humanity.

Thus none can properly be said to write history, but he who understands the human heart, and its whole train of affections and follies. Those affections and follies are properly the materials he has to work upon. The relations of great events may surprise indeed ; they may be calculated to instruct those very few who govern the million beneath, but the generality of mankind find the most real improvement from relations which are levelled to the general surface of life ; which tell, not how men learned to conquer, but how they endeavoured to live ; not how they gained the shout of the admiring crowd, but how they acquired the esteem of their friends and acquaintance.

Every man's own life would perhaps furnish the most pleasing materials for history, if he only had candour enough to be sincere, and skill enough to select such parts as once making him more prudent, might serve to render his readers more cautious. There are few who do not prefer a page of Montaigne or Colley Cibber, who candidly tell us what they thought of the world and the world thought of them, to the more stately memoirs and transactions of Europe, where we see kings pretending to immortality, that are now almost forgotten, and statesmen planning frivolous negotiations, that scarce outlive the signing.

It were to be wished that ministers and kings were left to write their own histories; they are truly useful to few but themselves; but for men who are contented with more humble stations, I fancy such truths only are serviceable as may conduct them safely through life. That knowledge which we can turn to our real benefit should be most eagerly pursued. Treasures which we cannot use but little increase the happiness or even the pride of the possessor.

I profess to write the history of a man placed in the middle ranks of life; of one, whose vices and virtues were open to the eye of the most undiscerning spectator; who was placed in public view, without power to repress censure, or command adulation; who had too much merit not to become remarkable, yet too much folly to arrive at greatness. I attempt the character of one, who was just such a man as probably you or I may be, but with this difference, that he never performed an action which the world did not know, or ever formed a wish which he did not take pains to divulge. In short, I have chosen to write the life of the noted Mr. Nash, as it will be the delineation of a mind without disguise, of a man ever assiduous without industry, and pleasing to his superiors, without any superiority of genius or understanding.

Yet if there be any who think the subject of too little

importance to command attention, and had rather gaze at the actions of the great, than be directed in guiding their own, I have one undeniable claim to their attention. Mr. Nash was himself a king. In this particular, perhaps no biographer has been so happy as I. They who are for a delineation of men and manners may find some satisfaction that way, and those who delight in adventures of kings and queens, may perhaps find their hopes satisfied in another

It is a matter of very little importance who were the parents, or what was the education, of a man who owed so little of his advancement to either. He seldom boasted of family or learning, and his father's name and circumstances were so little known, that Doctor Cheyne used frequently to say, that Nash had no father. The Duchess of Marlborough one day rallying him in public company upon the obscurity of his birth, compared him to Gil Blas, who was ashamed of his father : ' No, ' Madam,' replied Nash, ' I seldom mention my father in ' company, not because I have any reason to be ashamed ' of him, but because he has some reason to be ashamed ' of me.'

However, though such anecdotes be immaterial, to go on in the usual course of history, it may be proper to observe, that Richard Nash, Esq., the subject of this memoir, was born in the town of Swansea, in Glamorganshire, on the 18th of October, in the year 1674.[1] His father was a gentleman, whose principal income arose

[1] This account of his birth and parentage is confirmed by the following memorandum, written by Mr. Nash himself in a book belonging to Mr. Charles Morgan, at the Coffee-House in Bath ; whence it was transcribed by George Scott, Esq. ; to whom we are indebted for this and many other anecdotes respecting the life of Mr. Nash.

' My father was a Welch Gentleman, my mother niece to Col. Poyer, who was murdered by Oliver for defending Pembroke. I was born Oct. 18, 1674, in Swansey, Glamorganshire.'

from a partnership in a glass-house ; his mother was niece to Colonel Poyer, who was killed by Oliver Cromwell, for defending Pembroke Castle against the rebels. He was educated under Mr. Maddocks at Carmarthen School, and from thence sent to Jesus College, in Oxford, in order to prepare him for the study of the law. His father had strained his little income to give his son such an education; but from the boy's natural vivacity, he hoped a recompense from his future preferment. In college, however, he soon showed that though much might be expected from his genius, nothing could be hoped from his industry. A mind strongly turned to pleasure, always is first seen at the University : there the youth first finds himself freed from the restraint of tutors, and being treated by his friends in some measure as a man, assumes the passions and desires of riper age, and discovers in the boy, what are likely to be the affections of his maturity.

The first method Mr. Nash took to distinguish himself at college was not by application to study, but by his assiduity in intrigue. In the neighbourhood of every University there are girls who with some beauty, some coquetry, and little fortune, lie upon the watch for every raw amorous youth, more inclined to make love than to study. Our hero was quickly caught, and went through all the mazes and adventures of a college intrigue, before he was seventeen ; he offered marriage, the offer was accepted, but the whole affair coming to the knowledge of his tutor, his happiness, or perhaps · his future misery, was prevented, and he was sent home from college, with necessary advice to him, and proper instructions to his father.[1]

[1] Since the publication of the first edition of this book, notice has been taken in some of the newspapers of Mr. Nash's leaving the University without discharging a small debt which he owed to the college where he was placed, and which stands on their books to this

When a man knows his power over the fair sex, he generally commences their admirer for the rest of life. That triumph which he obtains over one, only makes him the slave of another ; and thus he proceeds, conquering and conquered, to the closing of the scene. The army seemed the most likely profession in which to display this inclination ' for gallantry ; he therefore purchased a pair of colours, commenced a professed admirer of the sex, and dressed to the very edge of his finances. But the life of a soldier is more pleasing to the spectator at a distance than to the person who makes the experiment. Mr. Nash soon found that a red coat alone would never succeed, that the company of the fair sex is not to be procured without expense, and that his scanty commission could never procure him the proper reimbursements. He found too that the profession of arms required attendance and duty, and often encroached upon those hours he could have wished to dedicate to softer purposes. In short, he soon became disgusted with the life of a soldier, quitted the army, entered his name as a student in the Temple books, and here went to the very summit of second-rate luxury. Though very poor he was very fine ; he spread the little gold he had, in the most ostentatious manner, and though the gilding was but thin, he laid it on as far as it would go. They who know the town, cannot be

day. This is a circumstance which we were informed of before the publication of our former edition ; but as our business was to write the life of Mr. Nash, and not to settle his accounts, it seemed to us too immaterial to deserve any particular notice : besides, had we paid any regard to this, we ought also to have taken some notice of another anecdote, communicated to us, which was, that when he was sent from college he left behind him a pair of boots, two plays, a tobacco-box, and a fiddle, which had engaged more of his attention than either the public or private lectures. But as this, as well as the other, could afford neither entertainment nor edification, they were purposely omitted.

unacquainted with such a character as I describe ; one, who, though he may have dined in private upon a banquet served cold from a cook's shop, shall dress at six for the side-box ; one of those, whose wants are only known to their laundress and tradesmen, and their fine clothes to half the nobility ; who spend more in chair hire, than housekeeping ; and prefer a bow from a Lord, to a dinner from a Commoner.

In this manner Mr. Nash spent some years about town, till at last his genteel appearance, his constant civility, and still more, his assiduity, gained him the acquaintance of several persons qualified to lead the fashion both by birth and fortune. To gain the friendship of the young nobility, little more is requisite than much submission and very fine clothes ; dress has a mechanical influence upon the mind, and we naturally are awed into respect and esteem at the elegance of those, whom even our reason would teach us to contemn. He seemed early sensible of human weakness in this respect ; he brought a person genteelly dressed to every assembly ; he always made one of those who are called very good company, and assurance gave him an air of elegance and ease.

When King William was upon the throne, Mr. Nash was a member of the Middle Temple. It had been long customary for the Inns of Court to entertain our monarchs upon their accession to the crown, or some such remarkable occasion, with a revel and pageant. In the earlier periods of our history, poets were the conductors of these entertainments ; plays were exhibited, and complimentary verses were then written ; but by degrees the pageant alone was continued, Sir John Davis being the last poet that wrote verses upon such an occasion, in the reign of James I.

This ceremony, which has been at length totally

discontinued, was last exhibited in honour of King William, and Mr. Nash was chosen to conduct the whole with proper decorum. He was then but a very young man, but we see at how early an age he was thought proper to guide the amusements of his country, and be the *Arbiter Elegantiarum* of his time ; we see how early he gave proofs of that spirit of regularity, for which he afterwards became famous, and showed an attention to those little circumstances, of which, though the observ- ance be trifling, the neglect has often interrupted men of the greatest abilities in the progress of their fortunes.

In conducting this entertainment, Nash had an opportunity of exhibiting all his abilities, and King William was so well satisfied with his performance, that he made him an offer of knighthood. This, however, he thought proper to refuse, which in a person of his disposition seems strange. ' Please your Majesty,' replied he, when the offer was made him, ' if you intend to ' make me a knight, I wish it may be one of your poor ' Knights of Windsor, and then I shall have a fortune ' at least able to support my title.' Yet we do not find that the King took the hint of increasing his fortune ; perhaps he could not : he had at that time numbers to oblige, and he never cared to give money without important services.

But though Nash acquired no riches by his late office, yet he gained many friends, or what is more easily obtained, many acquaintance, who often answer the end as well. In the populous city where he resided, to be known was almost synonymous with being in the road to fortune. How many little things do we see, without merit, or without friends, push themselves forward into public notice, and by self-advertising, attract the attention of the day. The wise despise them, but the public are not all wise. Thus they succeed, rise upon the wing of folly, or of fashion, and by their success give a new sanction to effrontery.

But beside his assurance, Mr. Nash had in reality some merit and some virtues. He was, if not a brilliant, at least an easy companion. He never forgot good manners, even in the highest warmth of familiarity, and, as I hinted before, never went in a dirty shirt to disgrace the table of his patron or his friend. These qualifications might make the furniture of his head; but for his heart, that seemed an assemblage of the virtues which display an honest benevolent mind, with the vices which spring from too much good nature. He had pity for every creature's distress, but wanted prudence in the application of his benefits. He had generosity for the wretched in the highest degree, at a time when his creditors complained of his justice. He often spoke falsehoods, but never had any of his harmless tales tinctured with malice.

An instance of his humanity is told us in the *Spectator*, though his name is not mentioned. When he was to give in his accompts to the Masters of the Temple, among other articles, he charged ' For making one man ' happy, £10.' Being questioned about the meaning of so strange an item, he frankly declared, that happening to overhear a poor man declare to his wife and a large family of children, that £10 would make him happy, he could not avoid trying the experiment. He added, that if they did not choose to acquiesce in his charge, he was ready to refund the money. The Masters, struck with such an uncommon instance of good nature, publicly thanked him for his benevolence, and desired that the sum might be doubled as a proof of their satisfaction.

Another instance of his unaccountable generosity, and I shall proceed. In some transactions with one of his friends, Mr. Nash was brought in debtor twenty pounds. His friend frequently asked for the money, and was as often denied. He found at last, that assiduity was likely to have no effect, and therefore contrived an honourable method of getting back his money without dissolving the friendship that subsisted between them. One day, returning from Nash's chamber with the usual assurance of being paid to-morrow, he went to one of their mutual acquaintance, and related the frequent disappointments he had received, and the little hopes he had of being ever paid. 'My design,' continues he, ' is that you should go, and try to borrow twenty pounds ' from Nash, and bring me the money. I am apt to ' think he will lend to you, though he will not pay me. ' Perhaps we may extort from his generosity, what ' I have failed to receive from his justice.' His friend obeys, and going to Mr. Nash, assured him, that, unless relieved by his friendship, he should certainly be undone; he wanted to borrow twenty pounds, and had tried all his acquaintance without success. Mr. Nash, who had, but some minutes before, refused to pay a just debt, was in raptures at thus giving an instance of his friendship, and instantly lent what was required. Immediately upon the receipt, the pretended borrower goes to the real creditor, and gives him the money, who met Mr. Nash the day after ; our hero, upon seeing him, immediately began his usual excuses, that the billiard-room had stripped him, that he was never so damnably out of cash ; but that in a few days—' My dear sir, be ' under no uneasiness,' replied the other, ' I would not ' interrupt your tranquillity for the world ; you lent ' twenty pounds yesterday to our friend of the back ' stairs, and he lent it to me ; give him your receipt, and ' you shall have mine.' ' Perdition seize thee,' cried Nash, 'thou hast been too many for me. You demanded ' a debt, he asked a favour ; to pay thee, would not

' increase our friendship, but to lend him was procuring
' a new friend, by conferring a new obligation.'

Whether men, at the time I am now talking of, had
more wit than at present, I will not take upon me to
determine ; but certain it is, they took more pains
to show what they had. In that age, a fellow of
high humour would drink no wine but what was
strained through his mistress's smock. He would eat
a pair of her shoes tossed up in a fricassee. He would
swallow tallow-candles instead of toasted cheese, and
even run naked about town, as it was then said, to divert
the ladies. In short, that was the age of such kind of
wit as is the most distant of all others from wisdom.

Mr. Nash, as he sometimes played tricks with others,
upon certain occasions received very severe retaliations.
Being at York, and having lost all his money, some of
his companions agreed to equip him with fifty guineas,
upon this proviso, that he would stand at the great door
of the Minster, in a blanket, as the people were coming
out of church. To this proposal he readily agreed, but
the Dean passing by, unfortunately knew him. ' What,'
cried the divine, ' Mr. Nash, in masquerade ? ' ' Only
' a Yorkshire penance, Mr. Dean, for keeping bad
' company,' says Nash, pointing to his companions.

Some time after this, he won a wager of still greater
consequence, by riding naked through a village upon
a cow. This was then thought a harmless frolic; at
present it would be looked upon with detestation.

He was once invited by some gentlemen of the navy
on board a man-of-war, that had sailing orders for the
Mediterranean. This was soon after the affair of the
revels, and being ignorant of any design against him, he
took his bottle with freedom. But he soon found, to
use the expression then in fashion, that he was absolutely
bitten. The ship sailed away before he was aware of

his situation, and he was obliged to make the voyage in the company where he had spent the night.

Many lives are often passed without a single adventure, and I do not know of any in the life of our hero that can be called such, except what we are now relating. During this voyage, he was in an engagement, in which his particular friend was killed by his side, and he himself wounded in the leg. For the anecdote of his being wounded, we are solely to trust to his own veracity; but most of his acquaintance were not much inclined to believe him, when he boasted on those occasions. Telling one day of the wound he had received for his country, in one of the public rooms at Bath (Wiltshire's, if I don't forget), a lady of distinction, that sat by, said it was all false. 'I protest, Madam,' replied he, 'it is true; 'and if I cannot be believed, your Ladyship may, if 'you please, receive farther information, and feel the 'ball in my leg.'

Mr. Nash was now fairly for life entered into a new course of gaiety and dissipation, and steady in nothing but in pursuit of variety. He was thirty years old, without fortune, or useful talents to acquire one. He had hitherto only led a life of expedients, he thanked chance alone for his support, and having been long precariously supported, he became, at length, totally a stranger to prudence, or precaution. Not to disguise any part of his character, he was now, by profession, a gamester, and went on from day to day, feeling the vicissitudes of rapture and anguish, in proportion to the fluctuations of fortune.

At this time, London was the only theatre in England, for pleasure, or intrigue. A spirit of gaming had been introduced in the licentious age of Charles II, and had by this time thriven surprisingly. Yet all its devastations were confined to London alone. To this great mart of every folly, sharpers from every country daily arrived, for the winter, but were obliged to leave the kingdom at the approach of summer, in order to open a new campaign at Aix, Spa, or the Hague. Bath, Tunbridge, Scarborough, and other places of the same kind here, were then frequented only by such as really went for relief ; the pleasures they afforded were merely rural, the company splenetic, rustic, and vulgar. In this situation of things, people of fashion had no agreeable summer retreat from the town, and usually spent that season amidst a solitude of country squires, parsons' wives, and visiting tenants, or farmers ; they wanted some place where they might have each other's company, and win each other's money, as they had done during the winter in town.

To a person who does not thus calmly trace things to their source, nothing will appear more strange, than how the healthy could ever consent to follow the sick to those places of spleen, and live with those, whose disorders are ever apt to excite a gloom in the spectator. The truth is, the gaming-table was properly the salutary font to which such numbers flocked. Gaming will ever be the pleasure of the rich, while men continue to be men; while they fancy more happiness in being possessed of what they want, than they experience pleasure in the fruition of what they have. The wealthy only stake those riches, which give no real content, for an expectation of riches, in which they hope for satisfaction. By this calculation, they cannot lose happiness, as they begin with none ; and they hope to gain it, by being possessed of something they have not had already.

Probably upon this principle, and by the arrival of Queen Anne there for her health, about the year 1703, the city of Bath became in some measure frequented by people of distinction. The company was numerous enough to form a country dance upon the bowling green; they were amused with a fiddle and hautboy, and diverted with the romantic walks round the city. They usually sauntered in fine weather in the grove, between two rows of sycamore trees. Several learned physicians, Doctor Jordan and others, had even then praised the salubrity of the wells, and the amusements were put under the direction of a master of the ceremonies.

Captain Webster was the predecessor of Mr. Nash. This I take to be the same gentleman whom Mr. Lucas describes in his history of the lives of the gamesters, by which it appears, that Bath, even before the arrival of Mr. Nash, was found a proper retreat for men of that profession. This gentleman, in the year 1704, carried the balls to the town hall, each man paying half a guinea each ball.

Still, however, the amusements of this place were neither elegant, nor conducted with delicacy. General society among people of rank or fortune was by no means established. The nobility still preserved a tincture of Gothic haughtiness, and refused to keep company with the gentry at any of the public entertainments of the place. Smoking in the rooms was permitted; gentlemen and ladies appeared in a disrespectful manner at public entertainments in aprons and boots. With an eagerness common to those whose pleasures come but seldom, they generally continued them too long; and thus they were rendered disgusting by too free an enjoyment. If the company liked each other, they danced till morning; if any person lost at cards, he insisted on continuing the game till luck should turn. The lodgings for visitants were paltry, though expensive; the dining-rooms and other chambers were floored with boards, coloured brown with soot and small beer, to hide the dirt; the walls were covered with unpainted wainscot; the furniture corresponded with the meanness of the architecture ; a few oak chairs, a small looking-glass, with a fender and tongs, composed the magnificence of these temporary habitations. The city was in itself mean and contemptible : no elegant buildings, no open streets, nor uniform squares. The Pump-house was without any director ; the chairmen permitted no gentlemen or ladies to walk home by night without insulting them ; and to add to all this, one of the greatest physicians of his age conceived a design of ruining the city, by writing against the efficacy of the waters. It was from a resentment of some affronts he had received there, that he took this resolution ; and accordingly published a pamphlet, by which he said, *he would cast a toad into the spring.*

In this situation of things it was, that Mr. Nash first came into that city, and hearing the threat of this physician, he humorously assured the people, that if they would give him leave, he would charm away the poison of the Doctor's toad, as they usually charmed the venom of the Tarantula, by music. He therefore was immediately empowered to set up the force of a band of music, against the poison of the Doctor's reptile ; the company very sensibly increased, Nash triumphed, and the sovereignty of the city was decreed to him by every rank of people.

We are now to behold this gentleman as arrived at a new dignity for which nature seemed to have formed him ; we are to see him directing pleasures, which none had better learned to share ; placed over rebellious and refractory subjects, that were to be ruled only by the force of his address, and governing such as had been accustomed to govern others. We see a kingdom beginning with him, and sending off Tunbridge as one of its colonies.

But to talk more simply, when we talk at best of trifles. None could possibly conceive a person more fit to fill this employment than Nash : he had some wit, as I have said once or twice before ; but it was of that sort which is rather happy than permanent. Once a week he might say a good thing ; this the little ones about him took care to divulge ; or if they happened to forget the joke, he usually remembered to repeat it himself. In a long intercourse with the world he had acquired an impenetrable assurance ; and the freedom with which he was received by the great, furnished him with vivacity, which could be commanded at any time, and which some mistook for wit. His former intercourse among people of fashion in town, had let him into most of the characters of the nobility ; and he was acquainted with many of their private intrigues. He understood rank and precedence with the utmost exactness, was fond of show and finery himself, and generally set a pattern of it to others. These were his favourite talents, and he was the favourite of such as had no other.

But to balance these, which some may consider as foibles, he was charitable himself, and generally shamed his betters into a similitude of sentiment, if they were not naturally so before. He was fond of advising those young men, who, by youth and too much money, are taught to look upon extravagance as a virtue. He was an enemy to rudeness in others, though in the latter part of his life he did not much seem to encourage a dislike of it by his own example. None talked with more humanity of the foibles of others, when absent, than he, nor kept those secrets with which he was entrusted more inviolably. But above all (if moralists will allow it among the number of his virtues) though he gamed high, he always played very fairly. These were his qualifications. Some of the nobility regarded him as an inoffensive, useful companion, the size of whose understanding was, in general, level with their own ; but their little imitators admired him as a person of fine sense, and great good breeding. Thus people became fond of ranking him in the number of their acquaintance, told over his jests, and Beau Nash at length became the fashionable companion.

His first care, when made master of the ceremonies, or King of Bath, as it is called, was to promote a music subscription, of one guinea each, for a band which was to consist of six performers, who were to receive a guinea a week each for their trouble. He allowed also two guineas a week for lighting and sweeping the rooms, for which he accounted to the subscribers by receipt.

The Pump-house was immediately put under the care of an officer, by the name of the *Pumper* ; for which he paid the corporation an annual rent. A row of new houses was begun on the south side of the gravel walks, before which a handsome pavement was then made for the company to walk on. Not less than seventeen or eighteen hundred pounds was raised this year, and in the beginning of 1706, by subscription, and laid out in repairing the roads near the city. The streets began to be better paved, cleaned and lighted, the licences of the chairmen were repressed, and, by an Act of Parliament procured on this occasion, the invalids, who came to drink or bathe, were exempted from all manner of toll, as often as they should go out of the city for recreation.

The houses and streets now began to improve, and ornaments were lavished upon them even to profusion. But in the midst of this splendour the company still were obliged to assemble in a booth to drink tea and chocolate, or to game. Mr. Nash undertook to remedy this inconvenience. By his direction, one Thomas

Harrison erected a handsome Assembly-house for these purposes. A better band of music was also procured, and the former subscription of one guinea was raised to two. Harrison had three guineas a week for the room and candles, and the music two guineas a man. The money Mr. Nash received and accounted for with the utmost exactness and punctuality. To this house were also added gardens for people of rank and fashion to walk in ; and the beauty of the suburbs continued to increase, notwithstanding the opposition that was made by the corporation, who, at that time, looked upon every useful improvement, particularly without the walls, as dangerous to the inhabitants within.

His dominion was now extensive and secure, and he determined to support it with the strictest attention. But, in order to proceed in everything like a king, he was resolved to give his subjects a law, and the following rules were accordingly put up in the Pump-room.

RULES *to be observed at* BATH.

1. THAT a visit of ceremony at first coming and another at going away, are all that are expected or desired, by ladies of quality and fashion,—except impertinents.

2. That ladies coming to the ball appoint a time for their footmen coming to wait on them home, to prevent disturbance and inconveniences to themselves and others.

3. That gentlemen of fashion never appearing in a morning before the ladies in gowns and caps, show breeding and respect.

4. That no person take it ill that any one goes to another's play, or breakfast, and not theirs ;—except captious by nature.

5. That no gentleman give his ticket for the balls

to any but gentlewomen.—N.B. Unless he has none of his acquaintance.

6. That gentlemen crowding before the ladies at the ball, show ill manners ; and that none do so for the future,—except such as respect nobody but themselves.

7. That no gentleman or lady takes it ill that another dances before them ;—except such as have no pretence to dance at all.

8. That the elder ladies and children be content with a second bench at the ball, as being past or not come to perfection.

9. That the younger ladies take notice how many eyes observe them. N.B. This does not extend to the *Have-at-alls.*

10. That all whisperers of lies and scandal, be taken for their authors.

11. That all repeaters of such lies, and scandal, be shunned by all company ;—except such as have been guilty of the same crime.

N.B. Several men of no character, old women and young ones of questioned reputation, are great authors of lies in these places, being of the sect of levellers.

These laws were written by Mr. Nash himself, and, by the manner in which they are drawn up, he undoubtedly designed them for wit. The reader, however, it is feared, will think them dull. Poor Nash was not born a writer ; for whatever humour he might have in conversation, he used to call a pen his torpedo ; whenever he grasped it, it numbed all his faculties.

But were we to give laws to a nursery, we should make them childish laws ; his statutes, though stupid, were addressed to fine gentlemen and ladies, and were probably received with sympathetic approbation. It is certain, they were in general religiously observed by his subjects, and executed by him with impartiality; neither rank nor fortune shielded the refractory from his resentment.

The balls, by his directions, were to begin at six, and to end at eleven. Nor would he suffer them to continue a moment longer, lest invalids might commit irregularities, to counteract the benefit of the waters. Everything was to be performed in proper order. Each ball was to open with a minuet, danced by two persons of the highest distinction present. When the minuet concluded, the lady was to return to her seat, and Mr. Nash was to bring the gentleman a new partner. This ceremony was to be observed by every succeeding couple, every gentleman being obliged to dance with two ladies till the minuets were over, which generally continued two hours. At eight, the country dances were to begin; ladies of quality, according to their rank, standing up first. About nine o'clock a short interval was allowed for rest, and for the gentlemen to help their partners to tea. That over, the company were to pursue their amusements till the clock struck eleven. Then the master of the ceremonies entering the ballroom, ordered the music to desist, by lifting up his finger. The dances discontinued, and some time allowed for becoming cool, the ladies were handed to their chairs.

Even the Royal Family themselves had not influence enough to make him deviate from any of these rules. The Princess Amelia once applying to him for one dance more, after he had given the signal to withdraw, he assured Her Royal Highness, that the established rules of Bath resembled the laws of Lycurgus, which would admit of no alteration, without an utter subversion of all his authority.

He was not less strict with regard to the dresses, in which ladies and gentlemen were to appear. He had the strongest aversion to a white apron, and absolutely

excluded all who ventured to come to the assembly
dressed in that manner. I have known him on a ball
night strip even the Duchess of Q——, and throw her
apron at one of the hinder benches among the ladies'
women ; observing, that none but Abigails appeared in
white aprons. This from another would be insult, in
him it was considered as a just reprimand ; and the
good-natured duchess acquiesced in his censure, and with
great good sense, and good humour, begged his Majesty's
pardon.

But he found more difficulty in attacking the gentlemen's irregularities ; and for some time strove, but in
vain, to prohibit the use of swords. Disputes arising
from love or play, were sometimes attended with fatal
effects. To use his own expression, he was resolved to
hinder people from doing *what they had no mind to* ;
but for some time without effect. However, there
happened about that time a duel between two gamesters,
whose names were Taylor and Clarke, which helped to
promote his peaceable intentions. They fought by
torchlight in the grove ; Taylor was run through the
body, but lived seven years after, at which time his
wound breaking out afresh, it caused his death. Clarke
from that time pretended to be a Quaker, but the ortho-
dox brethren never cordially received him among their
number ; and he died at London, about eighteen years
after, in poverty and contrition. From that time it was
thought necessary to forbid the wearing of swords at
Bath, as they often tore the ladies' clothes, and frighted
them, by sometimes appearing upon trifling occasions.
Whenever therefore Nash heard of a challenge given,
or accepted, he instantly had both parties arrested. The
gentlemen's boots also made a very desperate stand
against him, the country squires were by no means
submissive to his usurpations; and probably his authority

alone would never have carried him through, had he not reinforced it with ridicule. He wrote a song upon the occasion, which, for the honour of his poetical talents, the world shall see.

FRONTINELLA'S *invitation to the Assembly.*

Come, one and all, to Hoyden Hall,
For there 's the assembly this night ;
  None but prude fools,
  Mind manners and rules ;
We Hoydens do decency slight.

Come, Trollops and Slatterns,
Cock'd hats and white aprons,
This best our modesty suits ;
  For why should not we
  In dress be as free
As Hogs-Norton squires in boots ?

The keenness, severity, and particularly the good rhymes of this little *morceau*, which was at that time highly relished by many of the nobility at Bath, gained him a temporary triumph. But to push his victories, he got up a puppet-show, in which Punch came in booted and spurred, in the character of a country squire. He was introduced as courting his mistress, and having obtained her consent to comply with his wishes, upon going to bed, he is desired to pull off his boots. ' My ' boots ! ' replies Punch, ' why, madam, you may as well ' bid me pull off my legs ; I never go without boots, I ' never ride, I never dance, without them ; and this ' piece of politeness is quite the thing at Bath. We ' always dance at our town in boots, and the ladies often ' move minuets in riding-hoods.' Thus he goes on, till his mistress, grown impatient, kicks him off the stage.

From that time few ventured to appear at the assem-

blies in Bath in a riding-dress ; and whenever any
gentleman, through ignorance, or haste, appeared in the
rooms in boots, Nash would make up to him, and,
bowing in an arch manner, would tell him, that he had
forgot his horse. Thus he was at last completely
victorious.

.   *Dolisque coacti*
Quos neque Tydides nec Larissaeus Achilles
Non anni domuere decem.

He began therefore to reign without a rival, and like
other kings had his mistresses, flatterers, enemies and
calumniators. The amusements of the place however
wore a very different aspect from what they did formerly.
Regularity repressed pride, and that lessened, people
of fortune became fit for society. Let the morose and
grave censure an attention to forms and ceremonies,
and rail at those, whose only business it is to regulate
them ; but though ceremony is very different from
politeness, no country was ever yet polite, that was
not first ceremonious. The natural gradation of breeding
begins in savage disgust, proceeds to indifference,
improves into attention, by degrees refines into ceremonious observance, and the trouble of being ceremonious at length produces politeness, elegance and
ease. There is therefore some merit in mending society,
even in one of the inferior steps of this gradation ; and
no man was more happy in this respect than Mr. Nash.
In every nation there are enough who have no other
business or care, but that of buying pleasure ; and he
taught them, who bid at such an auction, the art of
procuring what they sought, without diminishing the
pleasure of others.

The city of Bath, by such assiduity, soon became
the theatre of summer amusements for all people of
fashion ; and the manner of spending the day there

must amuse any, but such as disease or spleen had made uneasy to themselves. The following is a faint picture of the pleasures that scene affords. Upon a stranger's arrival at Bath, he is welcomed by a peal of the Abbey bells, and in the next place, by the voice and music of the city waits. For these civilities the ringers have generally a present made them of half a guinea ; and the waits of half a crown, or more, in proportion to the person's fortune, generosity, or ostentation. These customs, though disagreeable, are however generally liked, or they would not continue. The greatest incommodity attending them is the disturbance the bells must give the sick. But the pleasure of knowing the name of every family that comes to town recompenses the inconvenience. Invalids are fond of news, and upon the first sound of the bells, everybody sends out to inquire for whom they ring.

After the family is thus welcomed to Bath, it is the custom for the master of it to go to the public places, and subscribe two guineas at the assembly-houses towards the balls and music in the Pump-house, for which he is entitled to three tickets every ball night. His next subscription is a crown, half a guinea, 'or a guinea, according to his rank and quality, for the liberty of walking in the private walks belonging to Simpson's Assembly-house ; a crown or half a guinea is also given to the booksellers, for which the gentleman is to have what books he pleases to read at his lodgings. And at the Coffee-house another subscription is taken for pen, ink and paper, for such letters as the subscriber shall write at it during his stay. The ladies too may subscribe to the booksellers, and to a house by the Pump-room, for the advantage of reading the news, and for enjoying each other's conversation.

Things being thus adjusted, the amusements of the

day are generally begun by bathing, which is no un-
pleasing method of passing away an hour or so.

The baths are five in number. On the south-west
side of the Abbey church is the King's Bath, which is an
oblong square; the walls are full of niches, and at every
corner are steps to descend into it : this bath is said to
contain 427 tons and 50 gallons of water; and on its
rising out of the ground over the springs, it is sometimes
too hot to be endured by those who bathe therein.
Adjoining to the King's Bath there is another, called the
Queen's Bath; this is of a more temperate warmth,
as borrowing its water from the other.

In the south-west part of the city are three other
baths, viz. : The Hot Bath, which is not much inferior
in heat to the King's Bath, and contains 53 tons 2 hogsheads and 11 gallons of water. The Cross Bath, which
contains 52 tons 3 hogsheads and 11 gallons; and the
Leper's Bath, which is not so much frequented as the
rest.

The King's Bath (according to the best observations)
will fill in about nine hours and a half; the Hot Bath in
about eleven hours and a half; and the Cross Bath in
about the same time.

The hours for bathing are commonly between six
and nine in the morning; and the baths are every
morning supplied with fresh water; for when the
people have done bathing, the sluices in each bath are
pulled up, and the water is carried off by drains into
the river Avon.

In the morning the lady is brought in a close chair,
dressed in her bathing clothes, to the bath : and, being
in the water, the woman who attends presents her
with a little floating dish like a basin : into which the
lady puts a handkerchief, a snuff-box, and a nosegay.
She then traverses the bath; if a novice, with a guide;

if otherwise, by herself; and having amused herself thus while she thinks proper, calls for her chair, and returns to her lodgings.

˙ The amusement of bathing is immediately succeeded by a general assembly of people at the Pump-house, some for pleasure, and some to drink the hot waters. Three glasses, at three different times, is the usual portion for every drinker; and the intervals between every glass are enlivened by the harmony of a small band of music, as well as by the conversation of the gay, the witty, or the forward.

From the Pump-house the ladies, from time to time, withdraw to a female coffee-house, and from thence return to their lodgings to breakfast. The gentlemen withdraw to their coffee-houses, to read the papers, or converse on the news of the day, with a freedom and ease not to be found in the metropolis.

People of fashion make public breakfasts at the assembly-houses, to which they invite their acquaintances, and they sometimes order private concerts; or when so disposed, attend lectures upon the arts and sciences, which are frequently taught there in a pretty superficial manner, so as not to tease the understanding, while they afford the imagination some amusement. The private concerts are performed in the ballrooms, the tickets a crown each.

Concert breakfasts at the Assembly-house sometimes make also a part of the morning's amusement here, the expenses of which are defrayed by a subscription among the men. Persons of rank and fortune who can perform are admitted into the orchestra, and find a pleasure in joining with the performers.

Thus we have the tedious morning fairly over. When noon approaches, and church (if any please to go there) is done, some of the company appear upon the Parade, and other public walks, where they continue to chat and amuse each other, till they have formed parties for the play, cards, or dancing for the evening. Another part of the company divert themselves with reading in the booksellers' shops, or are generally seen tasting the air and exercise, some on horseback, some in coaches. Some walk in the meadows round the town, winding along the side of the river Avon and the neighbouring canal; while others are seen scaling some of those romantic precipices that overhang the city.

When the hour of dinner draws nigh, and the company is returned to their different recreations, the provisions are generally served with the utmost elegance and plenty. Their mutton, butter, fish, and fowl, are all allowed to be excellent, and their cookery still exceeds their meat.

After dinner is over, and evening prayers ended, the company meet a second time at the Pump-house. From this they retire to the walks, and from thence go to drink tea at the assembly-houses, and the rest of the evenings are concluded either with balls, plays or visits. A theatre was erected in the year 1705 by subscription, by people of the highest rank, who permitted their arms to be engraven on the inside of the house, as a public testimony of their liberality towards it. Every Tuesday and Friday evening is concluded with a public ball, the contributions to which are so numerous, that the price of each ticket is trifling. Thus Bath yields a continued rotation of diversions, and people of all ways of thinking, even from the libertine to the methodist, have it in their power to complete the day with employments suited to their inclinations.

In this manner every amusement soon improved under Mr. Nash's administration. The magistrates of the city found that he was necessary and useful, and took every opportunity of paying the same respect to his fictitious royalty, that is generally extorted by real power. The same satisfaction a young lady finds upon being singled out at her first appearance, or an applauded poet on the success of his first tragedy, influenced him. All admired him as an extraordinary character ; and some who knew no better, as a very fine gentleman ; he was perfectly happy in their little applause, and affected at length something particular in his dress, behaviour and conversation.

His equipage was sumptuous, and he usually travelled to Tunbridge in a post chariot and six greys, with outriders, footmen, French horns, and every other appendage of expensive parade. He always wore a white hat, and, to apologize for this singularity, said, he did it purely to secure it from being stolen ; his dress was tawdry, though not perfectly genteel ; he might be considered as a beau of several generations, and in his appearance he, in some measure, mixed the fashions of the last age with those of the present. He perfectly understood elegant expense, and generally passed his time in the very best company, if persons of the first distinction deserve that title.

But I hear the reader now demand, what finances were to support all this finery, or where the treasures, that gave him such frequent opportunities of displaying his benevolence, or his vanity ? To answer this, we must now enter upon another part of his character, his talents as a gamester ; for by gaming alone at that period, of which I speak, he kept up so very genteel an appearance. When he first figured at Bath, there were few laws against this destructive amusement. The gaming-table was the constant resource of despair and indigence, and the frequent ruin of opulent fortunes. Wherever people of fashion came, needy adventurers were generally

found in waiting. With such Bath swarmed, and
among this class Mr. Nash was certainly to be numbered
in the beginning, only with this difference, that he
wanted the corrupt heart, too commonly attending
a life of expedients ; for he was generous, humane and
honourable, even though by profession a gamester.

A thousand instances might be given of his integrity,
even in this infamous profession ; where his generosity
often impelled him to act in contradiction to his interest.
Wherever he found a novice in the hands of a sharper,
he generally forewarned him of the danger ; whenever he
found any inclined to play, yet ignorant of the game, he
would offer his services, and play for them. I remember
an instance to this effect, though too nearly concerned
in the affair to publish the gentleman's name of whom it
is related. In the year 1725, there came to Bath a giddy
youth, who had just resigned his fellowship at Oxford.
He brought his whole fortune with him there ; it was
but a trifle ; however, he was resolved to venture it all.
Good fortune seemed kinder than could be expected.
Without the smallest skill in play, he won a sum
sufficient to make any unambitious man happy. His
desire of gain increasing with his gains, in the October
following he was *at all*, and added four thousand pounds
to his former capital. Mr. Nash one night, after losing
a considerable sum to this undeserving son of fortune,
invited him to supper. 'Sir,' cried this honest, though
veteran gamester, 'perhaps you may imagine I have
'invited you, in order to have my revenge at home ;
'but, sir ! I scorn so inhospitable an action. I desired
'the favour of your company to give you some advice,
'which you will pardon me, sir, you seem to stand in
'need of. You are now high in spirits, and drawn away
'by a torrent of success. But there will come a time,
'when you will repent having left the calm of a college

' life for the turbulent profession of a gamester. Ill
' runs will come, as sure as day and night succeed each
' other. Be therefore advised, remain content with your
' present gains ; for be persuaded, that had you the
' Bank of England, with your present ignorance of gaming
' it would vanish like a fairy dream. You are a stranger
' to me, but to convince you of the part I take in your
' welfare, I'll give you fifty guineas, to forfeit twenty,
' every time you lose two hundred at one sitting.' The
young gentleman refused his offer, and was at last
undone !

The late Duke of B. being chagrined at losing a
considerable sum, pressed Mr. Nash to tie him up for
the future from playing deep. Accordingly, the beau
gave his Grace a hundred guineas, to forfeit ten thousand,
whenever he lost a sum to the same amount at play, in
one sitting. The Duke loved play to distraction, and
soon after at hazard lost eight thousand guineas, and
was going to throw for three thousand more ; when
Nash, catching hold of the dice-box, entreated his Grace
to reflect upon the penalty if he lost : the Duke for
that time desisted ; but so strong was the furor of play
upon him, that soon after, losing a considerable sum at
Newmarket, he was contented to pay the penalty.

When the late Earl of T——d was a youth, he was
passionately fond of play, and never better pleased than
with having Mr. Nash for his antagonist. Nash saw
with concern his lordship's foible, and undertook to
cure him, though by a very disagreeable remedy. Conscious of his own superior skill, he determined to engage
him in single play for a very considerable sum. His
lordship, in proportion as he lost his game, lost his
temper too ; and as he approached the gulf, seemed
still more eager for ruin. He lost his estate ; some
writings were put into the winner's possession ; his very

equipage was deposited as a last stake, and he lost that also. But, when our generous gamester had found his lordship sufficiently punished for his temerity, he returned all; only stipulating, that he should be paid five thousand pounds whenever he should think proper to make the demand. However, he never made any such demand during his lordship's life; but some time after his decease, Mr. Nash's affairs being in the wane, he demanded the money of his lordship's heirs, who honourably paid it without any hesitation.

But whatever skill Nash might have acquired by long practice in play, he was never formed by nature for a successful gamester. He was constitutionally passionate and generous. To acquire a perfection in that art, a man must be naturally phlegmatic, reserved and cool; every passion must learn to obey control; but he frequently was unable to restrain the violence of his, and was often betrayed by this means into unbecoming rudeness, or childish impertinence; was sometimes a minion of fortune, and as often depressed by adversity. While others made considerable fortunes at the gaming-table, he was ever in the power of chance; nor did even the intimacy with which he was received by the great, place him in a state of independence.

The considerable inconveniences that were found to result from a permission of gaming, at length attracted the attention of the legislature, and in the twelfth year of his late Majesty, the most prevalent games at that time were declared fraudulent and unlawful. Every age has had its peculiar modes of gaming. The games of Gleek, Primero, In and In, and several others now exploded, employed our sharping ancestors; to these succeeded the Ace of Hearts, Pharaoh, Basset, and Hazard, all games of chance like the former. But though in these the chances seemed equal to the novice, in general those who kept the bank were considerable winners. The Act therefore, passed upon this occasion, declared all such games and lotteries illicit, and directed, that all who should set up such games, should forfeit two hundred pounds, to be levied by distress on the offender's goods ; one-third to go to the informer, the residue to the poor.

The Act further declared, that every person who played in any place, except in the royal palace where His Majesty resided, should forfeit fifty pounds, and should be condemned to pay treble costs in case of an appeal.

This law was scarcely made, before it was eluded by the invention of divers fraudulent and deceitful games ; and a particular game, called Passage, was daily practised, and contributed to the ruin of thousands. To prevent this, the ensuing year it was enacted, that this and every other game invented, or to be invented, with one die, or more, or any other instrument of the same nature, with numbers thereon, should be subject to a similar penalty ; and at the same time, the persons playing with such instruments should be punished as above.

This amendment of the law soon gave birth to new evasions ; the game of Rolly Polly, Marlborough's Battles, but particularly the E O, were set up ; and strange to observe ! several of those very noblemen who had given their voices to suppress gaming, were the most ready to encourage it. This game was at first set up at Tunbridge. It was invented by one C——k, and carried on between him and one Mr. A——e, proprietor of the Assembly-room at that place ; and was reckoned extremely profitable to the bank, as it gained two and a half per cent. on all that was lost or won.

As all gaming was suppressed but this, Mr. Nash was

now utterly destitute of any resource that he could expect from his superior skill, and long experience in the art. The money to be gained in private gaming is at best but trifling, and the opportunity precarious. The minds of the generality of mankind shrink with their circumstances ; and Nash, upon the immediate prospect of poverty, was now mean enough (I will call it no worse) to enter into a base confederacy with those low creatures to evade the law, and to share the plunder. The occasion was as follows. The profits of the table were, as I observed, divided between C——k, the inventor, and A——e, the room-keeper. The first year's profits were extraordinary, and A——e the room-keeper now began to wish himself sole proprietor. The combinations of the worthless are ever of short duration. The next year, therefore, A——e turned C——k out of his room, and set up the game for himself. The gentlemen and ladies who frequented the Wells, unmindful of the immense profit gained by these reptiles, still continued to game as before ; and A——e was triumphing in the success of his politics, when he was informed, that C——k and his friends hired the crier to cry the game down. The consequences of this would have been fatal to A——e's interest, for by this means frauds might have been discovered which would deter even the most ardent lovers of play. Immediately, therefore, while the crier was yet upon the walks, he applied to Mr. Nash to stop these proceedings, and, at the same time, offered him a fourth share of the bank, which Mr. Nash was mean enough to accept. This is the greatest blot in his life, and this it is hoped will find pardon.

The day after, the inventor offered a half of the bank ; but this Mr. Nash thought proper to refuse, being pre-engaged to A——e. Upon which, being disappointed, he applied to one Mr J——e, and under his protection another table was set up, and the company seemed to be divided equally between them. I cannot reflect, without surprise, at the wisdom of the gentlemen and ladies, to suffer themselves to be thus parcelled out between a pack of sharpers, and permit themselves to be defrauded, without even the show of opposition. The company thus divided, Mr. Nash once more availed himself of their parties, and prevailed upon them to unite their banks, and to divide the gains into three shares, of which he reserved one to himself.

Nash had hitherto enjoyed a fluctuating fortune ; and, had he taken the advantage of the present opportunity, he might have been for the future not only above want, but even in circumstances of opulence. Had he cautiously employed himself in computing the benefits of the table, and exacting his stipulated share, he might have soon grown rich ; but he entirely left the management of it to the people of the rooms ; he took them (as he says in one of his memorials upon this occasion) to be honest, and never inquired what was won or lost ; and, it is probable, they were seldom assiduous in informing him. I find a secret pleasure in thus displaying the insecurity of friendships among the base. They pretended to pay him regularly at first, but he soon discovered, as he says, that at Tunbridge he had suffered to the amount of two thousand guineas.

In the meantime, as the E O table thus succeeded at Tunbridge, Mr. Nash was resolved to introduce it at Bath, and previously asked the opinion of several lawyers, who declared it no way illegal. In consequence of this, he wrote to Mrs. A——e, who kept one of the great rooms at Bath, acquainting her with the profits attending such a scheme, and proposing to have a fourth share with her and Mr. W——, the proprietor of the other room, for his authority, and protection. To this

Mr. W—— and she returned him for answer, that they would grant him a fifth share ; which he consented to accept. Accordingly, he made a journey to London, and bespoke two tables, one for each room, at the rate of fifteen pounds each table.

The tables were no sooner set up at Bath, than they were frequented with a greater concourse of gamesters than those at Tunbridge. Men of that infamous profession, from every part of the kingdom, and even other parts of Europe, flocked here to feed on the ruins of each other's fortune. This afforded another opportunity for Mr. Nash to become rich ; but, as at Tunbridge, he thought the people here also would take care of him, and therefore he employed none to look after his interest. The first year they paid him what he thought just ; the next, the woman of the room dying, her son paid him, and showed his books. Some time after the people of the rooms offered him one hundred pounds a year each for his share, which he refused ; every succeeding year they continued to pay him less and less ; till at length he found, as he pretends, that he had thus lost not less than twenty thousand pounds.

Thus they proceeded, deceiving the public and each other, till the legislature thought proper to suppress these seminaries of vice. It was enacted, that after the 24th of June, 1745, none should be permitted to keep a house, room or place, for playing, upon pain of such forfeitures as were declared in former Acts instituted for that purpose.

The legislature likewise amended a law, made in the reign of Queen Anne, for recovering money lost at play, on the oath of the winner. By this Act, no person was rendered incapable of being a witness ; and every person present at a gaming-table might be summoned by the magistrate who took cognizance of the affair.

No privilege of Parliament was allowed to those convicted of having gaming-tables in their houses. Those who lost ten pounds at one time, were liable to be indicted within six months after the offence was committed ; and being convicted, were to be fined five times the value of the sum won or lost, for the use of the poor. Any offender, before conviction, discovering another, so as to be convicted, was to be discharged from the penalties incurred by his own offences.

By this wise and just act, all Nash's future hopes of succeeding by the tables were blown up. He had now only the justice and generosity of his confederates to trust to ; but that he soon found to be a vain expectation ; for, if we can depend on his own memorials, what at one time they confessed, they would at another deny ; and though upon some occasions they seemed at variance with each other, yet when they were to oppose him, whom they considered as a common enemy, they generally united with confidence and success. He now therefore had nothing but a lawsuit to confide in for redress ; and this is ever the last expedient to retrieve a desperate fortune. He accordingly threw his suit into Chancery, and, by this means, the public became acquainted with what he had long endeavoured to conceal. They now found that he was himself concerned in the gaming-tables, of which he only seemed the conductor ; and that he had shared part of the spoil, though he complained of having been defrauded of a just share.

The success of his suit was what might have been naturally expected ; he had but at best a bad cause, and as the oaths of the defendants were alone sufficient to cast him in Chancery, it was not surprising that he was nonsuited. But the consequence of this affair was much more fatal than he had imagined ; it lessened him in the esteem of the public, it drew several enemies against him, and in some measure diminished the authority of any defence he could make. From that time (about the year 1745), I find this poor, good-natured, but misguided man involved in continual disputes, every day calumniated with some new slander, and continually endeavouring to obviate its effects.

Upon these occasions his usual method was, by printed bills handed about among his acquaintance, to inform the public of his most private transactions with some of those creatures with whom he had formerly associated; but these apologies served rather to blacken his antagonists, than to vindicate him. They were in general extremely ill written, confused, obscure, and sometimes unintelligible. By these, however, it appeared, that W—— was originally obliged to him for the resort of company to his room; that Lady H——, who had all the company before W——'s room was built, offered Mr. Nash a hundred pounds for his protection; which he refused, having previously promised to support Mrs. W——. It appears by these apologies, that the persons concerned in the rooms made large fortunes, while he still continued in pristine indigence; and that his nephew, for whom he had at first secured one of the rooms, was left in as great distress as he.

His enemies were not upon this occasion contented with aspersing him, as a confederate with sharpers: they even asserted, that he spent and embezzled the subscriptions of gentlemen and ladies, which were given for useful or charitable purposes. But to such aspersions he answered, by declaring, to use his own expression, before God and man, that he never diverted one shilling of the said subscriptions to his own use; nor was he ever thought to have done it, till new enemies started up against him. Perhaps the reader may be curious to see one of these memorials, written by himself; and

I will indulge his curiosity, merely to show a specimen of the style and manner of a man whose whole life was passed in a round of gaiety and conversation, whose jests were a thousand times repeated, and whose company was courted by every son and daughter of fashion. The following is particularly levelled against those, who, in the latter part of his life, took every opportunity to traduce his character.

A MONITOR.

' *For the Lord hateth lying and deceitful lips.*—PSALM.

'THE curse denounced in my motto, is sufficient to
' intimidate any person who is not quite abandoned in
' their evil ways, and who have any fear of God before
' their eyes ; everlasting burnings are a terrible reward
' for their misdoings ; and nothing but the most
' hardened sinners will oppose the judgements of heaven,
' being without end. This reflection must be shocking
' to such, as are conscious to themselves, of having
' erred from the sacred dictates of the Psalmist, and who
' following the blind impulse of passion, daily forging
' lies and deceit, to annoy their neighbour. But there
' are joys in heaven which they can never arrive at,
' whose whole study is to destroy the peace and harmony,
' and good order of society, in this place.'

This carries little the air of a bagatelle : it rather seems a sermon in miniature, so different are some men in the closet and in conversation. The following I have taken at random from a heap of other memorials, all tending to set his combination with the aforementioned partners in a proper light.

'E O was first set up in A——e room, the profits divided between one C——k (the inventor of the game) and A——e.

'The next year, A——e finding the game so advantageous, turned C——k out of his room, and set the
game up himself ; but C——k and his friends hired the
crier to cry the game down ; upon which A——e came
running to me to stop it, after he had cried it once, which
I immediately did, and turned the crier off the walks.

'Then A——e asked me to go a fourth with him in the
bank, which I consented to ; C——k next day took me
into his room which he had hired, and proffered me to
go half with him, which I refused, being engaged before
to A——e.

'J——e then set up the same game, and complained
that he had not half play at his room ; upon which
I made them agree to join their banks, and divide
equally the gain and loss, and I to go the like share in
the bank.

'I, taking them to be honest, never inquired what was
won or lost; and thought they paid me honestly, till it was
discovered that they had defrauded me of 2,000 guineas.

'I then arrested A——e, who told me I must go into
Chancery, and that I should begin with the people of
Bath, who had cheated me of ten times as much ; and
told my attorney, that J——e had cheated me of 500,
and wrote me word that I probably had it not under
his hand, which never was used in play.

'Upon my arresting A——e, I received a letter not to
prosecute J——e, for he would be a very good witness :
I wrote a discharge to J——e for £125 in full, though he
never paid me a farthing, upon his telling me, if his
debts were paid, he was not worth a shilling.

'Every article of this I can prove from A——e's own
mouth, as a reason that he allowed the bank-keepers
but 10 per cent. because I went 20 ; and his suborning
* * * * to alter his informations.

'RICHARD NASH.'

This gentleman's simplicity, in trusting persons whom he had no previous reasons to place confidence in, seems to be one of those lights into his character, which, while they impeach his understanding, do honour to his benevolence. The low and timid are ever suspicious ; but a heart impressed with honourable sentiments, expects from others sympathetic sincerity.

But now that we have viewed his conduct as a gamester, and seen him on that side of his character, which is by far the most unfavourable, seen him declining from his former favour and esteem, the just consequence of his quitting, though but ever so little, the paths of honour ; let me turn to those brighter parts of his life and character which gained the affection of his friends, the esteem of the corporation which he assisted, and may possibly attract the attention of posterity. By his successes we shall find, that figuring in life, proceeds less from the possession of great talents, than from the proper application of moderate ones.. Some great minds are only fitted to put forth their powers in the storm ; and the occasion is often wanting during a whole life for a great exertion : but trifling opportunities of shining are almost every hour offered to the little sedulous mind ; and a person thus employed, is not only more pleasing, but more useful in a state of tranquil society.

Though gaming first introduced him into polite company, this alone could hardly have carried him forward, without the assistance of a genteel address, much vivacity, some humour, and some wit. But once admitted into the circle of the Beau Monde, he then laid claim to all the privileges by which it is distinguished. Among others, in the early part of his life, he entered himself professedly into the service of the fair sex ; he set up for a man of gallantry and intrigue ; and if we can credit the boasts of his old age, he often succeeded. In fact, the business of love somewhat resembles the business of physic ; no matter for qualifications, he that makes vigorous pretensions to either is surest of success. Nature had by no means formed Mr. Nash for a Beau Garçon ; his person was clumsy, too large and awkward, and his features harsh, strong, and peculiarly irregular ; yet even, with those disadvantages, he made love, became a universal admirer of the sex, and was universally admired. He was possessed, at least, of some requisites of a lover. He had assiduity, flattery, fine clothes, and as much wit as the ladies he addressed. Wit, flattery, and fine clothes, he used to say, were enough to debauch a nunnery. But my fair readers of the present day are exempt from this scandal ; and it is no matter now, what he said of their grandmothers.

As Nestor was a man of three ages, so Nash sometimes humorously called himself a beau of three generations. He had seen flaxen bobs succeeded by majors, which in their turn gave way to negligents, which were at last totally routed by bags and ramilies. The manner in which gentlemen managed their amours, in these different ages of fashion, were not more different than their periwigs. The lover in the reign of King Charles was solemn, majestic, and formal. He visited his mistress in state ; languished for the favour, kneeled when he toasted his goddess, walked with solemnity, performed the most trifling things with decorum, and even took snuff with a flourish. The beau of the latter part of Queen Anne's reign was disgusted with so much formality ; he was pert, smart and lively ; his *billets doux* were written in a quite different style from that of his antiquated predecessor ; he was ever laughing at his own ridiculous situation ; till at last, he persuaded the lady to become as ridiculous as himself. The beau of the third age, in which Mr. Nash died, was still more extraordinary than either-; his whole secret in intrigue consisted in perfect indifference. The only way to make love now, I have heard Mr. Nash say, was to take no manner of notice of the lady, which method was found the surest way to secure her affections.

However these things be, this gentleman's successes in amour were in reality very much confined in the second and third age of intrigue ; his character was too public for a lady to consign her reputation to his keeping. But in the beginning of life, it is said, he knew the secret history of the times, and contributed himself to swell the page of scandal. Were I upon the present occasion to hold the pen of a novelist, I could recount some amours, in which he was successful. I could fill a volume with little anecdotes, which contain neither pleasure nor instruction ; with histories of professing lovers, and poor believing girls deceived by such professions. But such adventures are easily written, and as easily achieved. The plan even of fictitious novel is quite exhausted ; but truth, which I have followed here, and ever design to follow, presents in the affair of love scarce any variety. The manner in which one reputation is lost, exactly resembles that by which another is taken away. The gentleman begins at timid distance, grows more bold, becomes rude, till the lady is married or undone ; such is the substance of every modern novel ; nor will I gratify the pruriency of folly, at the expense of every other pleasure my narration may afford.

Mr. Nash did not long continue a universal gallant ; but in the earlier years of his reign, entirely gave up his endeavours to deceive the sex, in order to become the honest protector of their innocence, the guardian of their reputation, and a friend to their virtue.

This was a character he bore for many years, and supported it with integrity, assiduity and success. It was his constant practice to do everything in his power to prevent the fatal consequences of rash and inconsiderate love ; and there are many persons now alive, who owe their present happiness to his having interrupted the progress of an amour, that threatened to become unhappy, or even criminal, by privately making their guardians or parents acquainted with what he could discover. And his manner of disconcerting these schemes was such as generally secured him from the rage and resentment of the disappointed. One night, when I was in Wiltshire's room, Nash came up to a lady and her daughter, who were people of no inconsiderable fortune, and bluntly told the mother, *she had better be at home* : this was at that time thought an audacious piece of impertinence, and the lady turned away piqued and disconcerted. Nash, however, pursued her, and repeated the words again ; when the old lady, wisely conceiving there might be some hidden meaning couched under this seeming insolence, retired, and coming to her lodgings, found a coach and six at the door, which a sharper had provided to carry off her eldest daughter.

I shall beg leave to give some other instances of Mr. Nash's good sense and good nature on these occasions, as I have had the accounts from himself. At the conclusion of the treaty of peace at Utrecht, Colonel M—— was one of the thoughtless, agreeable, gay creatures, that drew the attention of the company at Bath. He danced and talked with great vivacity ; and when he gamed among the ladies, he showed, that his attention was employed rather upon their hearts than their fortunes. His own fortune however was a trifle, when compared to the elegance of his expense ; and his imprudence at last was so great, that it obliged him to sell an annuity, arising from his commission, to keep up his splendour a little longer.

However thoughtless he might be, he had the happiness of gaining the affections of Miss L——, whose father designed her a very large fortune. This lady was courted by a nobleman of distinction, but she refused his addresses, resolved upon gratifying rather her inclinations than her avarice. The intrigue went on successfully between her and the Colonel, and they both would certainly have been married, and been undone, had not Mr. Nash apprised her father of their intentions. The old gentleman recalled his daughter from Bath, and offered Mr. Nash a very considerable present, for the care he had taken, which he refused.

In the meantime Colonel M—— had an intimation how his intrigue came to be discovered; and by taxing Mr. Nash, found that his suspicions were not without foundation. A challenge was the immediate consequence, which the King of Bath, conscious of having only done his duty, thought proper to decline. As none are permitted to wear swords at Bath, the Colonel found no opportunity of gratifying his resentment, and waited with impatience to find Mr. Nash in town, to require proper satisfaction.

During this interval, however, he found his creditors became too importunate for him to remain longer at Bath; and his finances and credit being quite exhausted, he took the desperate resolution of going over to the Dutch army in Flanders, where he enlisted himself a volunteer. Here he underwent all the fatigues of a private sentinel, with the additional misery of receiving no pay, and his friends in England gave out, that he was shot at the battle of ——.

In the meantime the nobleman pressed his passion with ardour, but during the progress of his amour, the

young lady's father died, and left her heiress to a fortune
of fifteen hundred a year. · She thought herself now
disengaged from her former passion. An absence of two
years had in some measure abated her love for the
Colonel ; and the assiduity, the merit, and real regard of
the gentleman who still continued to solicit her, were
almost too powerful for her constancy. Mr. Nash, in
the meantime, took every opportunity of inquiring after
Colonel M——, and found, that he had for some time
been returned to England, but changed his name, in
order to avoid the fury of his creditors ; and that he
was entered into a company of strolling players, who
were at that time exhibiting at Peterborough.

He now therefore thought he owed the Colonel, in
justice, an opportunity of promoting his fortune, as he
had once deprived him of an occasion of satisfying his
love. Our Beau therefore invited the lady to be of a
party to Peterborough, and offered his own equipage,
which was then one of the most elegant in England, to
conduct her there. The proposal being accepted, the
lady, the nobleman, and Mr. Nash, arrived in town just
as the players were going to begin.

Colonel M——, who used every means of remaining
incognito, and who was too proud to make his distresses
known to any of his former acquaintance, was now
degraded into the character of Tom in the *Conscious
Lovers.* Miss L—— was placed in the foremost row of
the spectators, her lord on one side, and the impatient
Nash on the other ; when the unhappy youth appeared
in that despicable situation upon the stage. The
moment he came on, his former mistress struck his view,
but his amazement was increased when he saw her
fainting away in the arms of those who sat behind her.
He was incapable of proceeding, and scarce knowing
what he did, he flew and caught her in his arms.

'Colonel,' cried Nash, when they were in some measure recovered, 'you once thought me your enemy, 'because I endeavoured to prevent you both from 'ruining each other; you were then wrong, and you 'have long had my forgiveness. If you love well enough 'now for matrimony, you fairly have my consent, and 'd——n him, say I, that attempts to part you.' Their nuptials were solemnized soon after, and affluence added a zest to all their future enjoyments. Mr. Nash had the thanks of each, and he afterwards spent several agreeable days in that society, which he had contributed to render happy.

I shall beg the reader's patience, while I give another instance, in which he ineffectually offered his assistance and advice. This story is not from himself; but told us partly by Mr. Wood, the architect of Bath, as it fell particularly within his own knowledge; and partly from another memoir, to which he refers.

Miss Sylvia S—— was descended from one of the best families in the kingdom, and was left a large fortune upon her sister's decease. She had early in life been introduced into the best company, and contracted a passion for elegance and expense. It is usual to make the heroine of a story very witty, and very beautiful, and such circumstances are so surely expected, that they are scarce attended to. But whatever the finest poet could conceive of wit, or the most celebrated painter imagine of beauty, were excelled in the perfections of this young lady. Her superiority in both was allowed by all, who either heard, or had seen her. She was naturally gay, generous to a fault, good-natured to the highest degree, affable in conversation, and some of her letters, and other writings, as well in verse as prose, would have shone amongst those of the most celebrated wits of this, or any other age, had they been published.

But these great qualifications were marked by another, which lessened the value of them all. She was imprudent! But let it not be imagined, that her reputation or honour suffered by her imprudence ; I only mean, she had no knowledge of the use of money; she relieved distress, by putting herself into the circumstances of the object whose wants she supplied.

She was arrived at the age of nineteen, when the crowd of her lovers, and the continual repetition of new flattery, had taught her to think she could never be forsaken, and never poor. Young ladies are apt to expect a certainty of success, from a number of lovers ; and yet I have seldom seen a girl courted by a hundred lovers that found a husband in any. Before the choice is fixed, she has either lost her reputation, or her good sense ; and the loss of either is sufficient to consign her to perpetual virginity.

Among the number of this young lady's lovers was the celebrated S——, who, at that time, went by the name of *the good-natured man*. This gentleman, with talents that might have done honour to humanity, suffered himself to fall at length into the lowest state of debasement. He followed the dictates of every newest passion, his love, his pity, his generosity, and even his friendships were all in excess ; he was unable to make head against any of his sensations or desires, but they were in general worthy wishes and desires ; for he was constitutionally virtuous. This gentleman, who at last died in a jail, was at that time this lady's envied favourite.

It is probable that he, thoughtless creature, had no other prospect from this amour but that of passing the present moments agreeably. He only courted dissipation, but the lady's thoughts were fixed on happiness. At length, however, his debts amounting to a considerable sum, he was arrested, and thrown into prison. He endeavoured at first to conceal his situation from his beautiful mistress ; but she soon came to a knowledge of his distress, and took a fatal resolution of freeing him from confinement by discharging all the demands of his creditors.

Mr. Nash was at that time in London, and represented to the thoughtless young lady, that such a measure would effectually ruin both ; that so warm a concern for the interests of Mr. S——, would in the first place quite impair her fortune, in the eyes of our sex ; and what was worse, lessen her reputation in those of her own. He added, that thus bringing Mr. S—— from prison, would be only a temporary relief ; that a mind so generous as his would become bankrupt under the load of gratitude ; and instead of improving in friendship or affection, he would only study to avoid a creditor he could never repay ; that though small favours produce goodwill, great ones destroy friendship. These admonitions, however, were disregarded, and she too late found the prudence and truth of her adviser. In short, her fortune was by this means exhausted ; and, with all her attractions, she found her acquaintance began to disesteem her, in proportion as she became poor.

In this situation she accepted Mr. Nash's invitation of returning to Bath ; he promised to introduce her to the best company there, and he was assured that her merit would do the rest ; upon her very first appearance, ladies of the highest distinction courted her friendship and esteem ; but a settled melancholy had taken possession of her mind, and no amusements that they could propose were sufficient to divert it. Yet still, as if from habit, she followed the crowd in its levities, and frequented those places where all persons endeavour to forget themselves in the bustle of ceremony and show.

Her beauty, her simplicity, and her unguarded situation, soon drew the attention of a designing wretch, who at that time kept one of the rooms at Bath, and who thought that this lady's merit, properly managed, might turn to good account. This woman's name was Dame Lindsey, a creature, who, though vicious, was in appearance sanctified ; and, though designing, had some wit and humour. She began by the humblest assiduity to ingratiate herself with Miss S—— ; showed that she could be amusing as a companion, and by frequent offers of money, proved, that she could be useful as a friend. Thus, by degrees, she gained an entire ascendant over this poor, thoughtless, deserted girl ; and, in less than one year, namely about 1727, Miss S——; without ever transgressing the laws of virtue, had entirely lost her reputation. Whenever a person was wanting to make up a party for play at Dame Lindsey's, Sylvia, as she was then familiarly called, was sent for, and was obliged to suffer all those slights which the rich but too often let fall upon their inferiors in point of fortune.

In most, even the greatest, minds, the heart at last becomes level with the meanness of its condition ; but, in this charming girl, it struggled hard with adversity, and yielded to every encroachment of contempt with sullen reluctance.

But though in the course of three years she was in the very eye of public inspection, yet Mr. Wood, the architect, avers, that he could never, by the strictest observations, perceive her to be tainted with any other vice, than that of suffering herself to be decoyed to the gaming-table, and, at her own hazard, playing for the amusement and advantage of others. Her friend, Mr. Nash, therefore, thought proper to induce her to break off all connexions with Dame Lindsey, and to rent part of Mr. Wood's house, in Queen Square, where she behaved with the utmost complaisance, regularity, and virtue.

In this situation her detestation of life still continued ; she found that time would infallibly deprive her of part of her attractions, and that continual solicitude would impair the rest. With these reflections she would frequently entertain herself and an old faithful maid in the vales of Bath, whenever the weather would permit them to walk out. She would even sometimes start questions in company, with seeming unconcern, in order to know what act of suicide was easiest, and which was attended with the smallest pain. When tired with exercise, she generally retired to meditation, and she became habituated to early hours of sleep and rest. But when the weather prevented her usual exercise, and her sleep was thus more difficult, she made it a rule to rise from her bed, and walk about her chamber, till she began to find an inclination for repose.

This custom made it necessary for her to order a burning candle to be kept all night in her room. And the maid usually, when she withdrew, locked the chamber door, and pushing the key under it beyond reach, her mistress by that constant method lay undisturbed till seven o'clock in the morning, then she arose, unlocked the door, and rang the bell, as a signal for the maid to return.

This state of seeming piety, regularity, and prudence, continued for some time, till the gay, celebrated, toasted Miss Sylvia was sunk into a housekeeper to the gentleman at whose house she lived. She was unable to keep company for want of the elegances of dress, that are the usual passport among the polite, and she was too haughty to seem to want them. The fashionable, the amusing, and the polite in society now seldom visited her, and from being once the object of every eye, she was now deserted by all, and preyed upon by the bitter reflections of her own imprudence.

Mr. Wood, and part of his family, were gone to London. Miss Sylvia was left with the rest as a governess at Bath. She sometimes saw Mr. Nash, and acknowledged the friendship of his admonitions, though she refused to accept any other marks of his generosity, than that of advice. Upon the close of the day, in which Mr. Wood was expected to return from London, she expressed some uneasiness at the disappointment of not seeing him ; took particular care to settle the affairs of his family, and then as usual sat down to meditation. She now cast a retrospect over her past misconduct, and her approaching misery ; she saw, that even affluence gave her no real happiness, and from indigence she thought nothing could be hoped but lingering calamity. She at length conceived the fatal resolution of leaving a life in which she could see no corner for comfort, and terminating a scene of imprudence in suicide.

Thus resolved, she sat down at her dining-room window, and with cool intrepidity, wrote the following elegant lines on one of the panes of the window.

> O death ; thou pleasing end of human woe :
> Thou cure for life ! Thou greatest good below ?
> Still may'st thou fly the coward, and the slave,
> And thy soft slumbers only bless the brave.

She then went into company with the most cheerful serenity ; talked of indifferent subjects till supper, which she ordered to be got ready in a little library belonging to the family. There she spent the remaining hours, preceding bed-time, in dandling two of Mr. Wood's children on her knees. In retiring from thence to her chamber, she went into the nursery, to take her leave of another child, as it lay sleeping in the cradle. Struck with the innocence of the little babe's looks, and the consciousness of her meditated guilt, she could not avoid bursting into tears, and hugging it in her arms ; she then bid her old servant a good night, for the first time she had ever done so, and went to bed as usual.

It is probable she soon quitted her bed, and was seized with an alternation of passions, before she yielded to the impulse of despair. She dressed herself in clean linen, and white garments of every kind, like a bride-maid. Her gown was pinned over her breast, just as a nurse pins the swaddling clothes of an infant. A pink silk girdle was the instrument with which she resolved to terminate her misery, and this was lengthened by another made of gold thread. The end of the former was tied with a noose, and the latter with three knots, at a small distance from one another.

Thus prepared, she sat down again, and read ; for she left the book open at that place, in the story of Olympia, in the *Orlando Furioso* of Ariosto, where, by the perfidy and ingratitude of her bosom friend, she was ruined, and left to the mercy of an unpitying world. This tragical event gave her fresh spirits to go through her fatal purpose ; so, standing upon a stool, and flinging the girdle, which was tied round her neck, over a closet-door that opened into her chamber, she remained suspended. Her weight, however, broke the girdle, and the poor despairer fell upon the floor with such violence, that her fall awakened a workman that lay in the house, about half an hour after two o'clock.

Recovering herself, she began to walk about the room, as her usual custom was when she wanted sleep ; and the workman imagining it to be only some ordinary accident, again went to sleep. She once more, therefore, had recourse to a stronger girdle made of silver thread ; and this kept her suspended till she died.

Her old maid continued in the morning to wait as usual for the ringing of the bell, and protracted her patience, hour after hour, till two o'clock in the afternoon ; when the workmen at length entering the room through the window, found their unfortunate mistress still hanging, and quite cold. The coroner's jury being empanelled, brought in their verdict lunacy ; and her corpse was next night decently buried in her father's grave, at the charge of a female companion, with whom she had for many years an inseparable intimacy.

Thus ended a female wit, a toast, and a gamester ; loved, admired, and forsaken. Formed for the delight of society, fallen by imprudence into an object of pity. Hundreds in high life lamented her fate, and wished, when too-late, to redress her injuries. They who once had helped to impair her fortune, now regretted that they had assisted in so mean a pursuit. The little effects she had left behind were bought up with the greatest avidity, by those who desired to preserve some token of a companion, that once had given them such delight. The remembrance of every virtue she was possessed of was now improved by pity. Her former follies were few, but the last swelled them to a large amount. As she remains the strongest instance to posterity, that want of prudence, alone, almost cancels every other virtue.

In all this unfortunate lady's affairs Mr. Nash took a peculiar concern ; he directed her when they played, advised her when she deviated from the rules of caution, and performed the last offices of friendship after her decease, by raising the auction of her little effects.

But he was not only the assistant and the friend of the fair sex, but also their defender. He secured their persons from insult, and their reputations from scandal. Nothing offended him more, than a young fellow's pretending to receive favours from ladies he probably never saw; nothing pleased him so much, as seeing such a piece of deliberate mischief punished. Mr. Nash and one of his friends, being newly arrived at Tunbridge from Bath, were one day on the Walks, and seeing a young fellow of fortune, with whom they had some slight acquaintance, joined him. After the usual chat and news of the day was over, Mr. Nash asked him, how long he had been at the Wells, and what company was there? The other replied, he had been at Tunbridge a month; but as for company, he could find as good at a Tyburn ball. Not a soul was to be seen, except a parcel of gamesters and whores, who would grant the last favour, for a single stake at the Pharaoh bank. ' Look you ' there,' continued he, ' that Goddess of midnight, so ' fine, at t'other end of the Walks, by Jove, she was ' mine this morning for half a guinea. And she there, ' who brings up the rear with powdered hair and dirty ' ruffles, she 's pretty enough, but cheap, perfectly cheap; ' why, my boys, to my own knowledge, you may have ' her for a crown, and a dish of chocolate into the ' bargain. Last Wednesday night we were happy.' ' Hold there, sir,' cried the gentleman; ' as for your ' having the first lady, it is possible it may be true, and ' I intend to ask her about it, for she is my sister; but ' as to your lying with the other last Wednesday, I am ' sure you are a lying rascal—she is my wife, and we ' came here but last night.' The buck vainly asked pardon; the gentleman was going to give him proper chastisement; when Mr. Nash interposed in his behalf, and obtained his pardon, upon condition that he quitted Tunbridge immediately.

But Mr. Nash not only took care, during his administra- tion, to protect the ladies from the insults of our sex, but to guard them from the slanders of each other. He, in the first place, prevented any animosities that might arise from place and precedence, by being previously acquainted with the rank and quality of almost every family in the British dominions. He endeavoured to render scandal odious, by marking it as the result of envy and folly united. Not even Solon could have enacted a wiser law in such a society as Bath. The gay, the heedless, and the idle, which mostly compose the group of water-drinkers, seldom are at the pains of talking upon universal topics, which require comprehensive thought, or abstract reasoning. The adventures of the little circle of their own acquaintance, or of some names of quality and fashion, make up their whole conversation. But it is too likely, that when we mention those, we wish to depress them, in order to render ourselves more conspicuous ; scandal must therefore have fixed her throne at Bath, preferable to any other part of the kingdom. However, though these endeavours could not totally suppress this custom among the fair, yet they gained him the friendship of several ladies of distinction, who had smarted pretty severely under the lash of censure. Among this number was the old Duchess of Marlborough, who conceived a particular friendship for him, and which continued during her life. She frequently consulted him in several concerns of a private nature. Her letting leases, building bridges, or forming canals, were often carried on under his guidance ; but she advised with him particularly in purchasing liveries for the footmen ; a business to which she thought his genius best adapted. As anything relative to her may please the curiosity of such as delight in the anecdotes and letters of the great, however dull and insipid, I shall beg leave to present them with one or two of her letters, collected at a venture from several others to the same purpose.

To Mr. Nash, at the Bath.

Blenheim, Sept. 18, 1724.

MR. JENNENS will give you an account how little time I have in my power, and that will make my excuse for not thanking you sooner for the favour of your letter, and for the trouble you have given yourself in bespeaking the cloth, which I am sure will be good, since you have undertaken to order it. Pray ask Mrs. Jennens concerning the cascade, which will satisfy all your doubts in that matter ; she saw it play, which it will do in great beauty, for at least six hours together, and it runs enough to cover all the stones constantly, and is a hundred feet broad, which I am told is a much greater breadth than any cascade is in England ; and this will be yet better than it is, when it is quite finished ; this water is a great addition to this place, and the lake being thirty acres, out of which the cascade comes and falls into the canal that goes through the bridge, it makes that look as if it was necessary, which before seemed so otherwise.

I am

Your most humble Servant,

S.˙ MARLBOROUGH.

To Mr. Nash, at the Bath.

Marlborough House, May 17, 1735.

SIR,

I have received the favour of yours of the tenth of May, with that from Mr. Harvey. And by last post I received a letter from Mr. Overton, a sort of a bailiff and a surveyor, whom I have employed a great while upon my estates in Wiltshire. He is a very active and very useful man of his sort. He writes to me, that Mr. Harvey has been with him, and brought him a paper, which I sent you. He says, that finding he was a man that was desirous to serve me, he had assisted him all he could, by informations which he has given ; and that he should continue to assist him. I have writ to him that he did mighty well. There is likewise a considerable tenant of my Lord Bruce's, his name is Cannons, who has promised me his assistance towards recommending tenants for these farms. And if Mr. Harvey happens to know such a man, he may put him in mind of it. I am sure you do me all the good you can. And I hope you are sure that I shall always be sensible of the obligations I have to you, and ever be

Your most thankful and obliged
humble Servant,
S. MARLBOROUGH.

Mr. Harvey may conclude to take any prices that were given you in the paper. But as I know that we have been scandalously cheated, if he finds that anything can be let better than it has been let, I do not doubt but he will do it.

The Duchess of Marlborough seems not to be a much better writer than Mr. Nash, but she was worth many hundred thousand pounds, and that might console her. It may give splenetic philosophy, however, some scope for meditation, when it considers, what a parcel of stupid trifles the world is ready to admire.

Whatever might have been Mr. Nash's other excellences, there was one in which few exceeded him ; I mean his extensive humanity. None felt pity more strongly, and none made greater efforts to relieve distress. If I were to name any reigning and fashionable virtue in the present age, I think it should be charity. The numberless benefactions privately given, the various public solicitations for charity, and the success they meet with, serve to prove, that though we may fall short of our ancestors in other respects, yet in this instance we greatly excel them. I know not whether it may not be spreading the influence of Mr. Nash too widely to say, that he was one of the principal causes of introducing this noble emulation among the rich; but certain it is, no private man ever relieved the distresses of so many as he did.

Before gaming was suppressed, and in the meridian of his life and fortune, his benefactions were generally found to equal his other expenses. The money he got without pain, he gave away without reluctance; and whenever unable to relieve a wretch who sued for assistance, he has been often seen to shed tears. A gentleman of broken fortune, one day standing behind his chair, as he was playing a game of picquet for two hundred pounds, and observing with what indifference he won the money, could not avoid whispering these words to another who stood by, 'Heavens! how happy would all that money make me!' Nash, overhearing him, clapped the money into his hand; and cried, 'Go and be happy.'

About six and thirty years ago, a clergyman brought his family to Bath for the benefit of the waters. His wife laboured under a lingering disorder, which it was thought nothing but the Hot Wells could remove. The expenses of living there soon lessened the poor man's finances; his clothes were sold, piece by piece, to provide a temporary relief for his little family; and his appearance was at last so shabby, that, from the number of holes in his coat and stockings, Nash gave him the name of Doctor Cullender. Our beau, it seems, was rude enough to make a jest of poverty, though he had sensibility enough to relieve it. The poor clergyman combated his distresses with fortitude; and, instead of attempting to solicit relief, endeavoured to conceal them. Upon a living of thirty pounds˙ a year he endeavoured to maintain his wife and six children ; but all his resources at last failed him, and nothing but famine was seen in the wretched family. The poor man's circumstances were at last communicated to Nash ; who, with his usual cheerfulness, undertook to relieve him. On a Sunday evening, at a public tea-drinking at Harrison's, he went about to collect a subscription, and began it himself, by giving five guineas. By this means, two hundred guineas were collected in less than two hours, and the poor family raised from the lowest despondence into affluence and felicity. A bounty so unexpected had a better influence even upon the woman's constitution than all that either the physicians or the waters of Bath could produce, and she recovered. But his good offices did not rest here. He prevailed upon a nobleman of his acquaintance to present the Doctor with a living of a hundred and sixty pounds a year, which made that happiness, he had before produced, in some measure permanent.

In the severe winter, which happened in the year 1739, his charity was great, useful, and extensive. He frequently, at that season of calamity, entered the houses of the poor, whom he thought too proud to beg, and generously relieved them. The colliers were at this time peculiarly distressed ; and, in order to excite compassion, a number of them yoked themselves to a wagon loaded with coals, and drew it into Bath, and presented it to Mr. Nash. Their scheme had the proper effect. Mr. Nash procured them a subscription, and gave ten guineas towards it himself. The weavers also shared his bounty at that season. They came begging in a body into Bath, and he provided a plentiful dinner for their entertainment, and gave each a week's subsistence at going away.

There are few public charities to which he was not

a subscriber, and many he principally contributed to support. Among others, Mr. Annesley, that strange example of the mutability of fortune, and the inefficacy of our laws, shared his interest and bounty. I have now before me a well-written letter, addressed to Mr. Nash, in order to obtain his interest for that unhappy gentleman ; it comes from Mr. Henderson, a Quaker, who was Mr. Annesley's father's agent. This gentleman warmly espoused the young adventurer's interest, and, I am told. fell with him.

London, October 23, 1756.

My Good Friend,

When I had the honour of conversing with thee at Tunbridge, in September last, concerning that most singular striking case of Mr. Annesley, whom I have known since he was about six years old, I being then employed by the late Lord Baron of Altham, his father, as his agent. From what I know of the affairs of that family, I am well assured, that Mr. Annesley is the legitimate son of the late Lord Baron of Altham, and, in consequence thereof, is entitled to the honours and estates of Anglesey. Were I not well assured of his right to those honours and estates, I would not give countenance to his claim.—I well remember, that then then madest me a promise to assist him in soliciting a subscription, that was then begun at Tunbridge; but, as that place was not within the limits of thy province, thou couldest not promise to do much there. But thou saidst, that in case he would go to Bath in the season, thou wouldest then and there show how much thou wouldest be his friend.

And now, my good friend, as the season is come on, and Mr. Annesley now at Bath, I beg leave to remind thee of that promise ; and that thou wilt keep in full view the honour, the everlasting honour, that will naturally redound to thee from thy benevolence, and crown all the

good actions of thy life.—I say, now in the vale of life,
to relieve a distressed young nobleman, to extricate so
immense an estate, from the hands of oppression ; to
do this, will fix such a ray of glory on thy memory, as
will speak forth thy praise to future ages.—This with
great respect is the needful,

from thy assured Friend,

WILLIAM HENDERSON,

Be pleased to give my respects to Mr. Annesley and
his spouse.

Mr. Nash punctually kept his word with this gentleman ; he began the subscription himself with the utmost
liberality, and procured such a list of encouragers, as at
once did honour to Mr. Annesley's cause, and their own
generosity. What a pity it was, that this money, which
was given for the relief of indigence only, went to feed
a set of reptiles, who batten upon our weakness, miseries,
and vice.

It may not be known to the generality of my readers,
that the last act of the comedy, called *Esop*, which was
added to the French plot of Boursault, by Mr. Vanbrugh,
was taken from a story told of Mr. Nash, upon a similar
occasion. He had in the early part of life made proposals
of marriage to Miss V——, of D—— ; his affluence at
that time, and the favour which he was in with the
nobility, readily induced the young lady's father to
favour his addresses. However, upon opening the affair
to herself, she candidly told him, her affections were
placed upon another, and that she could not possibly
comply. Though this answer satisfied Mr. Nash, it was
by no means sufficient to appease the father ; and he
peremptorily insisted upon her obedience. Things were
carried to the last extremity ; when Mr. Nash undertook to settle the affair ; and desiring his favoured rival

to be sent for, with his own hand presented his mistress to him, together with a fortune equal to what her father intended to give her. Such an uncommon instance of generosity had an instant effect upon the severe parent; he considered such disinterestedness as a just reproach to his own mercenary disposition, and took his daughter once more into favour. I wish, for the dignity of history, that the sequel could be concealed; but the young lady ran away with her footman, before half a year was expired; and her husband died of grief.

In general, the benefactions of a generous man are but ill bestowed. His heart seldom gives him leave to examine the real distress of the object which sues for pity; his good nature takes the alarm too soon, and he bestows his fortune on only apparent wretchedness. The man naturally frugal, on the other hand, seldom relieves; but when he does, his reason, and not his sensations, generally find out the object. Every instance of his bounty is therefore permanent, and bears witness to his benevolence.

Of all the immense sums which Nash lavished upon real or apparent wretchedness, the effects, after a few years, seemed to disappear. His money was generally given to support immediate want, or to relieve improvident indolence, and therefore it vanished in an hour. Perhaps towards the close of life, were he to look round on the thousands he had relieved, he would find but few made happy, or fixed by his bounty in a state of thriving industry; it was enough for him, that he gave to those that wanted; he never considered, that charity to some might impoverish himself without relieving them; he seldom considered the merit or the industry of the petitioner; or he rather fancied, that misery was an excuse for indolence and guilt. It was a usual saying of his, when he went to beg for any person in distress, that they who could stoop to the meanness of solicitation, must certainly *want* the favour for which they petitioned.

In this manner, therefore, he gave away immense sums of his. own, and still greater, which he procured from others. His way was, when any person was proposed to him as an object of charity, to go round with his hat, first among the nobility, according to their rank, and so on, till he left scarce a single person unsolicited. They who go thus about to beg for others, generally find a pleasure in the task. They consider, in some measure, every benefaction they procure, as given by themselves, and have at once the pleasure of being liberal, without the self-reproach of being profuse.

But of all the instances of Mr. Nash's bounty, none does him more real honour than the pains he took in establishing a hospital at Bath, in which benefaction, however, Doctor Oliver had a great share. This was one of those well-guided charities, dictated by reason, and supported by prudence. By this institution the diseased poor might recover health, when incapable of receiving it in any other part of the kingdom. As the disorders of the poor, who could expect to find relief at Bath, were mostly chronical, the expense of maintaining them there was found more than their parishes thought proper to afford. They therefore chose to support them in a continual state of infirmity, by a small allowance at home, rather than be at the charge of an expensive cure. A hospital therefore at Bath, it was thought, would be an asylum, and a place of relief to those disabled creatures, and would, at the same time, give the physician more thorough insight into the efficacy of the waters, from the regularity with which such patients would be obliged to take them. These inducements therefore influenced Doctor Oliver, and Mr. Nash, to promote a subscription towards such a benefaction. The design was set on foot so early as the year 1711, but not completed till the year 1742. This delay, which seems surprising, was in fact owing to the want of a proper fund for carrying the work into execution. What I said above, of charity being the characteristic virtue of the present age, will be more fully evinced, by comparing the old and new subscriptions for this hospital. These will show the difference between ancient and modern benevolence. When I run my eye over the list of those who subscribed in the year 1723, I find the subscription in general seldom rise above a guinea each person ; so that, at that time, with all their efforts, they were unable to raise four hundred pounds ; but in about twenty years after, each particular subscription was greatly increased—ten, twenty, thirty pounds, being the most ordinary sums subscribed, and they soon raised above two thousand pounds for the purpose.

Thus, chiefly by the means of Doctor Oliver and Mr. Nash, but not without the assistance of the good Mr. Allen, who gave them the stone for building and other benefactions, this hospital was erected, and it is at present fitted up for the reception of patients, the cases most paralytic or leprous. The following conditions are observed previous to admittance.

' I. The case of the patient must be described by ' some physician, or person of skill, in the neighbour- ' hood of the place where the patient has resided for some ' time ; and this description, together with a certificate ' of the poverty of the patient, attested by some persons ' of credit, must be sent in a letter post-paid, directed ' to the register of the *General Hospital at Bath.*

' II. After the patient's case has been thus described, ' and sent, he must remain in his usual place or residence ' till he has notice of a vacancy, signified by a letter ' from the register.

' III. Upon the receipt of such a letter, the patient
' must set forward for Bath, bringing with him this
' letter, the parish certificate duly executed, and allowed
' by two justices, and three pounds caution-money, if
' from any part of England or Wales ; but if the patient
' comes from Scotland or Ireland, then the caution-
' money, to be deposited before admission, is the sum of
' five pounds.

' IV. Soldiers may, instead of parish certificates, bring
' a certificate from their commanding officers, signifying
' to what corps they belong, and that they shall be
' received into the same corps, when discharged from
' the Hospital, in whatever condition they are. But it is
' necessary that their cases be described, and sent
' previously, and that they bring with them three
' pounds caution-money.

' *Note.* The intention of the caution-money is to
' defray the expenses of returning the patients after they
' are discharged from the Hospital, or of their burial in
' case they die there. The remainder of the caution-
' money, after these expenses are defrayed, will be
' returned to the person who made the deposit.'

I am unwilling to leave this subject of his benevolence,
because it is a virtue in his character which must stand
almost single against a hundred follies ; and it deserves
the more to be insisted on, because it was large enough to
outweigh them all. A man may be a hypocrite safely
in every other instance, but in charity ; there are few
who will buy the character of benevolence at the rate
for which it must be acquired. In short, the sums he
gave away were immense ; and, in old age, when at
last grown too poor to give relief, *he gave*, as the poet
has it, *all he had, a tear* ; when incapable of relieving the
agonies of the wretched, he attempted to relieve his own
by a flood of sorrow.

The sums he gave and collected for the hospital, were great, and his manner of doing it was no less admirable. I am told that he was once collecting money in Wiltshire's room for that purpose, when a lady entered who is more remarkable for her wit than her charity, and not being able to pass by him unobserved, she gave him a pat with her fan, and said, ' You must put down a trifle for ' me, Nash, for I have no money in my pocket.' ' Yes, ' madam,' says he, ' that I will with pleasure, if your ' Grace will tell me when to stop ' : then taking a handful of guineas out of his pocket, he began to tell them into his white hat, one, two, three, four, five. ' Hold, hold,' says the Duchess, ' consider what you are about.' ' Consider your rank and fortune, madam,' says Nash, and continued telling, six, seven, eight, nine, ten. Here the Duchess called again, and seemed angry. ' Pray ' compose yourself, madam,' cried Nash, ' and don't ' interrupt the work of charity ; eleven, twelve, thirteen, ' fourteen, fifteen.' Here the Duchess stormed, and caught hold of his hand. ' Peace, madam,' says Nash ; ' you shall have your name written in letters of gold, ' madam, and upon the front of the building, madam. ' Sixteen, seventeen, eighteen, nineteen, twenty.' ' I ' won't pay a farthing more,' says the Duchess. ' Charity ' hides a multitude of sins,' replies Nash. ' Twenty-one, ' twenty-two, twenty-three, twenty-four, twenty-five.' ' Nash,' says she, ' I protest you frighten me out of my ' wits. L——d, I shall die ! ' ' Madam, you will never ' die with doing good ; and if you do, it will be the ' better for you,' answered Nash, and was about to proceed ; but perceiving her Grace had lost all patience, a parley ensued, when he, after much altercation, agreed to stop his hand, and compound with her Grace for thirty guineas. The Duchess, however, seemed displeased the whole evening ; and when he came to the table where she was playing, bid him, 'Stand farther, an ugly devil, for she hated the sight of him.' But her Grace afterwards, having a run of good luck, called Nash to her. 'Come,' says she, 'I will be friends with you, though you are ' a fool ; and to let you see I am not angry, there is ten ' guineas more for your charity. But this I insist on, ' that neither my name, nor the sum, shall be mentioned.'

From the hospital erected for the benefit of the poor, it is an easy transition to the monuments erected by him in honour of the great. Upon the recovery of the Prince of Orange, by drinking the Bath waters, Mr. Nash caused a small obelisk, thirty feet high, to be erected in a grove near the Abbey church, since called *Orange Grove*. This Prince's arms adorn the west side of the body of the pedestal. The inscription is on the opposite side, in the following words :

In memoriam
Sanitatis
Principi Auriaco
Aquarum thermalium potu,
Favente Deo,
Ovante Britannia,
Feliciter restitutæ,
M. DCC. XXXIV.

In English thus :

In memory
Of the happy restoration
Of the health of the
Prince of *Orange*,
Through the favour of God,
And to the great joy of Britain,
By drinking the *Bath* waters.
1734.

I find it a general custom, at all baths and spas, to

erect monuments of this kind to the memory of every prince who has received benefit from the waters. Aix, Spa, and Pisa, abound with inscriptions of this nature, apparently doing honour to the prince, but in reality celebrating the efficacy of their springs. It is wrong, therefore, to call such monuments instances of gratitude, though they may wear that appearance.

In the year 1738, the Prince of Wales came to Bath, who presented Mr. Nash with a large gold enamelled snuff-box ; and upon his departure, Nash, as King of Bath, erected an obelisk in honour of this prince, as he had before done for the Prince of Orange. This handsome memorial in honour of that good-natured prince is erected in Queen Square. It is enclosed with a stone balustrade, and in the middle of every side there are large iron gates. In the centre is the obelisk, seventy feet high, and terminating in a point. The expenses of this were eighty pounds ; and Mr. Nash was determined, that the inscription should answer the magnificence of the pile. With this view he wrote to Mr. Pope, at London, requesting an inscription. I should have been glad to have given Mr. Nash's letter upon this occasion ; the reader, however, must be satisfied with Pope's reply ; which is as follows.

SIR,

I have received yours, and thank your partiality in my favour. You say words cannot express the gratitude you feel for the favour of his R. H., and yet you would have me express what you feel, and in a few words. I own myself unequal to the task ; for even granting it possible to express an inexpressible idea, I am the worst person you could have pitched upon for this purpose, who have received so few favours from the great myself, that I am utterly unacquainted with what kind of thanks they like best. Whether the P—— most loves poetry or prose, I protest I do not know; but this I dare venture to affirm, that you can give him as much satisfaction in either as I can.

I am,

Sir,

Your affectionate Servant,

·A. POPE.

What Mr. Nash's answer to this *billet* was, I cannot take upon me to ascertain, but it was probably a perseverance in his former request. The following is the copy of Mr. Pope's reply to his second letter.

SIR,

I had sooner answered yours, but in the hope of procuring a properer hand than mine; and then in consulting with some, whose office about the P—— might make them the best judges, what sort of inscription to set up. Nothing can be plainer than the enclosed; it is nearly the common sense of the thing, and I do not know how to flourish upon it. But this you would do as well, or better yourself, and I dare say may mend the expression. I am truly,

Dear Sir,

Your affectionate Servant,

A. POPE.

I think I need not tell you my name should not be mentioned.

Such a letter as this was what might naturally be expected from Mr. Pope. Notwithstanding the seeming modesty towards the conclusion, the vanity of an applauded writer bursts through every line of it. The difficulty of concealing his hand from the clerks at the

Post Office, and the solicitude to have his name concealed, were marks of the consciousness of his own importance. It is probable, his hand was not so very well known, nor his letters so eagerly opened by the clerks of the Office, as he seems always to think. But in all his letters, as well as those of Swift, there runs a strain of pride, as if the world talked of nothing but themselves. ' Alas,' says he, in one of them, ' the day after I am dead, the ' sun will shine as bright as the day before, and the ' world will be as merry as usual ! ' Very strange, that neither an eclipse nor an earthquake should follow the loss of a poet !

The inscription referred to in this letter, was the same which was afterwards engraved on the obelisk ; and is as follows :

In memory of honours bestow'd,
And in gratitude for benefits conferred in this city,
By his Royal Highness
Frederick, Prince of Wales,
And his Royal Consort,
In the Year 1738,
This obelisk is erected by
Richard Nash, Esq.

I dare venture to say, there was scarce a Common Council-man in the corporation of Bath, but could have done this as well. Nothing can be more frigid ; though the subject was worthy of the utmost exertions of genius.

About this period every season brought some new accession of honour to Mr. Nash ; and the corporation now universally found, that he was absolutely necessary for promoting the welfare of the city ; so that this year seems to have been the meridian of his glory. About this time he arrived at such a pitch of authority, that

I really believe Alexander was not greater at Persepolis. The countenance he received from the Prince of Orange, the favour he was in with the Prince of Wales, and the caresses of the nobility, all conspired to lift him to the utmost pitch of vanity. The exultation of a little mind, upon being admitted to the familiarity of the great, is inexpressible. The Prince of Orange had made him a present of a very fine snuff-box. Upon this some of the nobility thought it would be proper to give snuff-boxes too ; they were quickly imitated by the middling gentry, and it soon became the fashion to give Mr. Nash snuff-boxes ; who had in a little time a number sufficient to have furnished a good toy-shop.

To add to his honours, there was placed a full-length picture of him, in Wiltshire's Ballroom, between the busts of Newton and Pope. It was upon this occasion that the Earl of Chesterfield wrote the following severe but witty epigram :

> Immortal Newton never spoke
>   More truth than here you'll find ;
> Nor Pope himself e'er penn'd a joke
>   Severer on mankind,

> This picture placed these busts between,
>   Gives satire its full strength ;
> Wisdom and Wit are little seen,
>   But Folly at full length.

There is also a full-length picture of Mr. Nash in Simpson's Ballroom ; and his statue at full length in the Pump-room, with a plan of the Bath Hospital in his hand. He was now treated in every respect like a great man ; he had his levee, his flatterers, his buffoons, his good-natured creatures, and even his dedicators. A trifling ill-supported vanity was his foible, and while he received the homage of the vulgar, and enjoyed the familiarity of the great, he felt no pain for the unpromising view of poverty that lay before him ; he enjoyed the world as it went, and drew upon content for the deficiencies of fortune. If a cringing wretch called him his Honour, he was pleased ; internally conscious, that he had the justest pretensions to the title. If a beggar called him my Lord, he was happy, and generally sent the flatterer off happy too. I have known him, in London, wait a whole day at a window in the Smyrna Coffee-house, in order to receive a bow from the Prince, or the Duchess of Marlborough, as they passed by where he was standing ; and he would then look round upon the company for admiration and respect.

But perhaps the reader desires to know, who could be low enough to flatter a man, who himself lived in some measure by dependence. Hundreds are ready upon those occasions. The very needy are almost ever flatterers. A man in wretched circumstances forgets his own value, and feels no pain in giving up superiority to every claimant. The very vain are ever flatterers ; as they find it necessary to make use of all their arts, to keep company with such as are superior to themselves. But particularly the prodigal are prone to adulation, in order to open new supplies for their extravagance. The poor, the vain, and extravagant, are chiefly addicted to this vice ; and such hung upon his good nature. When these three characters are found united in one person, the composition generally becomes a great man's favourite. It was not difficult to collect such a group in a city that was the centre of pleasure. Nash had them of all sizes, from the half-pay captain in laced clothes, to the humble boot-catcher at the Bear.

I have before me a bundle of letters, all addressed from a pack of flattering reptiles, to his Honour ; and even some printed dedications, in the same servile strain.

In these his Honour is complimented as the great encourager of the polite arts, as a gentleman of the most
accomplished taste, of the most extensive learning, and,
in short, of everything in the world. But perhaps it will
be thought wrong in me, to unveil the blushing muse, to
brand learning with the meanness of its professors, or to
expose scholars in a state of contempt.—For the honour
of letters, the dedications to Mr. Nash are not written
by scholars or poets, but by people of a different stamp.

Among this number was the highwayman, who was
taken after attempting to rob and murder Doctor
Hancock. He was called Poulter, *alias* Baxter, and
published a book, exposing the tricks of gamblers, thieves
and pickpockets. This he intended to have dedicated to
Mr. Nash ; but the generous patron, though no man
loved praise more, was too modest to have it printed.
However, he took care to preserve the manuscript,
among the rest of his papers. The book was entitled,
The discoveries of John Poulter, alias Baxter, who was
apprehended for robbing Doctor Hancock, of Salisbury, on
Claverton Down near Bath ; and who has since been
admitted king's evidence, and discovered a most numerous
gang of villains. Being a full account of all the robberies
he committed, and the surprising tricks and frauds he has
practised for the space of five years last past, in different
parts of England, particularly in the West. Written
wholly by himself. The dedication intended to be
prefixed is as follows, and will give a specimen of the
style of a highwayman and a gambler.

To the Honourable Richard Nash, Esq.
May it please your Honour,
    With humblest submission, I make bold to present
the following sheets to your Honour's consideration,
and well-known humanity. As I am industriously careful,

in respect to his Majesty, and good subjects, to put an end to the unfortunate misconducts of all I know, by bringing them to the gallows. To be sure some may censure, as if from self-preservation I made this ample discovery; but I communicate this to your Honour and gentry, whether the life of one person being taken away, would answer the end, as to let escape such a number of villains, who has been the ruining of many a poor family, for whom my soul is now much concerned. If my inclinations was ever so roguish inclined, what is it to so great a number of villains, when they consult together. As your Honour's wisdom, humanity, and interest are the friend of the virtuous, I make bold to lay, at your Honour's feet, the following lines, which will put every honest man upon his defence against the snares of the mischievous; and am, with the greatest gratitude, honoured Sir,

Your Honour's
Most truly devoted and obedient Servant,
JOHN POULTER, *alias* BAXTER.

Taunton Gaol,
June 2nd.

Flattery from such a wretch as this, one would think but little pleasing; however, certain it is, that Nash was pleased with it: he loved to be called your Honour, and Honourable; and the highwayman more than once experienced his generosity.

But since I have mentioned this fellow's book, I cannot repress an impulse to give an extract from it, however foreign from my subject. I take the following picture to be a perfectly humorous description of artful knavery affecting ignorance on one hand, and rustic simplicity pretending to great wisdom and sagacity on the other. It is an account of the manner in which countrymen are deceived by gamblers, at a game called

Pricking in the Belt, or the Old Nob. This is a leathern
strop, folded up double, and then laid upon a table ; if the
person who plays with a bodkin pricks into the loop of the
belt he wins ; if otherwise, he loses. However, by slipping
one end of the strop, the sharper can win with pleasure.

'There are generally four persons concerned in this
'fraud, one to personate a *Sailor*, called a *Legg Cull*,
'another called the *Capper*, who always keeps with the
'*Sailor* ; and two pickers up, or *Money-Droppers*, to
'bring in *Flats* or *Bubbles*. The first thing they do at
': a fair, is to look for a room clear of company, which the
'*Sailor* and *Capper* immediately take, while the *Money-*
'*Droppers* go out to look for a *Flat*. If they see a country-
'man, whose looks they like, one drops a shilling, or
'half a crown, just before him, and picking it up again,
'looks the man in the face, and says, I have found
'a piece of money, friend, did you see me pick it up ?
'The man says, yes : Then says the sharper, if you had
'found it, I would have had half, so I will do as I would
'be done unto ; come, honest friend, we will not part
'with dry lips. Then taking him into the room where
'the other two are, he cries, By your leave, gentlemen,
'I hope we don't disturb the company. No, cries the
'*Sailor* ; no, brothers ; Will you drink a glass of
'brandy, I don't like your weak liquors ; and then
'begins a discourse, by asking the *Capper* how far it is
'to *London* ; who replies, I don't know ; perhaps the
'gentleman there can tell you, directing his discourse to
'the *Flat* ; perhaps the *Flat* will answer, a hundred
'miles ; the *Sailor* cries, I can ride that in a day, ay,
'in four or five hours ; for, says he, my horse will run
'twenty knots an hour for twenty-four hours together :
'*Capper*, or the *Sailor's* supposed companion, says, I
'believe, *Farmer*, you have not got such a horse as the
'*Sailor* has ; the *Farmer* cries No, and laughs ; and

'then the *Sailor* says, I must go and get half a pint of
'brandy, for I am griped, and so leaves them. The
'*Capper*, affecting a look of wisdom in his absence,
'observes, that it is an old saying, and a true one, *that*
'*Sailors get their money like horses, and spend it like*
'*asses* ; as for that there *Sailor*, I never saw him till now,
'buying a horse of my man ; he tells me he has been
'at *Sea*, and has got about four hundred pounds prize-
'money, but I believe he will squander it all away, for he
'was gaming just now with a sharping fellow, and lost
'forty shillings, at a strange game of pricking in a
'string. Did either of you ever see it, gentlemen ?
'continued the *Capper* ; if you two are willing, I will
'ask him to show it, for we may as well win some of
'his money as any body else : The *Flat* and the *Dropper*
'cry, Do. Then in comes the *Sailor*, staggering as if
'drunk, and cries, What cheer, brothers ? I have just
'seen a pretty girl in the fair, and went in to drink with
'her, we made a bargain, and I gave her a six and
'thirty shilling piece, but an old b—h, her mother, came
'and called her away, but I hope she will come back
'to me presently ; then the *Capper* laughs, and says,
'Have you got your money of her again ? The *Sailor*
'says, No ; but she will come to me, I'm sure ; then they
'all laugh. This is done to deceive the *Flat* : then says
'the *Capper*, What have you done with the stick and
'the string, *Sailor* ? he answers, What, that which
'I bought of the boys ? I have got it here, but will
'not sell it, and then he pulls out the Old Nobb, saying,
'What do you think I gave for it ? I ga e but six-pence,
'and as much brandy as the two boys could drink ; it
'is made out of a monkey's hide, as the boys told me,
'and they told me, there is a game to be played at it,
'which no body can do twice together ; I will go down
'aboard ship, and play with my Captain, and I do not

' fear but I shall win his ship and cargo : then they all
' laugh, and the *Sailor* makes up the Old Nobb, and the
' *Capper* lays a shilling, and pricks himself and wins ;
' the *Sailor* cries, You are a dab, I will not lay with you,
' but if you will call a stranger, I will lay again ; why
' if you think me a dab, as you call it, I will get this
' strange gentleman, or this (pointing to the *Flat*).
' Done, cries the *Sailor*, but you shall not tell him ; then
' he makes up the Nob, and *Capper* lays a shilling,
' *Flat* pricks, being permitted to go sixpence ; to which
' he agreeing, wins ; and *Capper* says to the *Flat*, Can
' you change me half a crown ? This is done to find the
' depth of his pocket ; if they see a good deal of gold,
' *Flat* must win three or four times ; if no gold, but
' twice. Sometimes, if the *Flat* has no money, the
' *Sailor* cries, I have more money than any man in the
' fair, and pulls out his purse of gold, and saith, Not
' one of you can beg, borrow, or steal half this sum in an
' hour for a guinea. *Capper* cries, I have laid out all
' mine ; *Farmer*, Can you ? I'll go your halves, if you
' think you can do it. The *Sailor* saith, you must not
' bring any body with you ; then the *Dropper* goes with
' the *Flat*, and saith, You must not tell your friend it is
' for a wager ; if you do, he will not lend it you. *Flat*
' goes and borrows it, and brings it to the *Sailor*, shows
' it him, and wins the wager ; then the *Sailor* pinches
' the Nob again, and the *Capper* whispers to the *Flat*,
' to prick out purposely this time, saying, it will make
' the *Sailor* more eager to lay on ; we may as well win
' his money as not, for he will spend it upon whores :
' *Flat*, with all the wisdom in the world, loses on purpose ;
' upon which the *Sailor* swears, pulls out all his money,
' throws it about the room, and cries, I know no man
' can win for ever, and then lays a guinea, but will
' not let him prick, but throws down five guineas ; and

'the *Capper* urging the *Flat*, and going his halves, the
' *Sailor* saith, my cabbin boy will lay as much as that;
' I'll lay no less than twenty guineas ; the·*Capper* cries,
' lay, *Farmer*, and take up forty; which, being certain of
' winning, he instantly complies with, and loses the
' whole. When he has lost, in order to advise him, the
' *Dropper* takes him by the arm, and hauls him out of
' doors, and the reckoning being in the mean time paid
' within, the *Capper* and *Sailor* follow after, and run
' another way. When they are out of sight, the *Dropper*
' saith to the *Flat*, Go you back, and play with the
' *Sailor* for a shilling, whilst I go and borrow money ;
' but when the *Flat* goes to the house, he finds them gone,
' and then he knows that he is bit, but not till he has
' dearly paid for it.'

By this fellow's discoveries Mr. Nash was enabled to
serve many of the nobility and gentry of his acquaint·
ance ; he received a list of all those houses of ill-fame
which harboured or assisted rogues, and took care to
furnish travellers with proper precautions to avoid them.
It was odd enough to see a gamester thus employed,
in detecting the frauds of gamblers.

Among the dedications, there is one from a professor
of cookery, which is more adulatory than the preceding.
It is prefixed to a work, intituled, *The complete preserver,
or a new method of preserving fruits, flowers, and other
vegetables, either with or without sugar, vinegar, or spirits,*
&c.

To the very Honourable *Richard Nash*, Esq.

HONOURED SIR,

As much as the oak exceeds the bramble, so
much do you exceed the rest of mankind, in benevolence,
charity, and every other virtue that adorns, ennobles,
and refines the human species. I have therefore made

bold to prefix your name, though without permission, to
the following work, which stands in need of such a patron,
to excuse its errors, with a candour, only known to such
a heart as your own ; the obligations I have received
at your hands, it is impossible for me ever to repay,
except by my endeavours, as in the present case, to
make known the many excellent virtues which you
possess. But what can my wit do to recommend such
a genius as yours: a single word, a smile from yourself,
outweighs all that I, or perhaps the best of our poets,
could express in writing to the compass of a year. It
would ill become my sex, to declare what power you have
over us, but your generosity is, even in this instance,
greater than your desire to oblige. The following sheets
were drawn up at my hours of leisure, and may be
serviceable to such of my sex, as are more willing to
employ their time in laudable occupations and domestic
economy, than in dress and dissipation. What reception
they may receive from your Honour, I am incapable of
telling; however, from your known candour and humanity,
I expect the most favourable.

I am, Honoured Sir,
Your most obedient,
and obliged humble Servant,
H. W.

A musician in his dedication still exceeds the other
two in adulation. However, though the matter may
be some impeachment on his sincerity, the manner in
which it is written reflects no disgrace upon his understanding.

To *Richard Nash*, Esq.

SIR,
The kind partiality of my friends prevailed with
me to present to the world these my first attempts in
musical composition ; and the generous protection you

have been pleased to afford me, makes it my indispensable duty to lay them at your feet. Indeed, to whom could I presume to offer them, but to the great encourager of all polite arts; for your generosity knows no bounds; nor are you more famed for that dignity of mind, which ennobles and gives a grace to every part of your conduct, than for that humanity and beneficence, which makes you the friend and benefactor of all mankind. To you, the poor and the rich, the diseased and the healthy, the aged and the young, owe every comfort, every conveniency, and every innocent amusement, that the best heart, the most skilful management, and the most accomplished taste can furnish. Even this age, so deeply practised in all the subtilties of refined pleasure, gives you this testimony: even this age, so ardently engaged in all the ways of the most unbounded charity, gives you this praise. Pardon me then, if, amidst the crowd of votaries, I make my humble offering, if I seize this first opportunity of publicly expressing the grateful sentiments of my own heart and profound respect, with which,

I am, Sir,

Your most obliged, most devoted,

and most obedient Servant,

J. G.

I fancy I have almost fatigued the reader, and I am almost fatigued myself, with the efforts of those elegant panegyrists; however, I can't finish this run of quotation, without giving a specimen of poetry, addressed to him upon a certain occasion; and all I shall say in its defence is, that those, who are pleased with the prose dedications, will not dislike the present attempt in poetry.

To Richard Nash, Esq.

On his sickness at Tunbridge.

Say, must the friend of human kind,
Of most refin'd—of most diffusive mind ;
Must Nash himself beneath these ailments grieve ?
He felt for all—He felt—but to relieve,
To heal the sick—the wounded to restore,
And bid desponding nature mourn no more.
Thy quick'ning warmth, O let thy patron feel,
Improve thy springs with double power to heal :
Quick, hither, all-inspiring health, repair,
And save the gay—and wretched from despair ;
Thou only Esra's drooping sons can'st cheer,
And stop the soft-ey'd virgin's trickling tear ;
In murmurs who their monarch's pains deplore ;
While sickness faints—and pleasure is no more ;
O let not death, with hasty strides advance,
Thou, mildest charity, avert the lance ;
His threat'ning power, celestial maid ! defeat ;
Nor take him with thee, to thy well-known seat ;
Leave him on earth some longer date behind,
To bless,—to polish,—and relieve mankind :
Come then, kind health, O quickly come away,
Bid Nash revive—and all the world be gay.

Such addresses as these were daily offered to our titular King. When in the meridian of power, scarce a morning passed, that did not increase the number of his humble admirers, and enlarge the sphere of his vanity.

The man, who is constantly served up with adulation, must be a first-rate philosopher, if he can listen without contracting new affectations. The opinion we form of ourselves, is generally measured by what we hear from others ; and when they conspire to deceive, we too readily concur in the delusion. Among the number of much applauded men in the circle of our own friends, we can recollect but few that have heads quite strong enough to bear a loud acclamation of public praise in their favour ; among the whole list, we shall scarce find one, that has not thus been made, on some side of his character, a coxcomb.

When the best head turns and grows giddy with praise, is it to be wondered that poor Nash should be driven by it almost into a phrenzy of affectation ? Towards the close of life he became affected. He chiefly laboured to be thought a sayer of good things ; and by frequent attempts was now and then successful, for he ever lay upon the lurch.

There never perhaps was a more silly passion, than this desire of having a man's jests recorded. For this purpose, it is necessary to keep ignorant or ill-bred company, who are only fond of repeating such stories ; in the next place, a person must tell his own jokes, in order to make them more universal ; but what is worst of all, scarce a joke of this kind succeeds, but at the expense of a man's good nature ; and he who exchanges the character of being thought agreeable, for that of being thought witty, makes but a very bad bargain.

The success Nash sometimes met with led him on, when late in life, to mistake his true character. He was really agreeable, but he chose to be thought a wit. He therefore indulged his inclination, and never mattered how rude he was, provided he was thought comical. He thus got the applause he sought for, but too often found enemies, where he least expected to find them. Of all the jests recorded of him, I scarce find one that is not marked with petulance ; he said whatever came uppermost, and in the number of his remarks it might naturally be expected that some were worth repeating ; he threw often, and sometimes had a lucky cast.

In a life of almost hinety years, spent in the very point of public view, it is not strange, that five or six sprightly things of his have been collected, particularly as he took every opportunity of repeating them himself. His usual way, when he thought he said anything clever, was to strengthen it with an oath, and to make up its want of sentiment by asseveration and grimace. For many years he thus entertained the company at the coffee-house with old stories, in which he always made himself the principal character. Strangers liked this well enough ; but they who were used to his conversation found it insupportable. One story brought on another, and each came in the same order that it had the day preceding. But this custom may be rather ascribed to the peculiarity of age, than a peculiarity of character ; it seldom happens, that old men allure, at least by novelty ; age that shrivels the body contracts the understanding ; instead of exploring new regions, they rest satisfied in the old, and walk around the circle of their former discoveries. His manner of telling a story, however, was not displeasing, but few of those he told are worth transcribing. Indeed it is the manner, which places the whole difference between the wit of the vulgar, and of those who assume the name of the polite ; one has in general as much good sense as the other ; a story transcribed from the one, will be as entertaining as that copied from the other ; but in conversation, the manner will give charms even to stupidity. The following is the story which he most frequently told, and pretty much in these words. Suppose the company to be talking of a German war, or Elizabeth Canning, he would begin thus : ' I'll tell you something to that purpose
' that I fancy will make you laugh. A covetous old par-
' son, as rich as the Devil, scraped a fresh acquaintance
' with me several years ago at Bath. I knew him when

'he and I were students at Oxford, where we both
'studied damnationly hard, but that's neither here nor
'there. Well. Very well. I entertained him at my
'house in John's Court. (No, my house in John's
'Court was not built then) but I entertained him with
'all that the city could afford; the rooms, the music,
'and everything in the world. Upon his leaving Bath,
'he pressed me very hard to return the visit; and
'desired me to let him have the pleasure of seeing me
'at his house in Devonshire. About six months after,
'I happened to be in that neighbourhood, and was
'resolved to see my old friend, from whom I expected
'a very warm reception. Well: I knocks at his door,
'when an old queer creature of a maid came to the
'door, and denied him. I suspected, however, that he
'was at home; and going into the parlour, what should
'I see, but the Parson's legs up the chimney, where he
'had thrust himself to avoid entertaining me. This
'was very well. "My dear," says I to the maid, "it is
'very cold, extreme cold indeed, and I am afraid
'I have got a touch of my ague; light me the fire, if you
'please." "La, sir," says the maid, who was a modest
'creature to be sure, "the chimney smokes monstrously;
'you could not bear the room for three minutes together."
'By the greatest good luck there was a bundle of straw
'in the hearth, and I called for a candle. The candle
'came. "Well, good woman," says I, "since you
'won't light me a fire, I'll light one for myself," and in
'a moment the straw was all in a blaze. This quickly
'unkennelled the old fox; there he stood in an old
'rusty nightgown, blessing himself, and looking like—
'a—hem—egad.'

He used to tell surprising stories of his activity when
young. 'Here I stand, gentlemen, that could once leap
'forty-two feet, upon level ground, at three standing

' jumps, backward or forward.   One, two, three, dart
' like an arrow out of a bow.   But I am old now.   I
' remember I once leaped for three hundred guineas with
' Count Klopstock, the great leaper, leaping-master to the
' Prince of Passau ; you must all have heard of him.
' First he began with the running jump, and a most
' damnable bounce it was, that's certain : everybody
' concluded that he had the match hollow ; when only
' taking off my hat, stripping off neither coat, shoes, nor
' stockings, mind me, I fetches a run, and went beyond
' him one foot, three inches and three quarters, measured,
' upon my soul, by Captain Pately's own standard.'

But in this torrent of insipidity, there sometimes were
found very severe satire, strokes of true wit, and lines of
humour, *cum fluerent lutulentus, &c.*   He rallied very
successfully, for he never felt another's joke ; and drove
home his own without pity.   With his superiors he was
familiar and blunt, the inferiority of his station secured
him from their resentment ; but the same bluntness
which they laughed at, was by his equals regarded as
insolence.   Something like a familiar boot-catcher at an
inn, a gentleman would bear that joke from him, for
which a brother boot-catcher would knock him down.

Among other stories of Nash's telling, I remember one,
which I the more cheerfully repeat, as it tends to correct
a piece of impertinence that reigns in almost every
country assembly. The principal inhabitants of a market-
town, at a great distance from the capital, in order to
encourage that harmony which ought to subsist in
society, and to promote a mutual intercourse between
the sexes, so desirable to both, and so necessary for
all, had established a monthly assembly in the Town
Hall, which was conducted with such decency, decorum,
and politeness, that it drew the attention of the gentlemen and ladies in the neighbourhood ; and a nobleman

and his family continually honoured them with their presence. This naturally drew others, and in time the room was crowded with, what the world calls, good company, and the assembly prospered, till some of the new-admitted ladies took it into their heads, that the tradesmen's daughters were unworthy of their notice, and therefore refused to join hands with them in the dance. This was complained of by the town ladies, and that complaint was resented by the country gentlemen, who, more pert than wise, publicly advertised, that they would not dance with tradesmen's daughters. This the most eminent tradesmen considered as an insult on themselves, and being men of worth, and able to live independently, they in return advertised that they would give no credit out of their town, and desired all others to discharge their accounts. A general uneasiness ensued ; some writs were actually issued out, and much distress would have happened, had not my Lord, who sided with no party, kindly interfered and composed the difference. The assembly, however, was ruined, and the families, I am told, are not friends yet, though this affair happened thirty years ago.

Nothing debases human nature so much as pride—This Nash knew, and endeavoured to stifle every emotion of it at Bath. When he observed any ladies so extremely delicate and proud of a pedigree, as to only touch the back of an inferior's hand in the dance, he always called to order, and desired them to leave the room, or behave with common decency ; and when any ladies and gentlemen drew off, after they had gone down a dance, without standing up till the dance was finished, he made up to them, and after asking whether they had done dancing, told them, they should dance no more unless they stood up for the rest ; and on these occasions he always was as good as his word.

Nash, though no great wit, had the art of sometimes
saying rude things with decency, and rendering them
pleasing by an uncommon turn.—But most of the good
things attributed to him, which have found their way
into the jest-books, are no better than puns; the
smartest things I have seen are against him. One day
in the grove, he joined some ladies, and asking one of
them, who was crooked, whence she came? she replied,
' Straight from London.' ' Confound me, madam,' said
he, ' then you must have been damnably warped by the
' way.'

She soon, however, had ample revenge. Sitting the
following evening in one of the rooms, he once more
joined her company, and with a sneer and a bow, asked
her, if she knew her Catechism, and could tell the name
of Tobit's dog? ' His name, sir, was Nash,' replied the
lady, ' and an impudent dog he was.' This story is told
in a celebrated romance; I only repeat it here to have
an opportunity of observing, that it actually happened.

Queen Anne once asked him, why he would not accept
of knighthood? To which he replied, lest Sir William
Read, the mountebank, who had been just knighted,
should call him brother.

A house in Bath was said to be haunted by the
Devil, and a great noise was made about it; when Nash,
going to the minister of St. Michael's, entreated him to
drive the Devil out of Bath for ever, if it were only to
oblige the ladies.

Nash used sometimes to visit the great Doctor Clarke.
The Doctor was one day conversing with Locke, and two
or three more of his learned and intimate companions,
with that freedom, gaiety and cheerfulness, which is
ever the result of innocence. In the midst of their
mirth and laughter, the Doctor, looking from the
window, saw Nash's chariot stop at the door. ' Boys,

' boys,' cried the philosopher, to his friends, ' let us now
' be wise, for here is a fool coming.'

Nash was one day complaining in the following manner
to the Earl of Chesterfield of his bad luck at play.
' Would you think it, my Lord, that damned bitch
' fortune, no later than last night, tricked me out of
' 500. Is it not surprising,' continued he, ' that my luck
' should never turn, that I should thus eternally be
' mauled ? ' ' I don't wonder at your losing money,
' Nash,' says his lordship, ' but all the world is surprised
' where you get it to lose.'

Doctor Cheney once, when Nash was ill, drew up
a prescription for him, which was sent in accordingly.
The next day the Doctor coming to see his patient,
found him up and well; upon which he asked, if he had
followed his prescription ? ' Followed your prescription,'
cried Nash, ' No.—Egad, if I had, I should have broke my
neck, for I flung it out of the two pair stairs window.'

It would have been well, had he confined himself to such
sallies ; but as he grew old he grew insolent, and seemed,
in some measure, insensible of the pain his attempts to be
a wit gave others. Upon asking a lady to dance a minuet;
if she refused, he would often demand, if she had got
bandy legs. He would attempt to ridicule natural de-
feets ; he forgot the deference due to birth and quality,
and mistook the manner of settling rank and precedence
upon many occasions. He now seemed no longer fashionable among the present race of gentry ; he grew peevish
and fretful, and they who only saw the remnant of
a man, severely returned that laughter upon him, which
he had once lavished upon others.

Poor Nash was no longer the gay, thoughtless, idly
industrious creature he once was ; he now forgot how
to supply new modes of entertainment, and became too
rigid, to wind with ease through the vicissitudes of

fashion. The evening of his life began to grow cloudy. His fortune was gone, and nothing but poverty lay in prospect. To embitter his hopes, he found himself abandoned by the great, whom he had long endeavoured to serve ; and was obliged to fly to those of humbler stations for protection, whom he once affected to despise. He now began to want that charity, which he had never refused to any ; and to find, that a life of dissipation and gaiety, is ever terminated by misery and regret.

Even his place of master of the ceremonies (if I can trust the papers he has left behind him) was sought after. I would willingly be tender of any living reputation ; but these papers accuse Mr. Quin of endeavouring to supplant him. He has even left us a letter, which he supposed was written by that gentleman, soliciting a Lord for his interest upon the occasion. As I choose to give Mr. Quin an opportunity of disproving this, I will insert the letter, and, to show the improbability of its being his, with all its faults, both of style and spelling. I am the less apt to believe it written by Mr. Quin, as a gentleman, who has mended Shakespeare's plays so often, would surely be capable of something more correct than the following. It was sent, as it should seem, from Mr. Quin to a nobleman, but left open for the perusal of an intermediate friend. It was this friend who sent a copy of it to Mr. Nash, who caused it to be instantly printed, and left among his other papers.

The letter from the intermediate friend to Nash,
is as follows.

London, October 8, 1760.

DEAR NASH,

Two posts ago I received a letter from Quin, the old player, covering one to my Lord, which he left open for my perusal, which after reading he desired I might seal up and deliver. The request he makes is so extra-ordinary, that it has induced me to send you the copy of his letter to my Lord, which is as follows.

MY DER LORD,[1]

Old beaux Knash has mead himselfe so dissagree-able to all the companey that comes here to Bath that the corperatian of this city have it now under thier consideration to remove him from beeing master of the cereymoines, should he be continuead the inhabitants of thiss city will be rueind, as the best companey declines to come to Bath on his acc^{t}t.

Give me leave to show to your Lords'hip how he beheaved at the firs't ball he had here thiss' season which was Tus'day las't. A younge Lady was as'ked to dance a minueat she begg the gent^m would be pleased to exquise here, as' she did not chuse to dance; upon thiss' old Nash called out so as to be head by all the companey in the room, G— dam yo, Madam, what buis-ness have yo here if yo do not dance, upon which the Lady was so afrighted, she rose and danced, the ress'et of the companey was so much offended at the rudness of Nash that not one Lady more, would dance a minueat that night. In country dances' no person of note danced except two boys' Lords S—— and T——, the res't of the companey that danced waire only the families of

[1] Can any one, who has read what precedes and what follows this letter, suppose that we thought it was written by Mr. Quin, or that it would give any uneasiness either to him or his friends ?—The letter was really found among Mr. Nash's papers, as the Editor can at any time prove, and it was inserted here, to show what artifices were used, by those who had more levity than good nature, to impose upon a poor old man, and to embitter his last moments.

This Note has been rendered necessary, by a piece of criticism without candour, and an epigram without wit, which appeared on this occasion, in the public papers.

all the habberdas'hers' machinukes and inkeepers in the three kingdoms' brushed up and colexted togither.

I have known upon such an occaison as' thiss' seventeen Dutchess' and Contiss' to be at the opening of the ball at Bath now not one. This man by his' pride and extravagancis has out-lived his' reasein it would be happy for thiss' city that he was ded ; and is, now only fitt to reed Shirlock upon death by which he may seave his soul and gaine more than all the proffits he can make, by his white hatt, suppose it was to be died red :

The fav^r I have now to reques't by what I now have wrote yo ; is' that your Lordship will speke to Mr. Pitt, for to recommend me to the corporeatian of this city to succede this old sinner as master of the cerremonies and yo will much oblige,

My Lord your
Lord^s and Hu^c
Ob^t Ser^t.

N.B. There were some other private matters and offers in Quin's letter to my Lord, which do not relate to you.

Here Nash, if I may be permitted the use of a polite and fashionable phrase, was humm'd ; but he experienced such rubs as these, and a thousand other mortifications every day. He found poverty now denied him the indulgence not only of his favourite follies, but of his favourite virtues. The poor now solicited him in vain ; he was himself a more pitiable object than they. The child of the public seldom has a friend, and he who once exercised his wit at the expense of others, must naturally have enemies. Exasperated at last to the highest degree, an unaccountable whim struck him ; poor Nash was resolved to become an author ; he who, in the vigour of manhood, was incapable of the task, now at the impotent age of eighty-six, was determined to write his own history! From the many specimens already given of his style, the reader will not much regret that the historian was interrupted in his design. Yet as Montaigne observes, as the adventures of an infant, if an infant could inform us of them, would be pleasing; so the life of a beau, if a beau could write, would certainly serve to regale curiosity.

Whether he really intended to put this design in execution, or did it only to alarm the nobility, I will not take upon me to determine; but certain it is, that his friends went about collecting subscriptions for the work, and he received several encouragements from such as were willing to be politely charitable. It was thought by many, that this history would reveal the intrigues of a whole age; that he had numberless secrets to disclose; but they never considered, that persons of public character, like him, were the most unlikely in the world to be made partakers of those secrets which people desired the public should not know. In fact, he had few secrets to discover, and those he had, are now buried with him in the grave.

He was now past the power of giving or receiving pleasure, for he was poor, old and peevish; yet still he was incapable of turning from his former manner of life to pursue his happiness. The old man endeavoured to practise the follies of the boy, he spurred on his jaded passions after every trifle of the day; tottering with age he would be ever an unwelcome guest in the assemblies of the youthful and gay; and he seemed willing to find lost appetite among those scenes where he was once young.

An old man thus striving after pleasure is indeed an object of pity; but a man at once old and poor, running on in this pursuit, might excite astonishment. To see

a being both by fortune and constitution rendered incapable of enjoyment, still haunting those pleasures he
was no longer to share in ; to see one of almost ninety
settling the fashion of a lady's cap, or assigning her
place in a country dance ; to see him unmindful of his
own reverend figure, or the respect he should have for
himself, toasting demireps, or attempting to entertain
the lewd and idle ; a sight like this might well serve
as a satire on humanity ; might show that man is the
only preposterous creature alive, who pursues the shadow
of pleasure without temptation.

But he was not permitted to run on thus without
severe and repeated reproof. The clergy sent him frequent calls to reformation ; but the asperity of their
advice in general abated its intended effects ; they
threatened him with fire and brimstone, for what he,
had long been taught to consider as foibles, and not
vices ; so, like a desperate debtor, he did not care to
settle an account, that, upon the first inspection, he
found himself utterly unable to pay. Thus begins one
of his monitors.

'This admonition comes from your friend, and one
'that has your interest deeply at heart : It comes on
'a design altogether important, and of no less conse-
'quence than your everlasting happiness : so that it
'may justly challenge your careful regard. It is not to
'upbraid or reproach, much less to triumph and insult
'over your misconduct or misery ; no, 'tis pure bene-
'volence, it is disinterested goodwill prompts me to
'write ; I hope therefore I shall not raise your resent-
'ment. Yet be the consequence what it will, I cannot
'bear to see you walk in the paths that lead to death,
'without warning you of the danger, without sounding
'in your ear the lawful admonition, " Return and live !
' " Why do you such things ? I hear of your evil dealings

' " by all this people." I have long observed and pitied
' you ; and must tell you plainly, sir, that your present
' behaviour is not the way to reconcile yourself to God.
' You are so far from making atonement to offended
' justice, that each moment you are aggravating the
' future account, and heaping up an increase of His
' anger. As long as you roll on in a continued circle of
' sensual delights and vain entertainments, you are dead
' to all the purposes of piety and virtue. You are as
' odious to God as a corrupt carcass that lies putrefying
' in the churchyard. You are as far from doing your
' duty, or endeavouring after salvation, or restoring
' yourself to the Divine favour, as a heap of dry bones
' nailed up in a coffin is from vigour and activity.—
' Think, sir, I conjure you, think upon this, if you have
' any inclination to escape the fire that will never be
' quenched. Would you be rescued from the fury and
' fierce anger of God ? Would you be delivered from
' weeping and wailing, and incessant gnashing of teeth ?
' sure you would ! But be certain, that this will never
' be done by amusements, which at best are trifling and
' impertinent ; and for that, if for no other reason,
' foolish and sinful. 'Tis by seriousness ; 'tis by retire-
' ment and mourning, you must accomplish this great
' and desirable deliverance. You must not appear at
' the head of every silly diversion, you must enter into
' your closet, and shut the door ; commune with your
' own heart, and search out its defects. The pride of
' life and all its superfluity of follies must be put away.
' You must make haste, and delay not to keep every
' injunction of heaven. You must always remember,
' that mighty sinners must be mightily penitent, or else
' mightily tormented. Your example and your projects
' have been extremely *prejudicial* ; I wish I could not
' say, *fatal* and *destructive*, to many. For this there is

' no amends but an alteration of your conduct, as signal
' and remarkable as your *person* and *name.*

    ' If you do not by this method remedy in some degree
' the evils that you have sent abroad, and prevent the
' mischievous consequences that may ensue—wretched
' will you be, wretched above all men to eternity. The
' blood of souls will be laid to your charge ; God's
' jealousy, like a consuming flame, will smoke against
' you ; as you yourself will see in that day, when the
' mountains shall quake, and the hills melt, and the
 earth be burnt up at His presence.

    ' Once more then I exhort you as a friend ; I beseech
' you as a brother; I charge you as a messenger from
' God, in His own most solemn words ; " Cast away
' "from you your transgressions ; make you a new heart,
' "and a new spirit ; so iniquity shall not be your ruin."

    ' Perhaps you may be disposed to contemn this, and
' its serious purport ; or to recommend it to your com-
' panions as a subject for raillery. Yet let me tell you
' beforehand, that for this, as well as for other things,
' God will bring you to judgement. He sees me now
' I write : He will observe you while you read. He notes
' down my words ; He will also note down your conse-
' quent procedure. Not then upon me, not upon me ; but
' upon your own soul, will the neglecting or despising my
' sayings turn. " If thou be wise, thou shalt be wise for
' "thyself ; if thou scornest, thou alone shalt bear it." '

Thus we see a variety of causes concurred to embitter
his departing life. The weakness and infirmities of
exhausted nature, the admonitions of the grave, who
aggravated his follies into vices ; the ingratitude of his
dependants, who formerly flattered his fortunes ; but
particularly the contempt of the great, many of whom
quite forgot him in his wants ; all these hung upon his
spirits and soured his temper, and the poor man of

pleasure might have terminated his life very tragically, had not the Corporation of Bath charitably resolved to grant him ten guineas the first Monday of every month. This bounty served to keep him from actual necessity, though far too trifling to enable him to support the character of a gentleman. Habit, and not nature, makes almost all our wants ; and he who had been accustomed in the early parts of life to affluence and prodigality, when reduced to a hundred and twenty-six pounds a year, must pine in actual indigence.

In this variety of uneasiness his health began to fail. He had received from nature a robust and happy constitution, that was scarce even to be impaired by intemperance. He even pretended, among his friends, that he never followed a single prescription in his life ; however, in this he was one day detected on the Parade ; for boasting there of his contempt and utter disuse of medicine, unluckily the water of two blisters, which Dr. Oliver had prescribed, and which he then had upon each leg, oozed through his stockings, and betrayed him. His aversion to physic, however, was frequently a topic of raillery between him and Doctor Cheney, who was a man of some wit and breeding. When Cheney recommended his vegetable diet, Nash would swear that his design was to send half the world grazing like Nebuchadnezzar. ' Aye,' Cheney would reply, ' Nebuchadnezzar ' was never such an infidel as thou art. It was but last ' week, gentlemen, that I attended this fellow in a fit of ' sickness ; there I found him rolling up his eyes to ' heaven, and crying for mercy ; he would then swallow ' my drugs like breast-milk, yet you now hear him, ' how the old dog blasphemes the faculty.' What Cheney said in jest was true, he feared the approaches of death more than the generality of mankind, and was generally very devout while it threatened him. Though he was somewhat the libertine in action, none believed or trembled more than he ; for a mind neither schooled by philosophy, nor encouraged by conscious innocence, is ever timid at the appearance of danger.

For some time before his decease nature gave warning of his approaching dissolution.. The worn machine had run itself down to an utter impossibility of repair ; he saw that he must die, and shuddered at the thought. His virtues were not of the great, but the amiable kind ; so that fortitude was not among the number. Anxious, timid, his thoughts still hanging on a receding world, he desired to enjoy a little longer that life, the miseries of which he had experienced so long. The poor unsuccessful gamester husbanded the wasting moments, with an increased desire to continue the game, and to the last eagerly wished for one yet more happy throw. He died at his house in St. John's Court, Bath, on the 12th of February, 1761, aged eighty-seven years, three months, and some days.

His death was sincerely regretted by the city, to which he had been so long and so great a benefactor. The day after he died, the Mayor of Bath called the Corporation together, where they granted fifty pounds towards burying their sovereign with proper respect. After the corpse had lain four days, it was conveyed to the Abbey church in that city, with a solemnity somewhat peculiar to his character. About five the procession moved from his house ; the charity girls two and two preceded, next the boys of the charity school singing a solemn occasional hymn.[1] Next marched the

---

[1] *The Hymn sung at his Funeral.*

I

Most unhappy are we here,
Full of sin and full of fear,
Ever weary, ne'er at rest,
When, O Lord, shall we be blest ?

city music, and his own band sounding at proper intervals a dirge. Three clergymen immediately preceded the coffin, which was adorned with sable plumes, and the pall supported by the six senior aldermen. The masters of the Assembly-rooms followed as chief mourners ; the beadles of that hospital, which he had contributed so largely to endow, went next ; and last of all, the poor patients themselves, the lame, the emaciated, and the feeble, followed their old benefactor to his grave, shedding unfeigned tears, and lamenting themselves in him.

The crowd was so great, that not only the streets were filled, but, as one of the journals in a rant expresses it, ' even the tops of the houses were covered with spectators ; ' each thought the occasion affected themselves most ; ' as when a real king dies, they asked each other, *where* ' *shall we find such another* ; sorrow sat upon every face, ' and even children lisped that their Sovereign was no

II

Earth's a clog, a pageant life,
Fill'd with folly, guilt, and strife ;
Till we all unite in Thee,
With ourselves we disagree.

III

What's our comfort here below ?
Empty bubble, transient show ;
Wrapt in the body's vile disguise,
None truly is until he dies.

IV

Here we dwell, but not at home,
To other worlds ordain'd to roam ;
Yet still we seek for joys that waste,
Fleeting as the vernal blast.

V

Lord remove these shadows hence,
Give us faith instead of sense ;
Teach us here in life to die,
That we may live eternally.

' more. The awfulness of the solemnity made the deepest
' impression on the minds of the distressed inhabitants.
' The peasant discontinued his toil, the ox rested from
' the plough, all nature seemed to sympathize with their
' loss, and the muffled bells rung a peal of Bob Major.'

Our deepest solemnities have something truly
ridiculous in them : there is somewhat ludicrous in the
folly of historians, who thus declaim upon the death of
kings and princes, as if there was anything dismal, or
anything unusual in it. ' For my part,' says Poggi, the
Florentine, ' I can no more grieve for another's death,
' than I could for my own. I have ever regarded death
' as a very trifling affair ; nor can black staves, long
' cloaks, or mourning coaches, in the least influence my
' spirits. Let us live here as long, and as merrily as we
' can ; and when we must die, why, let us die merrily too,
' but die so as to be happy.'

The few things he was possessed of were left to his
relations. A small library of well-chosen books, some
trinkets and pictures, were his only inheritance. Among
the latter (besides the box given him by the Prince of
Wales), were a gold box, which was presented to him
by the Countess of Burlington, with Lady Euston's
picture in the lid ; an étui, mounted in gold, with a
diamond to open it, and ornamented with another
diamond at the top, given him by the Princess-dowager
of Wales. He had also a silver terene, which was given
him by the Princess Amelia ; and some other things of
no great value. The rings, watches, and pictures, which
he formerly received from others, would have come
to a considerable amount ; but these his necessities had
obliged him to dispose of : some family pictures, however, remained, which were sold by advertisement, for
five guineas each, after Mr. Nash's decease.

It was natural to expect, that the death of a person
so long in the eye of the public, must have produced

a desire in several to delineate his character, or deplore his loss. He was scarce dead, when the public papers were filled with elegies, groans and characters ; and before he was buried, there were epitaphs ready made to inscribe on his stone. I remember one of those character writers, and a very grave one too, after observing, alas ! that Richard Nash, Esq. was no more, went on to assure us, that he was *sagacious, debonair, and commode* ; and concluded with gravely declaring, *that impotent posterity would in vain fumble to produce his fellow.* Another, equally sorrowful, gave us to know, *that he was indeed a man* ; an assertion, which I fancy none will be so hardy as to contradict. But the merriest of all the lamentations made upon this occasion was that where he is called, *A constellation of the heavenly sphere.*

One thing, however, is common almost with each of them, and that is, that Venus, Cupid, and the Graces, are commanded to weep ; and that Bath shall never find such another.

But though he was satirized with the praises of those, yet there were some of real abilities who undertook to do justice to his character, to praise him for his virtues, and acknowledge his faults. I need scarcely mention, that Doctor Oliver and Doctor King are of this number. They had honoured him with their friendship while living, and undertook to honour his memory when dead. As the reader may choose to compare their efforts upon the same subject, I have subjoined them, and perhaps many will find in either enough, upon so unimportant a subject as Mr. Nash's life, to satisfy curiosity. The first published, was that by Doctor Oliver, written with much good sense, and still more good nature. But the reader will consider, that he has assumed in his motto the character of a panegyrist, and spares his friend's faults, though he was too candid entirely to pass them over in silence.

A faint Sketch of the Life, Character, and Manners,
of the late Mr. Nash.

Imperium in Imperio.——
De mortuis nil nisi bonum.

Bath, February 13, 1761.

This morning died
RICHARD NASH, Esq.
Aged eighty-eight.
He was by birth a gentleman, an ancient Briton ;
By education, a student of Jesus College, in Oxford ;
By profession —— . ——   ——
His natural genius was too volatile for any.
He tried the army and the law ;
But soon found his mind superior to both—
He was *born to govern,*
Nor was his dominion, like that of other legislators,
Over the servility of the vulgar,
But over the pride of the noble, and the opulent.
His public character was great,
As it was self-built, and self-maintained :
His private amiable,
As it was grateful, beneficent, and generous.
By the force of genius
He erected the city of Bath into a province of pleasure,
And became, by universal consent,
Its legislator, and ruler.
He planned, improved, and regulated all the amuse-
ments of the place ;
His fundamental law was, that of good breeding ;
Hold sacred decency, and decorum,
His constant maxim :
Nobody, howsoever exalted
By beauty, blood, titles, or riches,

Could be guilty of a breach of it, unpunished——
The penalty, *his disapprobation*, and *public shame.*
To maintain the sovereignty he had established,
He published rules of behaviour,
Which, from their propriety, acquired the force of laws ;
And which the highest never infringed, without im-
mediately undergoing the public censure.
He *kept the men in order* ; most wisely,
By prohibiting the wearing swords in his dominions ;
By which means
He prevented sudden passion from causing
The bitterness of unavailing repentance,——
In all quarrels he was chosen the Umpire——
And so just were his decisions,
That peace generally triumphed,
Crowned with the mutual thanks of both parties.
He *kept the ladies in good humour* ; most effectually
By a nice observance of the rules of place and prece-
dence ;
By ordaining scandal to be the infallible mark
Of a foolish head, and a malicious heart,
Always rendering more suspicious
The reputation of her who propagated it,
Than that of the person abused.
Of the young, the gay, the heedless fair,
Just launching into the dangerous sea of pleasure,
He was ever, unsolicited (*sometimes unregarded*),
The kind protector :
Humanely correcting even their mistakes in dress,
As well as improprieties in conduct :
Nay, often warning them,
Though at the hazard of his life,
Against the artful snares of designing men,
Or an improper acquaintance with women of doubtful
characters.

Thus did he establish his government on pillars
Of honour and politeness,
Which could never be shaken :
And maintained it, for full half a century,
With reputation, honour, and undisputed authority,
Beloved, respected, and revered.
Of his private character, be it the first praise,
That, while by his conduct, the highest ranks became
his subjects,
He himself became
The servant of the poor and the distressed :
Whose cause he ever pleaded amongst the rich,
And enforced with all the eloquence of a good example :
They were ashamed not to relieve those wants,
To which they saw him administer with
So noble an heart, and so liberal an hand.
Nor was his munificence confined to particulars,
He being, to all the public charities of this city,
A liberal benefactor ;
Not only by his own most generous subscriptions,
But, by always assuming, in their behalf, the character of
A sturdy beggar ;
Which he performed with such an authoritative address
To all ranks, without distinction,
That few of the worst hearts had courage to refuse,
What their own inclinations would not have prompted
them to bestow.
Of a noble public spirit,
And
A warm grateful heart,
The obelisk in the grove,
And
The beautiful needle in the square,
Are magnificent testimonies
The One

Erected to preserve the memory of a
Most interesting event to his country,
The restitution of health, by the healing waters of this
place,
To the illustrious Prince of Orange,
Who came hither in a most languishing condition :
The Other,
A noble offering of thanks
To the late Prince of WALES, and his royal Consort,
For favours bestowed,
And honours by them conferred, on this city.

His long and peaceful reign of
Absolute power
Was so tempered by his
Excessive good-nature,
That no instance can be given either of his own cruelty,
Or of his suffering that of others, to escape
Its proper reward.
Example unprecedented amongst absolute monarchs.

R E A D E R.

This *monarch* was a *man,*
And had his foibles, and his faults ;
Which we would wish covered with the veil of good
nature,
Made of the same piece with his own :
But, truth forceth us unwillingly to confess,
His passions were strong ;
Which, as they fired him to act strenuously in good,
Hurried him to some excesses of evil.
His fire, not used to be kept under by an early restraint,
Burst out too often into flaming acts,
Without waiting for the cool approbation of his judge-
ment.

His generosity was so great,
That Prudence often whispered him, in vain,
That she feared it would enter the neighbouring confines
of profusion :
His charity so unbounded,
That the severe might suspect it sometimes to be.
The offspring of folly, or ostentation.

With all these,
Be they foibles, follies, faults, or frailties,
It will be difficult to point out,
Amongst his cotemporary Kings of the whole earth,
More than ONE
Who hath fewer, or less pernicious to mankind.
His existence
(For life it scarcely might be called)
Was spun out to so great an age, that
The *man*
Was sunk, like many former heroes, in
The weakness and infirmities of exhausted nature ;
The unwilling tax all animals must pay
For multiplicity of days.
Over his closing scene,
Charity long spread her all-covering mantle,
And dropped the curtain,
Before the poor actor, though he played his part,
Was permitted to quit the stage.
Now may she protect his memory !
Every friend of Bath,
Every lover of decency, decorum, and good breeding,
Must sincerely deplore
The loss of so excellent a governor ;
And join in the most fervent wishes (would I could say
hopes !)

That there may soon be found a man
Able and worthy,
To succeed him.

The reader sees in what alluring colours Mr. Nash's character is drawn ; but he must consider, that an intimate friend held the pencil ; the Doctor professes to say nothing of the dead but what was good ; and such a maxim, though it serves his departed friend, is but badly calculated to improve the living. Dr. King in his Epitaph, however, is still more indulgent; he produces him as an example to kings, and prefers his laws even to those of Solon, or Lycurgus.

EPITAPHIUM RICHARDI NASH, ARMIGERI.
H. S. E.
RICHARDUS NASH
Obscuro loco natus,
Et nullis ortus majoribus :
Cui tamen
(O rem miram, et incredibilem !)
Regnum opulentissimum florentissimumque
Plebs, proceres, principes,
Liberis suis suffragiis
Ultro detulerunt,
Quod et ipse summa cum dignitate tenuit,
Annos plus quinquaginta,
Universo populo consentiente, approbante, plaudente.
Una voce praeterea, unoque omnium ordinum consensu,
Ad imperium suum adjuncta est
Magni nominis [1] Provincia :
Quam admirabili consilio et ratione
Per se, non unquam per legatos, administravit ;

[1] Tunbridge.

Eam quotannis invisere dignatus,
Et apud provinciales, quoad necesse fuit,
Solitus manere.

In tanta fortuna
Neque fastu turgidus Rex incessu patuit,
Neque, tyrannorum more, se jussit coli,
Aut amplos honores, titulosque sibi arrogavit ;
Sed cuncta insignia, etiam regium diadema rejiciens,
Caput contentus fuit ornare
GALERO ALBO,
Manifesto animi sui candoris signo.

LEGISLATOR prudentissimus,
Vel Solone et Lycurgo illustrior
Leges, quascunque voluit,
Statuit, fixit, promulgavit :
Omnes quidem cum civibus suis,
Tum vero hospitibus, advenis, peregrinis,
Gratas, jucundas, utiles.

VOLUPTATUM arbiter et minister,
Sed gravis, sed elegans, sed urbanus,
Et in summa comitate satis adhibens severitatis,
Imprimis curavit,
Ut in virorum et foeminarum coetibus
Nequis impudenter faceret,
Neque in iis quid inesset
Impuritatis, clamoris, tumulti.

CIVITATEM hanc celeberrimam,
Delicias suas,
Non modo pulcherrimis aedificiis auxit,
Sed praeclara disciplina et moribus ornavit :
Quippe nemo quisquam
To PREPON melius intellexit, excoluit, docuit.

Justus, liberalis, benignus, facetus,
Atque amicus omnibus, praecipue miseris et egenis,
Nullos habuit inimicos,
Praeter magnos quosdam ardeliones,
Et declamatores eos tristes et fanaticos,
Qui generi humano sunt inimicissimi.

Pacis et patriae amans,
Concordiam, felicem et perpetuam,
In regno suo constituit,
Usque adeo,
Ut nullus alteri petulanter maledicere,
Aut facto nocere auderet ;
Neque, tanquam sibi metuens,
In publicum armatus prodire.

Fuit quanquam potentissimus,
Omnia arbitrio suo gubernans :
Haud tamen ipsa libertas
Magis usquam floruit
Gratia, gloria, auctoritate.
Singulare enim temperamentum invenit,
(Rem magnae cogitationis,
Et rerum omnium fortasse difficillimam)
Quo ignobiles cum nobilibus, pauperes cum divitibus,
Indocti cum doctissimis, ignavi cum fortissimis
Acquari se putarent,
Rex Omnibus Idem.

Quicquid Peccaverit,
(Nam peccamus omnes)
In seipsum magis, quam in alios,
Et errore, aut imprudentia magis quam scelere, aut
improbitate,
Peccavit ;

Nusquam vero ignoratione decori, aut honesti,
Neque ita quidem usquam,
Ut non veniam ab humanis omnibus
Facile impetrarit.

HUJUS vitae morumque exemplar
Si caeteri reges, regulique,
Et quotquot sunt regnorum praefecti,
Imitarentur ;
(Utinam ! iterumque utinam !)
Et ipsi essent beati,
Et cunctae orbis regiones beatissimae.

TALEM virum, tantumque ademptum
Lugeant musae, charitesque !
Lugeant Veneres, Cupidinesque !
Lugeant omnes juvenum et nympharum chori !
Tu vero, O BATHONIA,
Ne cesses tuum lugere
Principem, praeceptorem, amicum, patronum ;
Heu, heu, numquam posthac
Habitura parem !

The following translation of this Epitaph will give
the English reader an idea of its contents, though not
of its elegance.

THE EPITAPH OF RICHARD NASH, ESQ.

Here lies
RICHARD NASH,
Born in an obscure village,
And from mean ancestors.
To whom, however,
Strange to relate,
Both the vulgar, and the mighty,

Without bribe or compulsion,
Unanimously gave
A kingdom, equally rich and flourishing.
A kingdom which he governed
More than fifty years,
With universal approbation and applause.
To his empire also was added,
By the consent of all orders,
A celebrated province [1]
Which he ever swayed with great prudence,
Not by delegated power, but in person.
He deigned to visit it every year,
And while the necessities of state demanded his presence,
He usually continued there.
In such greatness of fortune
His pride discovered itself by no marks of dignity ;
Nor did he ever claim the honours of prostration.
Despising at once titles of adulation,
And laying aside all royal splendour,
Wearing not even the diadem,
He was content with being distinguished only by the
ornamental ensign
Of a white hat ;
A symbol of the candour of his mind.
He was a most prudent legislator,
And more remarkable even than Solon or Lycurgus.
He at once established and authorized
Whatever laws were thought convenient,
Which were equally serviceable to the city,
And grateful to strangers,
Who made it their abode.
He was at once a provider and a judge of pleasures,
But still conducted them with gravity and elegance,
And repressed licentiousness with severity.

---

[1] Tunbridge.

His chief care was employed
In preventing obscenity or impudence
From offending the modesty or the morals
Of the Fair Sex,
And in banishing from their assemblies
Tumult, clamour, and abuse.
He not only adorned this city,
Which he loved,
With beautiful structures,
But improved it by his example ;
As no man knew, no man taught, what was *becoming*
Better than he.
He was just, liberal, kind, and facetious,
A friend to all, but particularly to the poor.
He had no enemies,
Except some of the trifling great,
Or dull declaimers, foes to all mankind.
Equally a lover of peace and of his country,
He fixed a happy and lasting concord
In his kingdom,
So that none dare convey scandal, or injure by open
violence the universal peace,
Or even by carrying arms appear prepared for war,
With impunity.

But though his power was boundless,
Yet never did liberty flourish more, which he promoted,
Both by his authority, and cultivated for his fame.
He found out the happy secret
(A thing not to be considered without surprise)
Of uniting the vulgar and the great,
The poor and the rich,
The learned and ignorant,
The cowardly and the brave,
In the bonds of society, an equal king to all.

Whatever his faults were,
For we have all faults,
They were rather obnoxious to himself than others ;
They arose neither from imprudence nor mistake,
Never from dishonesty or corrupt principle,
But so harmless were they,
That though they failed to create our esteem,
Yet can they not want our pardon.

Could other kings and governors
But learn to imitate his example,
(Would to heaven they could !)
Then might they see themselves happy,
And their people still enjoying
more true felicity.

Ye Muses and Graces mourn
His death ;
Ye powers of love, ye choirs
of youth and virgins,
But thou, O Bathonia, more than the rest,
Cease not to weep,
Your king, your teacher, patron, friend,
Never, ah, never, to behold
His equal.

Whatever might have been justly observed of Mr. Nash's superiority as a governor, at least it may be said, that few contemporary kings have met with such able panegyrists. The former enumerates all his good qualities with tenderness ; and the latter enforces them with impetuosity. They both seem to have loved him, and honourably paid his remains the last debt of friendship. But a cool biographer, unbiased by resentment or regard, will probably find nothing in the man either truly great, or strongly vicious. His virtues were all amiable, and more adapted to procure friends than admirers, they were more capable of raising love than esteem. He was naturally endued with good sense ; but by having been long accustomed to pursue trifles, his mind shrunk to the size of the little objects on which it was employed. His generosity was boundless, because his tenderness and his vanity were in equal proportion ; the one impelling him to relieve misery, and the other to make his benefactions known. In all his actions, however virtuous, he was guided by sensation and not by reason ; so that the uppermost passion was ever sure to prevail. His being constantly in company had made him an easy though not a polite companion. He chose to be thought rather an odd fellow, than a well-bred man ; perhaps that mixture of respect and ridicule, with which his mock royalty was treated, first inspired him with this resolution. The foundations of his empire were laid in vicious compliance, the continuance of his reign was supported by a virtuous impartiality. In the beginning of his authority, he in reality obeyed those whom he pretended to govern ; towards the end, he attempted to extort a real obedience from his subjects, and supported his right by prescription. Like a monarch Tacitus talks of, they complied with him at first because they loved, they obeyed at last because they feared him. He often led the rich into new follies, in order to promote the happiness of the poor, and served the one at the expense of the other. Whatever his vices were, they were of use to society ; and this neither Petronius, nor Apicius, nor Tigellius, nor any other professed voluptuary, could say. To set him up, as some do, for a pattern of imitation, is wrong, since all his virtues received a tincture from the neighbouring folly ; to denounce peculiar judgements against him, is equally unjust, as his faults raise rather our mirth than our detestation. He was fitted for the station in which fortune placed him. It required no great abilities to fill it, and few of great abilities but would have disdained the employment. He led a life of vanity, and long mistook it for happiness. Unfortunately he was taught at last to know, that a man of pleasure leads the most unpleasant life in the world.

A Letter from Mr. **** in Tunbridge, to Lord —— in London; found among the Papers of Mr. Nash, and prepared by him for the press.

MY LORD,

What I foresaw has arrived; poor Jenners, after losing all his fortune, has shot himself through the head. His losses to Bland were considerable, and his playing soon after with Spedding contributed to hasten his ruin. No man was ever more enamoured of play, or understood it less. At whatever game he ventured his money, he was most usually the dupe, and still foolishly attributed to his bad luck, those misfortunes that entirely proceeded from his want of judgement.

After finding that he had brought on himself irreparable indigence and contempt, his temper, formerly so sprightly, began to grow gloomy and unequal; he grew more fond of solitude, and more liable to take offence at supposed injuries; in short, for a week before he shot himself, his friends were of opinion that he meditated some such horrid design. He was found in his chamber fallen on the floor, the bullet having glanced on the bone, and lodged behind his right eye.

You remember, my Lord, what a charming fellow this deluded man was once. How benevolent, just, temperate, and every way virtuous; the only faults of his mind arose from motives of humanity; he was too easy, credulous and good-natured, and unable to resist temptation, when recommended by the voice of friendship. These foibles the vicious and the needy soon perceived, and what was at first a weakness they soon perverted into guilt; he became a gamester, and continued the infamous profession, till he could support the miseries it brought with it no longer.

I have often been not a little concerned to see the

first introduction of a young man of fortune to the gaming-table. With what eagerness his company is courted by the whole fraternity of sharpers ; how they . find out his most latent wishes, in order to make way to his affections by gratifying them ; and continue to hang upon him with the meanest degree of condescension. The youthful dupe, no way suspecting, imagines himself surrounded by friends and gentlemen, and incapable of even suspecting that men of such seeming good sense, and so genteel an appearance, should deviate from the laws of honour, walks into the snare, nor is he undeceived till schooled by the severity of experience.

As I suppose no man would be a gamester unless he hoped to win, so I fancy it would be easy to reclaim him, if he was once effectually convinced, that by continuing to play he must certainly lose. Permit me, my Lord, to attempt this task, and to show, that no young gentleman by a year's run of play, and in a mixed company, can possibly be a gainer.

Let me suppose in the first place, that the chances on both sides are equal, that there are no marked cards, no pinching, shuffling, nor hiding ; let me suppose that the players also have no advantage of each other in point of judgement, and still further let me grant, that the party is only formed at home, without going to the usual expensive places of resort frequented by gamesters. Even with all these circumstances in the young gamester's favour, it is evident he cannot be a gainer. With equal players after a year's continuance of any particular game it will be found, that, whatever has been played for, the winnings on either side are very inconsiderable, and most commonly nothing at all. Here then is a year's anxiety, pain, jarring, and suspense, and nothing gained ; were the parties to sit down and professedly play for nothing, they would contemn the proposal ; they would call it trifling away time, and one of the most insipid amusements in nature ; yet in fact, how do equal players differ ? It is allowed that little or nothing can be gained ; but much is lost ; our youth, our time, those moments that may be laid out in pleasure or improvement, are foolishly squandered away, in tossing cards, fretting at ill-luck, or, even with a run of luck in our favour, fretting that our winnings are so small.

I have now stated gaming in that point of view in which it is alone defensible, as a commerce carried on with equal advantage and loss to either party, and it appears, that the loss is great, and the advantage but small. But let me suppose the players not to be equal, but the superiority of judgement in our own favour. A person who plays under this conviction, however, must give up all pretensions to the approbation of his own mind, and is guilty of as much injustice as the thief who robbed a blind man because he knew he could not swear to his person.

But in fact, when I allowed the superiority of skill on the young beginner's side, I only granted an impossibility. Skill in gaming, like skill in making a watch, can only be acquired by long and painful industry. The most sagacious youth alive was never taught at once all the arts and all the niceties of gaming. Every passion must be schooled by long habit into caution, and phlegm ; the very countenance must be taught proper discipline ; and he who would practise this art with success, must practise on his own constitution all the severities of a martyr, without any expectation of the reward. It is evident therefore every beginner must be a dupe, and can only be expected to learn his trade by losses, disappointments, and dishonour.

If a young gentleman therefore begins to game, the commencements are sure to be to his disadvantage ; and all that he can promise himself is, that the company he keeps, though superior in skill, are above taking advantage of his ignorance, and unacquainted with any sinister arts to correct fortune. But this, however, is but a poor hope at best, and what is worse, most frequently a false one. In general, I might almost have said always, those who live by gaming, are not beholding to chance alone for their support, but take every advantage which they can practise without danger of detection. I know many are apt to say, and I have once said so myself, that after I have shuffled the cards, it is not in the power of a sharper to pack them ; but at present I can confidently assure your Lordship, that such reasoners are deceived. I have seen men, both in Paris, the Hague, and London, who, after three deals, could give whatever hands they pleased to all the company. However, the usual way with sharpers is to correct fortune thus but once in a night, and to play in other respects without blunder or mistake, and a perseverance in this practice always balances the year in their favour.

It is impossible to enumerate all the tricks and arts practised upon cards ; few but have seen those bungling poor fellows who go about at coffee-houses, perform their clumsy feats, and yet, indifferently as they are versed in the trade, they often deceive us ; when such as these are possessed of so much art, what must not those be, who have been bred up to gaming from their infancy, whose hands are not like those mentioned above, rendered callous by labour, who have continual practice in the trade of deceiving, and where the eye of the spectator is less upon its guard.

Let the young beginner only reflect by what a variety of methods it is possible to cheat him, and perhaps it will check his confidence. His antagonists may act by signs and confederacy, and this he can never detect;

they may cut to a particular card after three or four hands have gone about, either by having that card pinched, or broader than the rest, or by having an exceeding fine wire thrust between the folds of the paper, and just peeping out at the edge. Or the cards may be chalked with particular marks, which none but the sharper can understand, or a new pack may be slipped in at a proper opportunity. I have known myself in Paris, a fellow thus detected with a tin case, containing two packs of cards concealed within his shirt sleeve, and which, by means of a spring, threw the cards ready packed into his hands. These and a hundred other arts may be practised with impunity, and escape detection.

The great error lies in imagining every fellow with a laced coat to be a gentleman. The address and transient behaviour of a man of breeding are easily acquired, and none are better qualified than gamesters in this respect. At first, their complaisance, civility, and apparent honour is pleasing, but upon examination, few of them will be found to have their minds sufficiently stored with any of the more refined accomplishments, which truly characterize the man of breeding. This will commonly serve as a criterion to distinguish them, though there are other marks which every young gentleman of fortune should be apprised of. A sharper, when he plays, generally handles and deals the cards awkwardly like a bungler ; he advances his bets by degrees, and keeps his antagonist in spirits by small advantages and alternate success at the beginning ; to show all his force at once, would but fright the bird he intends to decoy ; he talks of honour and virtue, and his being a gentleman, and that he knows great men, and mentions his coal-mines, and his estate in the country ; he is totally divested of that masculine confidence which is the attendant of real fortune ; he turns, yields, assents, smiles, as he hopes will be most pleasing to his destined prey ; he is afraid of meeting a shabby acquaintance, particularly if in better company ; as he grows richer, he wears finer clothes ; and if ever he is seen in an undress, it is most probable he is without money ; so that seeing a gamester growing finer each day, is a certain symptom of his success.

The young gentleman who plays with such men for considerable sums, is sure to be undone, and yet we seldom see even the rook himself make a fortune. A life of gaming must necessarily be a life of extravagance : parties of this kind are formed in houses where the whole profits are consumed ; and while those who play mutually ruin each other, they only who keep the house or the table acquire fortunes. Thus gaming may readily ruin a fortune, but has seldom been found to retrieve it. The wealth which has been acquired with industry and hazard, and preserved for ages by prudence and fore- sight, is swept away on a sudden ; and when a besieging sharper sits down before an estate, the property is often transferred in less time than the writings can be drawn to secure the possession. The neglect of business, and the extravagance of a mind which has been taught to covet precarious possession, brings on premature destruc- tion ; though poverty may fetch a compass and go somewhat about, yet will it reach the gamester at last ; and though his ruin be slow, yet it is certain.

A thousand instances could be given of the fatal tendency of this passion, which first impoverishes the mind, and then perverts the understanding. Permit me to mention one, not caught from report, or dressed up by fancy, but such as has actually fallen under my own observation, and of the truth of which, I beg your Lordship may rest satisfied.

At Tunbridge, in the year 1715, Mr. J. Hedges made

a very brilliant appearance ; he had been married about two years to a young lady of great beauty and large fortune ; they had one child, a boy, on whom they bestowed all that affection which they could spare from each other. He knew nothing of gaming, nor seemed to have the least passion for play ; but he was unacquainted with his own heart ; he began by degrees to bet at the tables for trifling sums, and his soul took fire at the prospect of immediate gain ; he was soon surrounded with sharpers, who with calmness lay in ambush for his fortune, and coolly took advantage of the precipitancy of his passions.

His lady perceived the ruin of her family approaching, but, at first, without being able to form any scheme to prevent it. She advised with his brother, who, at that time, was possessed of a small fellowship in Cambridge. It was easily seen, that whatever passion took the lead in her husband's mind, seemed to be there fixed unalterably ; it was determined, therefore, to let him pursue fortune, but previously take measures to prevent the pursuits being fatal.

Accordingly every night this gentleman was a constant attender at the hazard table ; he understood neither the arts of sharpers, nor even the allowed strokes of a connoisseur, yet still he played. The consequence is obvious; he lost his estate, his equipage, his wife's jewels, and every other movable that could be parted with, except a repeating watch. His agony upon this occasion was inexpressible ; he was even mean enough to ask a gentleman, who sat near, to lend him a few pieces, in order to turn his fortune ; but this prudent gamester, who plainly saw there were no expectations of being repaid, refused to lend a farthing, alleging a former resolution against lending. Hedges was at last furious with the continuance of ill-success, and pulling out his watch,

asked if any person in company would set him sixty
guineas upon it : the company were silent ; he then
demanded fifty; still no answer ; he sunk to forty,
thirty, twenty; finding the company still without answering, he cried out, ' By G—d, it shall never go for less,' and
dashed it against the floor, at the same time attempting to
dash out his brains against the marble chimney-piece.

This last act of desperation immediately excited the
attention of the whole company ; they instantly gathered
round, and prevented the effects of his passion ; and
after he again became cool, he was permitted to return
home, with sullen discontent, to his wife. Upon his
entering her apartment, she received him with her usual
tenderness and satisfaction ; while he answered her
caresses with contempt and severity ; his disposition
being quite altered with his misfortunes. ' But, my dear
' Jemmy,' says his wife, ' perhaps you don't know the
' news I have to tell ; *My Mamma's old uncle is dead,*
' *the messenger is now in the house, and you know his*
' *estate is settled upon you.*' This account seemed only
to increase his agony, and looking angrily at her, he
cried, ' There you lie, my dear, his estate is not settled
' upon me.' ' I beg your pardon,' says she, ' I really
' thought it was, at least you have always told me so.'
' No,' returned he, ' as sure as you and I are to be
' miserable here, and our children beggars hereafter,
' I have sold the reversion of it this day, and have lost
' every farthing I got for it at the hazard table.' ' What,
' all ! ' replied the lady. ' Yes, every farthing,' returned
he, ' and I owe a thousand pounds more than I have
' to pay.' Thus speaking, he took a few frantic steps
across the room. When the lady had a little enjoyed
his perplexity, ' No, my dear,' cried she, ' you have
' lost but a trifle, and you owe nothing. Our brother
' and I have taken care to prevent the effects of your

'rashness, and are actually the persons who have won
'your fortune ; we employed proper persons for this
'purpose, who brought their winnings to me ; your
'money, your equipage, are in my possession, and here
'I return them to you, from whom they were unjustly
'taken. I only ask permission to keep my jewels, and
'to keep you, my greatest jewel, from such dangers for
'the future.' Her prudence had the proper effect : he
ever after retained a sense of his former follies, and
never played for the smallest sums, even for amusement.

Not less than three persons in one day, fell a sacrifice
at Bath, to this destructive passion. Two gentlemen
fought a duel, in which one was killed, and the other
desperately wounded ; and a youth of great expectation,
and excellent disposition, at the same time ended his
own life by a pistol. If there be any state that deserves
pity, it must be that of a gamester ; but the state of
a dying gamester is of all situations the most deplorable.

There is another argument which your Lordship, I
fancy, will not entirely despise; beauty, my Lord, I own
is at best but a trifle, but such as it is, I fancy few
would willingly part with what little they have. A man
with a healthful complexion, how great a philosopher
soever he be, would not willingly exchange it for a sallow
hectic phiz, pale eyes, and a sharp wrinkled visage.
I entreat you only to examine the faces of all the noted
gamblers round one of our public tables ; have you ever
seen anything more haggard, pinched, and miserable ?
and it is but natural that it should be so. The succession
of passions flush the cheek with red, and all such flushings
are ever succeeded by consequent paleness; so that
a gamester contracts the sickly hue of a student, while
he is only acquiring the stupidity of a fool.

Your good sense, my Lord, I have often had an
occasion of knowing, yet how miserable is it to be in

a set of company where the most sensible is ever the least skilful : your footman, with a little instruction, would, I dare venture to affirm, make a better and more successful gamester than you ; want of passions, and low cunning, are the two great arts ; and it is peculiar to this science alone, that they who have the greatest passion for it, are of all others the most unfit to practise it.

Of all the men I ever knew, Spedding was the greatest blockhead, and yet the best gamester : he saw almost intuitively the advantage on either side, and ever took it ; he could calculate the odds in a moment, and decide upon the merits of a cock or a horse, better than any man in England ; in short, he was such an adept in gaming, that he brought it up to a pitch of sublimity it had never attained before ; yet, with all this, Spedding could not write his own name. What he died worth, I cannot tell ; but of this I am certain, he might have possessed a ministerial estate, and that won from men, famed for their sense, literature, and patriotism.

If, after this description, your Lordship is yet resolved to hazard your fortune at gaming, I beg you would advert to the situation of an old and luckless gamester. Perhaps there is not in nature a more deplorable being : his character is too well marked, he is too well known to be trusted. A man that has been often a bankrupt, and renewed trade upon low compositions, may as well expect extensive credit as such a man. His reputation is blasted, his constitution worn, by the extravagance and ill hours of his profession ; he is now incapable of alluring his dupes, and like a superannuated savage of the forest, he is starved for want of vigour to hunt after prey.

Thus gaming is the source of poverty, and still worse, the parent of infamy and vice. It is an inlet to debauchery ; for the money thus acquired is but little valued. Every gamester is a rake, and his morals worse than his mystery. It is his interest to be exemplary in every scene of debauchery, his prey is to be courted with every guilty pleasure ; but these are to be changed, repeated, and embellished, in order to employ his imagination, while his reason is kept asleep ; a young mind is apt to shrink at the prospect of ruin ; care must be taken to harden his courage, and make him keep his rank ; he must be either found a libertine, or he must be made one. And when a man has parted with his money like a fool, he generally sends his conscience after it like a villain, and the nearer he is to the brink of destruction, the fonder does he grow of ruin.

Your friend and mine, my Lord, had been thus driven to the last reserve : he found it impossible to disentangle his affairs, and look the world in the face ; impatience at length threw him into the abyss he feared, and life became a burthen, because he feared to die. But I own that play is not always attended with such tragical circumstances : some have had courage to survive their losses, and go on content with beggary ; and sure those misfortunes, which are of our own production, are of all others most pungent. To see such a poor disbanded being an unwelcome guest at every table, and often flapped off like a fly, is affecting ; in this case the closest alliance is forgotten, and contempt is too strong for the ties of blood to unbind.

But however fatal this passion may be in its consequence, none allures so much in the beginning ; the person once listed as a gamester, if not soon reclaimed, pursues it through his whole life ; no loss can retard, no danger awaken him to common sense ; nothing can terminate his career but want of money to play, or of honour to be trusted.

Among the number of my acquaintance, I knew but of two who succeeded by gaming ; the one a phlegmatic heavy man, who would have made a fortune in whatever way of life he happened to be placed ; the other who had lost a fine estate in his youth by play, and retrieved a greater at the age of sixty-five, when he might be justly said, to be past the power of enjoying it. One or two successful gamesters are thus set up in an age to allure the young beginner ; we all regard such, as the highest prize in a lottery, unmindful of the numerous losses that go to the accumulation of such infrequent success.

Yet I would not be so morose, as to refuse your youth all kinds of play : the innocent amusements of a family must often be indulged, and cards allowed to supply the intervals of more real pleasure ; but the sum played for in such cases should always be a trifle ; something to call up attention, but not engage the passions. The usual excuse for laying large sums is, to make the players attend to their game ; but in fact, he that plays only for shillings, will mind his cards equally well, with him that bets guineas ; for the mind, habituated to stake large sums, will consider them as trifles at last ; and if one shilling could not exclude indifference at first, neither will a hundred in the end.

I have often asked myself, how it is possible that he who is possessed of competence, can ever be induced to make it precarious by beginning play with the odds against him ; for wherever he goes to sport his money, he will find himself overmatched and cheated. Either at White's, Newmarket, the Tennis-Court, the Cock-Pit, or the Billiard-Table, he will find numbers who have no other resource, but their acquisitions there ; and if such men live like gentlemen, he may readily conclude it must be on the spoils of his fortune, or the fortunes of ill-judging men like himself. Was he to attend but a moment to their manner of betting at those places, he would readily find the gamester seldom proposing bets but with the advantage in his own favour. A man of honour continues to lay on the side on which he first won ; but gamesters shift, change, lie upon the lurch, and take every advantage, either of our ignorance or neglect.

In short, my Lord, if a man designs to lay out his fortune in quest of pleasure, the gaming table is, of all other places, that where he can have least for his money. The company are superficial, extravagant, and un-entertaining ; the conversation flat, debauched, and absurd ; the hours unnatural, and fatiguing ; the anxiety of losing is greater than the pleasure of winning ; friendship must be banished from that society, the members of which are intent only on ruining each other ; every other improvement, either in knowledge or virtue, can scarce find room in that breast which is possessed by the spirit of play ; the spirits become vapid, the con-stitution is enfeebled, the complexion grows pale ; till, in the end, the mind, body, friends, fortune, and even the hopes of futurity sink together ! Happy, if nature terminates the scene, and neither justice nor suicide are called in to accelerate her tardy approach.

I am,

my Lord, &c.

Among other Papers in the custody of Mr. Nash, was the following angry Letter, addressed to him in this manner.

To RICHARD NASH, ESQ.

King of Bath.

SIRE,

I must desire your Majesty to order the enclosed to be read to the great Mr. Hoyle, if he be found in any part of your dominions. You will perceive that it is a panegyric on his manifold virtues, and that he is thanked more particularly for spending his time so much to the emolument of the public, and for obliging the world with a book more read than the Bible, and which so eminently tends to promote Christian knowledge, sound morality, and the happiness of mankind.

(The enclosed we have omitted, as it contains a satire on gaming, and may probably give offence to our betters.)

This author, however (continues the letter-writer), has not set forth half the merits of the piece under consideration, nor is the great care which he has taken to prevent our reading any other book, instead of this, been sufficiently taken notice of : *beware of counterfeits; these books are not to be depended on unless signed by E. Hoyle,* is a charitable admonition. As you have so much power at Bath, and are absolute, I think you should imitate other great monarchs, by rewarding those with honours who have been serviceable in your state; and I beg that a new order may be established for that purpose. Let him who has done nothing but game all his life, and has reduced the most families to ruin and beggary, be made a *Marshal of the Black Ace;* and those who are every day making proselytes to the tables, have the honour of knighthood conferred on them, and be distinguished by the style and title of *Knights of the four Knaves.*

The moment I came into Bath, my ears were saluted with the news of a gentleman's being plundered at the gaming table, and having lost his senses on the occasion. The same day a duel was fought between two gentlemen gamesters on the Downs, and in the evening another hanged himself at the Bear ; but first wrote a note, which was found near him, importing that he had injured the best of friends. These are the achievements of your *Knights of the four Knaves.* The Devil will pick the bones of all gamesters, that's certain !—Ay ! and of duellers too ! but in the meantime let none think that duelling is a mark of courage ; for I know it is not.

A person served under me in Flanders who had fought four duels, and depended so much on his skill, the strength of his arm, and the length of his sword, that he would take up a quarrel for anybody; yet, in the field, I never saw one behave so like a poltroon. If a few of these gamesters and duellers were gibbeted, it might perhaps help to amend the rest. I have often thought, that the only way, or at least, the most effectual way, to prevent duelling, would be to hang both parties, the living and the dead, on the same tree;[1] and if the

[1] A scheme to prevent duelling, similar to this, was attempted by Gustavus Adolphus; and is thus recorded by the writer of his life.

'In one of the Prussian Campaigns, when the irrational practice 'of duelling arose to a considerable height in the Swedish army, 'not only amongst persons of rank and fashion, but even amongst 'common soldiers, this prince published a severe edict, and de-'nounced death against every delinquent. Soon after a quarrel 'arose between two officers of very high command, and as they knew 'the king's firmness in preserving his word inviolable, they agreed to 'request an audience, and besought his permission to decide the 'affair like men of honour. His Majesty took fire in a moment, but 'repressed his passion with such art, that they easily mistook him; 'of course with some reluctance, but under the appearance of pitying 'brave men, who thought their reputation injured, he told them, 'that he blamed them much for their mistaken notions, concerning 'Fame and Glory; yet as this unreasonable determination appeared 'to be the result of deliberate reflection, to the best of their deluded 'capacity, he would allow them to decide the affair at the time and 'place specified: "and, gentlemen," said he, "I will be an eye-'witness myself of your extraordinary valour and prowess."

'At the hour appointed Gustavus arrived, accompanied by 'a small body of infantry, whom he formed into a circle round the 'combatants. "Now," says he, "fight till one man dies;" and 'calling the executioner of the army to him (or the provost-marshal, 'as the language then ran), "Friend," added he, "the instant one is 'killed, behead the other before my eyes."

'Astonished with such inflexible firmness, the two generals, after 'pausing a moment, fell down on their knees, and asked the king's 'forgiveness, who made them embrace each other, and give their 'promise to continue faithful friends to their last moments; as 'they did with sincerity and thankfulness.'

winner and the loser were treated in the same manner, it would be better for the public ; since the tucking up of a few R——ls might be a warning to others, and save many a worthy family from destruction.

I am yours, &c.

The author of this letter appears to have been very angry, and not without reason ; for, if I am rightly informed, his only son was ruined at Bath, and by sharpers. But why is Nash to be blamed for this ? It must be acknowledged, that he always took pains to prevent the ruin of the youth of both sexes, and had so guarded against duelling, that he would not permit a sword to be worn in Bath.

As the heart of a man is better known by his private than public actions, let us take a view of Nash in domestic life ; among his servants and dependants, where no gloss was required to colour his sentiments and disposition, nor any mask necessary to conceal his foibles. Here we shall find him the same open-hearted, generous, good-natured man we have already described ; one who was ever fond of promoting the interests of his friends, his servants, and dependants, and making them happy. In his own house no man perhaps was more regular, cheerful, and beneficent than Mr. Nash. His table was always free to those who sought his friendship, or wanted a dinner ; and after grace was said, he usually accosted the company in the following extraordinary manner, to take off all restraint and ceremony : 'Come, gentlemen, 'eat and welcome ; spare, and the Devil choke you.' I mention this circumstance for no other reason but because it is well known, and is consistent with the singularity of his character and behaviour.

As Mr. Nash's thoughts were entirely employed in the affairs of his government, he was seldom at home but at the time of eating or of rest. His table was well served, but his entertainment consisted principally of plain dishes. Boiled chicken and roast mutton were his favourite meats, and he was so fond of the small sort of potatoes, that he called them English pine-apples, and generally eat them as others do fruit, after dinner. In drinking he was altogether as regular and abstemious. Both in this, and in eating, he seemed to consult Nature, and obey only her dictates. Good small beer, with or without a glass of wine in it, and sometimes wine and water, was his drink at meals, and after dinner he generally drank one glass of wine. He seemed fond of hot suppers, usually supped about nine or ten o'clock, upon roast breast of mutton and his potatoes, and soon after supper went to bed ; which induced Dr. Cheney to tell him jestingly, *that he behaved like other brutes, and lay down as soon as he had filled his belly.* ' Very true,' replied Nash, ' and this prescription I had from my neighbour's ' cow, who is a better physician than you, and a superior ' judge of plants, notwithstanding you have written so ' learnedly on the vegetable diet.'

. Nash generally arose early in the morning, being seldom in bed after five ; and to avoid disturbing the family and depriving his servants of their rest, he had the fire laid after he was in bed, and in the morning lighted it himself, and sat down to read some of his few but well-chosen books. After reading some time, he usually went to the Pump-room and drank the waters ; then took a walk on the parade, and went to the coffee-house to breakfast ; after which, till two o'clock (his usual time of dinner), his hours were spent in arbitrating differences amongst his neighbours, or the company resorting to the wells ; directing the diversions of the day, in visiting the new-comers, or receiving friends at his own house, of which there were a great concourse till within six or eight years before his death.

His generosity and charity in private life, though not so conspicuous, was as great as that in public, and indeed far more considerable than his little income would admit of. He could not stifle the natural impulse which he had to do good, but frequently borrowed money to relieve the distressed ; and when he knew not conveniently where to borrow, he has been often observed to shed tears, as he passed through the wretched supplicants who attended his gate.

This sensibility, this power of feeling the misfortunes of the miserable, and his address and earnestness in relieving their wants, exalts the character of Mr. Nash, and draws an impenetrable veil over his foibles. His singularities are forgotten when we behold his virtues, and he who laughed at the whimsical character and behaviour of this Monarch of Bath, now laments that he is no more.

APPENDIX

BEAU TIBBS : A THIRD ESSAY
(*See* pp. 147, 151)

[From *The Citizen of the World*, Letter LXXI]

THE people of London are as fond of walking as our friends at Pekin of riding ; one of the principal entertainments of the citizens here in summer is to repair about nightfall to a garden not far from town, where they walk about, show their best clothes and best faces, and listen to a concert provided for the occasion.

I accepted an invitation a few evenings ago from my old friend, the man in black, to be one of a party that was to sup there ; and at the appointed hour waited upon him at his lodgings. There I found the company assembled and expecting my arrival. Our party consisted of my friend in superlative finery, his stockings rolled, a black velvet waistcoat which was formerly new, and his grey wig combed down in imitation of hair. A pawn-broker's widow, of whom, by the by, my friend was a professed admirer, dressed out in green damask, with three gold rings on every finger. Mr. Tibbs, the second-rate beau, I have formerly described ; together with his lady, in flimsy silk, dirty gauze instead of linen, and an hat as big as an umbrella.

Our first difficulty was in settling how we should set out. Mrs. Tibbs had a natural aversion to the water, and the widow being a little in flesh, as warmly protested against walking ; a coach was therefore agreed upon ; which being too small to carry five, Mr. Tibbs consented to sit in his wife's lap.

In this manner therefore we set forward, being entertained by the way with the bodings of Mr. Tibbs,

who assured us, he did not expect to see a single creature
for the evening above the degree of a cheesemonger;
that this was the last night of the gardens, and that
consequently we should be pestered with the nobility
and gentry from Thames Street and Crooked Lane;
with several other prophetic ejaculations probably
inspired by the uneasiness of his situation.

The illuminations began before we arrived, and I must
confess, that upon entering the gardens I found every
sense overpaid with more than expected pleasure; the
lights every where glimmering through the scarcely
moving trees; the full-bodied concert bursting on the
stillness of the night, the natural concert of the birds,
in the more retired part of the grove, vying with that
which was formed by art; the company gaily dressed,
looking satisfaction; and the tables spread with various
delicacies,—all conspired to fill my imagination with the
visionary happiness of the Arabian lawgiver, and lifted
me into an ecstasy of admiration. ' Head of Confucius,'
cried I to my friend, ' this is fine! this unites rural
'beauty with courtly magnificence! if we except the
'virgins of immortality that hang on every tree, and
'may be plucked at every desire, I don't see how this
'falls short of Mahomet's Paradise!' ' As for virgins,'
cries my friend, ' it is true, they are a fruit that don't
' much abound in our gardens here; but if ladies as plenty
'as apples in autumn, and as complying as any Houri of
'them all can content you, I fancy we have no need to
'go to heaven for Paradise.'

I was going to second his remarks, when we were called
to a consultation by Mr. Tibbs and the rest of the company, to know in what manner we were to lay out the
evening to the greatest advantage. Mrs. Tibbs was for
keeping the genteel walk of the garden, where she
observed there was always the very best company;

the widow, on the contrary, who came but once a season, was for securing a good standing place to see the water-works, which she assured us would begin in less than an hour at farthest ; a dispute therefore began, and as it was managed between two of very opposite characters, it threatened to grow more bitter at every reply. Mrs. Tibbs wondered ,how people could pretend to know the polite world who had received all their rudiments of breeding behind a counter ; to which the other replied, that though some people sat behind counters, yet they could sit at the head of their own tables too, and carve three good dishes of hot meat whenever they thought proper, which was more than some people could say for themselves, that hardly knew a rabbit and onions from a green goose and gooseberries.

It is hard to say where this might have ended, had not the husband, who probably knew the impetuosity of his wife's disposition, proposed to end the dispute by adjourning to a box, and try if there was anything to be had for supper that was supportable. To this we all consented, but here a new distress arose: Mr. and Mrs. Tibbs would sit in none but a genteel box, a box where they might see and be seen—one, as they expressed it, in the very focus of public view ; but such a box was not easy to be obtained, for though we were perfectly convinced of our own gentility, and the gentility of our appearance, yet we found it a difficult matter to persuade the keepers of the boxes to be of our opinion ; they chose to reserve genteel boxes for what they judged more genteel company.

At last however we were fixed, though somewhat obscurely, and supplied with the usual entertainment of the place. The widow found the supper excellent, but Mrs. Tibbs thought every thing detestable. ' Come, ' come, my dear,' cries the husband, by way of consolation,

' to be sure we can't find such dressing here as we have
' at Lord Crump's or Lady Crimp's ; but for Vauxhall
' dressing it is pretty good ; it is not their victuals indeed
' I find fault with, but their wine ; their wine,' cries he,
drinking off a glass, ' indeed, is most abominable.'

By this last contradiction the widow was fairly
conquered in point of politeness. She perceived now
that she had no pretensions in the world to taste ; her
very senses were vulgar, since she had praised detestable
custard, and smacked at wretched wine ; she was
therefore content to yield the victory, and for the rest
of the night to listen and improve. It is true, she would
now and then forget herself, and confess she was pleased,
but they soon brought her back again to miserable
refinement. She once praised the painting of the box
in which we were sitting, but was soon convinced that
such paltry pieces ought rather to excite horror than
satisfaction ; she ventured again to commend one of
the singers, but Mrs. Tibbs soon let her know, in the
style of a connoisseur, that the singer in question had
neither ear, voice, nor judgement.

Mr. Tibbs, now willing to prove that his wife's pretensions to music were just, entreated her to favour the
company with a song ; but to this she gave a positive
denial, ' for you know very well, my dear,' says she,
' that I am not in voice to-day, and when one's voice is
' not equal to one's judgement, what signifies singing ?
' besides, as there is no accompaniment, it would be but
' spoiling music.' All these excuses however were overruled by the rest of the company, who, though one
would think they already had music enough, joined in
the entreaty. But particularly the widow, now willing
to convince the company of her breeding, pressed so
warmly that she seemed determined to take no refusal.
At last then the lady complied, and after humming for

some minutes, began with such a voice, and such affectation, as I could perceive gave but little satisfaction to any except her husband. He sat with rapture in his eye, and beat time with his hand on the table.

You must observe, my friend, that it is the custom of this country, when a lady or gentleman happens to sing, for the company to sit as mute and motionless as statues. Every feature, every limb, must seem to correspond in fixed attention, and while the song continues, they are to remain in a state of universal petrifaction. In this mortifying situation we had continued for some time, listening to the song, and looking with tranquillity, when the master of the box came to inform us, that the water-works were going to begin. At this information I could instantly perceive the widow bounce from her seat ; but correcting herself, she sat down again, repressed by motives of good breeding. Mrs. Tibbs, who had seen the water-works an hundred times, resolving not to be interrupted, continued her song without any share of mercy, nor had the smallest pity on our impatience. The widow's face, I own, gave me high entertainment ; in it I could plainly read the struggle she felt between good breeding and curiosity ; she talked of the water-works the whole evening before, and seemed to have come merely in order to see them ; but then she could not bounce out in the very middle of a song, for that would be forfeiting all pretensions to high life, or high-lived company ever after : Mrs. Tibbs, therefore, kept on singing, and we continued to listen, till at last, when the song was just concluded, the waiter came to inform us that the water-works were over.

'The water-works over !' cried the widow ; 'the 'water-works over already, that's impossible, they can't be over so soon !'—'It is not my business,' replied the fellow, ' to contradict your ladyship ; I'll run again and

' see.' He went, and soon returned with a confirmation of the dismal tidings. No ceremony could now bind my friend's disappointed mistress. She testified her displeasure in the openest manner ; in short, she now began to find fault in turn, and at last insisted upon going home, just at the time that Mr. and Mrs. Tibbs assured the company that the polite hours were going to begin, and that the ladies would instantaneously be entertained with the horns.—Adieu.

Lightning Source UK Ltd.
Milton Keynes UK
UKOW05f1929250417
299899UK00018B/506/P